THE PRINCETON REVIEW

# Cracking the GRE Biology Subject Test

THE PRINCETON REVIEW

# Cracking the GRE Biology Subject Test

BY DEBORAH GUEST
AND THE STAFF OF THE PRINCETON REVIEW

2ND EDITION

RANDOM HOUSE, INC.
NEW YORK 1997
http://www.randomhouse.com

Princeton Review Publishing, L.L.C.
2315 Broadway
New York, NY 10024
E-mail: info@review.com



ISBN 0-679-78408-X
ISSN 1089-3687

Editor: Rachel Warren
Production Editor: Bruno Blumenfeld
Designer: Illeny Maaza
Production Supervisor: Chee Pae
Illustrations by: John Bergdahl and The Production Department of The Princeton Review

Manufactured in the United States of America on partially recycled paper.

9 8 7 6 5 4 3 2

2nd Edition

# ACKNOWLEDGMENTS

Heartfelt thanks go to Lynne Christensen, M.A., Martha Link, M.D., Kim Magloire, Elizabeth Secord, M.D., and Ted Silver, M.D., for their superb personal and professional support and their insightful contributions to the manuscript.

Thanks also to my editor Kristin Fayne-Mulroy, for her patience and calm, and to the Production staff of The Princeton Review: Illeny Maaza, John Bergdahl, Lisa Ruyter, Effie Hadjiioannou, Greta Englert, Robert McCormack, John Pak, and Christopher Thomas.

Finally, the author gratefully thanks the financial aid department of her alma mater, Columbia University, and the Helena Rubenstein Foundation for their Women Scholars in the Sciences funding, both of whose generous scholarships made it possible to get the best education she could have wanted.

# CONTENTS

# PART I

# Orientation

# 1

# Introduction

## No Time, No Space, No Point

Dust off those undergraduate biology textbooks and keep them nearby as you review for the GRE. This way, you can refer to a topic in more detail should you need to.

This book isn't going to teach you biology. If you're planning to take the GRE Biology Subject Test then you should already know plenty of biology. You must have sat through basic and upper-level biology courses and conducted countless lab experiments. Chances are, you've amassed (or have access to) a collection of textbooks on topics like cellular and molecular biology, biochemistry, immunology, comparative physiology, anatomy, genetics, developmental biology, botany, animal behavior, environmental science, natural resources, and ecology. If you need any more information about the topics that we touch upon in this book, refer to those books. We aren't saying that you might not need brushing up in some areas.

## If We Won't Teach You Biology, Then What Will We Do?

We know that you're serious about doing well on the GRE Biology Subject Test. Our job is to help you get the best score you're capable of getting. We'll start out by offering you tips and insights into the way that the test is set up; we'll teach you test-taking strategies that are designed for and proven to be effective on the GRE Biology Exam. Next, we'll help you figure out where to direct all of your mental energies. We'll coach you on the topics that are most likely to appear on the test, and we'll give you the opportunity to identify your weak and strong areas in biology. We won't stop there, though, like many GRE Biology review books do. We'll provide a concise review of key topics that you can expect to see on the test. After you've read and worked through the first part of the book you'll be ready to take on the full-length practice test.

After you complete the practice test, we'll explain clearly to you which answers are correct and why, as well as why the other answer choices are wrong. We don't cut any corners in our test explanation section the way other review books do. These things are all part of our master plan: to make you one of the best-prepared people to walk into the room on the day of the test.

## What, Exactly, Is ETS?

ETS is the Educational Testing Service. ETS sounds like a scholarly organization but in truth it's a business that's devoted to churning out standardized tests that are inflicted on you from their high school years, onward (remember the SAT?).

## What is the Princeton Review?

The Princeton Review is a test-coaching company based in New York City. We analyze actual standardized tests and use them to develop techniques for test-taking. We find the test's weaknesses, quirks, and patterns, and pass this information on to you. For this reason, after reading this book you'll be far better prepared to tackle ETS's tests than those people who are unfamiliar with their habits.

## About the GRE Biology Subject Test

The GRE Biology Subject Test consists of approximately 200 questions. The whole test is 170 minutes long, and consists of three distinct sections. The first section (questions 1-121) will consist of individual questions concerning specific biological concepts or terms. For each question, you will be asked to chose from a selection of five multiple-choice answers. In the second section (questions 122-149), a set of five terms, structures, or sets of data will be presented to you, and you'll be asked a series of questions about them. The third section (questions 150-200) will consist of experimental data in the form of a graph, chart, illustration, figure, or text. You'll be asked a series of questions related to that information, and each of the questions will be multiple-choice, with five answer choices.

**One thing's for sure:** on the GRE Biology test, you're going to see an experiment or a term or a concept that you've never seen before. But don't let that stop you from using the process of elimination to get rid of obviously wrong answers.

## What Does the Test Measure?

The test is designed to assess your qualifications as a potential graduate student in the field of biology. Since biology is a vast discipline and students across various colleges and even within one college may study entirely different aspects of biology, test questions are drawn up to broadly reflect the many different branches of biology. Because so many topics are covered on the test, you are not expected to know each and every subject tested. You have the benefit of being able to forgo answering a number of questions while still being able to achieve a high score.

At the same time that the exam tests your knowledge of biology, however, it also tests something else about you. Although ETS doesn't say so, the GRE Biology Subject Test is also a measure of your ability to perform on standardized tests.

## Who Writes the GRE Biology Test?

According to ETS, the test writers are professors who are recommended to them by the American Institute of Biological Sciences, the Botanical Society of America, the American Society of Zoologists, and the Ecological Society of America, along with a few other "subject-matter specialists."

650 | 650

## How Important is the Biology GRE?

This answer depends on what school you're talking about. Keep in mind that your scores on the GRE general test are considered as well as your GRE Bio scores. Some schools give equal weight to GRE scores, research experience, letters of recommendation, and undergraduate records when considering you as a potential candidate.

One ivy league school said that, first of all, they do not operate with a minimum cutoff score. Most students accepted to their program have a GRE score that ranges from as low as 550 to as high as 800. At the same time, the school noted, this doesn't mean that they haven't accepted applicants with scores below 550, or rejected applicants with scores of 780 or above. They tend to view recommendations, statements of purpose, and undergraduate records as more important than GRE Biology scores. And, yes, they believe that level of performance on the quantitative aspect of the general GRE test is a good indicator of how well a potential graduate student may perform in the program. However, they told us, if all other aspects of a student's qualifications are equal, the schools will look to the GRE Biology scores to cast the deciding vote.

So there you have it. Your GRE Biology scores probably will not single-handedly make or break your chances for acceptance. On the other hand, they count for something, and sometimes, depending on the school, they just may come through to save the day if you're balancing on the thin line between acceptance and rejection.

## What Score Should You Aim for?

The possible score range for most administrations of the test is from 200 up to 990. More realistically, though, the range in scores is usually from 430 to 810. Since for most tests a score of 870 puts you in the 99th percentile, scores above 900 are nearly impossible to get. And, as we mentioned above, the actual score you need in order to get into the school of your choice depends on the admissions policy of that school and on your other qualifications. Some schools establish minimum scores for admission, although the average score for admitted students is somewhat higher. Check with the schools of your choice for the numbers.

## What About Subscores?

Besides calculating your overall score and percentile, ETS will calculate three subscores. Subscore I indicates how you did on the Cellular and Molecular Biology section of the test, Subscore II evaluates your performance on Organismal Biology, and Subscore III records the damage you inflicted upon the Ecology and Evolution section. The subscores usually range from about 35 to 99 points.

## The Best Time to Take the Test

Make sure you take the test at least six weeks before your applications are due, in order to ensure that your scores will be released in time. Application deadlines for most schools occur in the range of dates from mid-December to mid-February.

## What About Guessing?

Guessing is good. Expect to do some aggressive guessing on this exam. We'll have more to say on this soon.

## How Many Times Should You Take the Test?

Once is probably enough; provided that you're prepared for it. Our job is to help prepare you.

## FIVE GUIDELINES TO HELP YOU PREPARE

1. Allow enough time to prepare—generally about six weeks.
2. Make it a social event. Assemble a study group.
3. Make studying for the test a daily habit, or as close to a daily habit as you can.
4. Practice our test-taking techniques. The more comfortable you feel with guessing and other techniques, the easier it will be for you to use them on the exam.
5. Get the practice test that's put out by ETS, called *Practicing to take the GRE Biology Test*. On the other hand, do NOT take practice tests from other sources. These can be confusing and may over- or underestimate the difficulty level of the exam. You can rely on the official GRE Biology test to give you an indication of the level of difficulty you'll see.

By taking ETS's practice test (we recommend that you do this about two weeks before the real exam) you'll get a chance to exercise your newly acquired knowledge and skills and pinpoint any topics that you may still be weak on. Once you determine your score be sure to look over each question with this idea in mind: *Based on everything I know about biology, did I earn as many points as I could have?* If the answer is no, look back through this book and you should be able to figure out why.

**As your test-taking confidence builds, you'll become bolder at taking chances, and you'll score more points.**

# CRACKING THE SYSTEM

## IMPROVING YOUR TEST-TAKING SKILLS

Not everyone does well on standardized tests. Some people thrive on them, but what if you're not one of those people? Should you throw in the towel and simply go in blindly, hoping for the best? Not by a long shot. There are many ways in which you can build up your test-taking confidence.

According to ETS, the GRE Biology test grills you on these things:

- Knowledge of basic vocabulary and facts in several biological fields at the equivalent of an upper-level course
- Conceptual understanding of biological ideas, relationships, and processes
- Understanding of basic scientific research, procedures, and tools
- Capacity to read, evaluate, and draw conclusions from unfamiliar laboratory and field studies
- Understanding of the connections among biological fields and between biological fields and cognate sciences

## What If You Suffer From Test Anxiety?

But there are a few other things that could affect your performance on the test. For instance, how well do you function under pressure? Can you prioritize? How's your test-taking stamina? Your ability to focus? Do a fear of failure and general self-doubt destroy your efforts? Luckily there's something you can do about these problems. You can, for instance, read up on them to get a better idea of what causes them and how to get a handle on them. You can also help to beat them with a few behavioral modifications. These are especially helpful for the actual day of the test.

Relax. Any technique designed to relax you, like yoga, meditation, or focusing on your breathing, will help ease the tension. Keep this in the back of your mind during those long 170 minutes when the test is in progress. A quick glance away from your test paper (and at your neighbor's!!! HA!) every so often will give your eyes a rest and help to keep you focused.

**So what should you bring to the test center? Your ticket, some form of identification, some number 2 pencils, an eraser, and your watch.**

Get a grip. Don't sweat over any one question–it's not worth it! If you think a question is too hard, move on. No single question is going to make or break your score or your career. And you can always return to it later, after you've covered more ground on the easier stuff. And if you really start to panic during the test, just remember that (1) you're probably doing better than you think, and (2) the rest of the test will offer you plenty of opportunities to gain points.

Remember that practice makes perfect. Before test day, map out the exact location of the test center. Know how to get there and know how long it takes to get there. Be sure, also, that you know what items you need to bring with you to the test. On test day, give yourself plenty of time to get there. Showing up late is not the way to begin the test. What's more, you don't want to run the risk of being turned away because you're late.

Go purchase yourself some attitude. Go in there on test day ready to kick some arse. By test day you will have finished this book. You'll have studied, reviewed, identified and worked on your weaknesses, and you'll have taken plenty of practice runs. You'll never be more ready to take the test. Armed with that knowledge, tackle the exam like you're the one in charge, because after all, you are.

## About Guessing

When it comes to guessing, ETS recommends this:

"If you have some knowledge of a question and are able to rule out one or more of the answer choices as incorrect, your chances of selecting the correct answer are improved, and answering such questions is likely to improve your score." (ETS, 1995)

That's a good start. Here's what we add to that advice: Get used to guessing! It's the best tool you've got to raise your score. If you're thinking right now *But what about the quarter-point ETS subtracts for each wrong answer?* we've got some more advice for you. The quarter-point penalty is meant to dissuade students from random guessing. Four wrong answers effectively cancel out one correct answer. Don't let that possibility discourage you, though. We're going to show you how to use guessing to your advantage every time. That involves POE, or the process of elimination.

## WE'LL SHOW YOU WHAT WE MEAN

Let's say you're faced with this question on the exam:

23. A measure of the volume of red blood cells per unit volume of blood is called (the)

(A) serum
(B) albumin
(C) platelets
(D) hematocrit
(E) plasma

What if you don't recognize any of the answer choices? What do you do? Apply the process of elimination (POE). See if you can eliminate one answer choice. From the dim recesses of your memory, you seem to recall that plasma is the watery, colorless part of blood, so chances are it isn't chock full of red blood cells. So you eliminate choice (E). Good move. Now you're down to four answer choices, and you can guess on this question. If you're on a roll, you may also notice that answer choice (C), "hematocrit," has the root heme- in it, and heme, as you may remember, is a component of hemoglobin—and hemoglobin is found in red blood cells! So you take a chance and opt for choice (C). Bingo. By going with your hunch, you score one full point.

*"The greater the difficulty, the greater the glory."*
*—Marcus Tullius Cicero*

The moral here is this: If you can eliminate even one answer choice, go for a guess. If you can eliminate two answer choices (and you often can), you have an even better chance of choosing the correct one.

Speaking of scoring, how does ETS calculate your test score?

## YOUR "RAW SCORE" VERSUS YOUR "SCALED SCORE"

To arrive at your "raw" test score, ETS takes the number of questions you answered correctly and subtracts from it one-fourth of the number of questions you answered incorrectly. Next, ETS takes that score and converts it to a "scaled" score, which generally ranges from 340 to 990.

Now, to calculate your percentile, ETS sees how your scaled score compares to the scaled scores of everyone else who took the same test and the scores that were achieved that year on different versions of the GRE Bio test. Take a look at the sample score conversion chart below to see what we mean. It shows how raw score, scaled score, and percentile for a typical administration of the test are related.

| RAW SCORE | SCALED SCORE | %-ILE |
|---|---|---|
| 168–200 | 990 | 99 |
| 166–167 | 980 | 99 |
| 163–165 | 970 | 99 |
| 161–162 | 960 | 99 |
| 158–160 | 950 | 99 |
| 155–157 | 940 | 99 |
| 153–154 | 930 | 99 |
| 150–152 | 920 | 99 |
| 148–149 | 910 | 99 |
| 145–147 | 900 | 99 |
| 143–144 | 890 | 99 |
| 140–142 | 880 | 99 |
| 137–139 | 870 | 99 |
| 135–136 | 860 | 98 |
| 132–134 | 850 | 98 |
| 130–131 | 840 | 97 |
| 127–129 | 830 | 97 |
| 124–126 | 820 | 96 |
| 122–123 | 810 | 95 |
| 119–121 | 800 | 94 |
| 117–118 | 790 | 93 |
| 114–116 | 780 | 92 |
| 112–113 | 770 | 90 |
| 109–111 | 760 | 89 |
| 106–108 | 750 | 87 |
| 104–105 | 740 | 85 |
| 101–103 | 730 | 83 |
| 99–100 | 720 | 81 |
| 96–98 | 710 | 79 |
| 93–95 | 700 | 76 |
| 91–92 | 690 | 74 |
| 88–90 | 680 | 71 |
| 86–87 | 670 | 68 |
| 83–85 | 660 | 66 |
| 80–82 | 650 | 63 |
| 78–79 | 640 | 59 |
| 75–77 | 630 | 56 |
| 73–74 | 620 | 53 |
| 70–72 | 610 | 49 |
| 68–69 | 600 | 46 |
| 65–67 | 590 | 43 |
| 62–64 | 580 | 39 |
| 60–61 | 570 | 36 |
| 57–59 | 560 | 33 |
| 55–56 | 550 | 30 |
| 52–54 | 540 | 27 |
| 49–51 | 530 | 24 |
| 47–48 | 520 | 21 |
| 44–46 | 510 | 19 |
| 42–43 | 500 | 16 |
| 39–41 | 490 | 14 |
| 37–38 | 480 | 12 |
| 34–36 | 470 | 10 |
| 31–33 | 460 | 9 |
| 29–30 | 450 | 8 |
| 26–28 | 440 | 6 |
| 24–25 | 430 | 5 |
| 21–23 | 420 | 4 |
| 18–20 | 410 | 3 |
| 16–17 | 400 | 2 |
| 13–15 | 390 | 2 |
| 11–12 | 380 | 1 |
| 8–10 | 370 | 1 |
| 6–7 | 360 | 1 |
| 3–5 | 350 | 1 |

## SETTING UP YOUR STRATEGY

The first step is to examine how you did on the practice test. Start by dividing the questions on the test into ones you know the answer to, ones you thought you knew the answer to, and ones you used POE on and guessed.

Now, based on your score on the practice test, your projected target score, and the score conversion chart we just showed you, work out some strategies for your test. Play around on paper with how many questions you would need to answer with reasonable certainty, and how many you would have to guess correctly on in order to reach your goal.

This is your chance to map out a few alternative approaches to the same target goal.

Target score range _____ _____

| | Performance on Practice Exam | Plan A | Plan B | Plan C |
|---|---|---|---|---|
| Know the answer | | | | |
| Pretty sure (right) | | | | |
| Pretty sure (wrong) | | | | |
| Guess (right) | | | | |
| Guess (wrong) | | | | |
| Questions Answered | | | | |
| Raw Score | | | | |
| Scaled Score | | | | |
| %-ile | | | | |

Now that you have a strategy in place, let's get you started on how to implement it.

## PACE YOURSELF

As you encounter each question on the test, immediately give it a rating of easy, medium, or hard. This is an easy job: Easy questions are easy to answer; medium questions are a little harder to figure out, but you could probably do them; and hard questions are the ones that you have no idea (at first glance) how to approach.

Now that you've labeled your questions, what are you going to do about them?

## THE THREE-PASS SYSTEM

The three-pass system allows you to squeeze out every possible point you can from the test. Why is it called the three-pass system? Because you will pass through the test three times. As incredible as this may sound, you actually have enough time to do this. What's more, you don't have to finish the test, you just need to score as many points as you possibly can. The three-pass system is supposed to be a tireless quest for points. Here's how it works:

On the first pass, you go through the entire test and answer all of the easy questions; on this pass you skip the medium and hard questions. As you go through the test on your first pass, you mark each question as either easy, medium, or hard. (Use the symbols below or make up your own if you want.)

- Place a check mark next to the easy questions that you've already answered. You're done with them and you can ignore them now.
- Draw a circle around the questions that look like they're only moderately difficult.
- Mark all of the hard questions with a question mark.

How long will the first pass take? Anywhere from one to two hours, depending on how well you know the test material. A word of advice here: Exercise caution on this pass; if you're not sure of the answer, it isn't an easy question.

On your second pass through the test attack the medium questions.

Now, in the time that you have left, do a third pass and revisit the hard questions. Here's where you should apply POE and *guess aggressively wherever you can.* By the end of your third pass, the only questions that should be left unanswered are ones for which you can't eliminate any answer choices.

## More On Being An Aggressive Test-Taker

We already covered general test-taking skills, pacing, guessing, and the process of elimination (POE). Now let's consider a few other tactics for approaching the questions. Luckily, ETS's biology test is not tricky; it's not designed to confuse or mislead you with obvious-looking answers that are wrong. That's good news for you, because it means you can follow your hunches if and when you have them.

Let's look at some ways to put your hunches to good use on the medium and hard questions.

Common sense and POE work hand in hand to win you points.

1. **Use common sense.** Using common sense can get you points you otherwise might have missed. To exercise common sense, you just need to decide which answer choice is reasonable or, before looking at the answer choices, what the logical answer to the question would be. On this test, you'll need to read actively and look for clues.

2. **Which one is not like the other?** Roughly twenty-five questions on your exam will ask you to identify which answer choice does *not* fit a given criterion. These questions have words like EXCEPT, LEAST, or NOT in them. Here's what you'll want to keep in mind about these questions: there are four correct answers and one incorrect one, and the incorrect answer is the one you're looking for. While this sounds very distracting, here's some good news: Built into these questions is something that you can use to your advantage every time.

The four correct answer choices must have something in common. This means that you just need to search for the answer that is different in some way from the others.

3. **Take the gamble.** Let's say that on a hard question, you've already eliminated one answer choice but you don't know which of the four remaining choices you should choose. Can you do anything to increase your odds of answering correctly? Yes. You can resort to this tactic: ETS tends to test concepts that they consider important. That means you should choose an answer choice that mentions something you recognize, or have heard of, over answer choices that concern something you've never seen before.

Now that you've acquired test-taking skills, you're ready to tackle the subject matter of the GRE Biology test. That means conducting a structured review. So let's head into the next section of the book.

# THE SUBJECT REVIEW

## WHAT YOU SHOULD KNOW

ETS has prepared a pretty handy checklist of subjects that are fair game on the Biology test. The data has been divided into the following categories and subcategories. Here's what they say you need to know:

## CELLULAR AND MOLECULAR BIOLOGY (33–34%)

ETS breaks this broad category into two major subdivisions:

1. Cellular Structure and Function (16–17%)
2. Molecular Biology and Molecular Genetics (16–17%)

Under Cellular Structure and Function, they list seven topics they expect you to know about:

I. Biological compounds
   A. Macromolecular structure and bonding
   B. Abiotic origin of macromolecules (origin of life)

II. Enzyme activity, receptor binding, and regulation

III. Major metabolic pathways and regulation
   A. Respiration, fermentation, and photosynthesis
   B. Synthesis and degradation of macromolecules
   C. Hormonal control and intracellular messengers

**If the sight of all these topics seems daunting, take heart: ETS doesn't expect you to know about each topic they list. You only need to know a percentage of the topics they think are important.**

IV. Membrane dynamics and cell surfaces
   A. Transport, endocytosis, and exocytosis
   B. Electrical potentials and transmitter substances
   C. Mechanisms of cell recognition, cell junctions, and plasmodesmata
   D. Cell wall and extracellular matrix

V. Organelles: Structure, function, synthesis, and targeting
   A. Nucleus, mitochondria, and plastids
   B. Endoplasmic reticulum and ribosomes
   C. Golgi apparatus and secretory vesicles
   D. Endosomes, lysosomes, peroxisomes, and vacuoles

**Don't forget to consult Word Watch at the end of the book for a quick review of terms ETS often presents on the exam.**

VI. Cytoskeleton, motility, and shape
   A. Actin-based systems
   B. Microtubule-based systems
   C. Intermediate filaments
   D. Bacterial flagella and movement

VII. Cell cycle
   A. Cell growth, division, and regulation

Under Molecular Biology and Molecular Genetics (16–17%), are listed nine topics that they expect you to know about:

I. Genetic foundations
   A. Mendelian inheritance and pedigree analysis
   B. Prokaryotic genetics (transformation, transduction, and conjugation)
   C. Genetic mapping

II. Chromatin and chromosomes
   A. Nucleosomes
   B. Karyotypes
   C. Chromosomal aberrations
   D. Polytene chromosomes

III. Genome sequence organization
   A. Introns and exons
   B. Single-copy and repetitive DNA
   C. Transposable elements

IV. Genome maintenance
   A. DNA replication
   B. DNA point mutation and repair

V. Gene expression and regulation in prokaryotes and eukaryotes: mechanisms
   A. The operon
   B. Promoters and enhancers
   C. Transcription factors
   D. RNA and protein synthesis
   E. Processing and modifications of both RNA and protein

VI. Gene expression and regulation: Effects
   A. Control of normal development
   B. Cancer and oncogenes

VII. Immunobiology
   A. Cellular basis of immunity
   B. Antibody diversity and synthesis
   C. Antigen-antibody interactions

VIII. Bacteriophages, animal viruses, and plant viruses
   A. Viral genome and assembly

IX. Recombinant DNA methodology
   A. Restriction endonucleases
   B. Blotting and hybridization
   C. Restriction fragment length polymorphisms
   D. DNA cloning, sequencing, and analysis
   E. Polymerase chain reaction

**Note the percentage of questions that ETS states will appear on the test for any one topic. These percentages will help you to gauge how much time you want to devote to reviewing a given topic.**

## Organismal Biology (33–34%)

ETS breaks this broad category into five major subdivisions:

1. Animal structure, function, and organization (9–10%)
2. Animal reproduction and development (5–6%)
3. Plant structure, function, and organization, with emphasis on flowering plants (6–7%)
4. Plant reproduction, growth, and development, with emphasis on flowering plants (4–5%)
5. Diversity of life (6–7%)

Within the broad subject of Animal structure, function, and organization, ETS expects you to be familiar with the following six topics:

I. Exchange with environment
   A. Digestion and nutrition
   B. Uptake and excretion
   C. Gas exchange
   D. Energy

II. Internal transport and exchange (including circulatory and gastrovascular systems)

III. Support and movement
   A. Support systems (external, internal, and hydrostatic)
   B. Movement systems (flagellar, ciliary, and muscular)

IV. Integration and control mechanisms
   A. Nervous and endocrine systems

V. Behavior
   A. Communication, orientation, learning, and instinct

VI. Metabolic rates
   A. Temperature, body size, and activity

Under Animal reproduction and Development are five important topics:

Don't overlook your classroom notes from old biology courses; they can help jump-start your memory as you review.

I. Reproductive structures

II. Meiosis, gametogenesis, and fertilization

III. Early development (including polarity, cleavage, and gastrulation)

IV. Developmental processes (including induction, determination, differentiation, morphogenesis, and metamorphosis)

V. External control mechanisms (including photoperiod)

For Plant structure, function, and organization, you should know about:

I. Tissues, tissue systems, and organs

II. Water transport (including absorption and transpiration)

III. Phloem transport and storage

IV. Mineral nutrition

V. Plant energetics (including respiration and photosynthesis)

For Plant reproduction, growth, and development, you are expected to be familiar with:

I. Reproductive structures

II. Meiosis and sporogenesis

III. Gametogenesis and fertilization

IV. Embryology and seed development

V. Meristems, growth, morphogenesis, and differentiation

VI. Control mechanisms (including hormones, photoperiod, and tropisms)

And finally, under the topic of Diversity of life, you should know something about the following:

I. Monera (archaebacteria and eubacteria, including cyanobacteria)
   A. Morphology, physiology, pathology, and identification (methodology)

II. Protista
   A. Protozoa (Mastigophora, Sarcodina, Ciliophora, and Sporozoa)
      Morphology, locomotion, physiology
   B. Other heterotrophic Protista
      Development of cellular slime molds
      Importance of Oomycota (decomposition, biodegradation, pathogenicity)
   C. Autotrophic Protista (Algae)
      Distinctive features of Chlorophyta, Phaeophyta, Rhodophyta, and Chrysophyta
      Patterns of cell division in Chlorophyta
      Importance (including role in nature and economic uses)

III. Fungi: Distinctive features of Zygomycota, Ascomycota, and Basidiomycota (including vegetative, asexual, and sexual reproduction)
   A. Generalized life cycles
   B. Importance (including decomposition, biodegradation, antibiotics, and pathogenicity)
   C. Lichens

IV. Animalia with emphasis on Porifera, Cnidaria, Platyhelminthes, Nematoda, Mollusca, Annelida, Arthropoda, Echinodermata, and Chordata
   A. Major distinguishing characteristics
   B. Phylogenetic relationships

V. Plantae with emphasis on Bryophyta, Pterophyta, Gymnosperms, and Angiosperms
   A. Alteration of generations
   B. Major distinguishing characteristics
   C. Phylogenetic relationships

**Remember, reviewing a little bit each day is more productive in the long run than a marathon cramming session near test-time.**

## ECOLOGY AND EVOLUTION (33–34%)

ETS breaks this broad category into two major subdivisions:

1. Ecology (16–17%)
2. Evolution (16–17%)

For Ecology, you are expected to be familiar with the following:

I. Environment/organism interaction
   A. Biogeographic patterns
   B. Adaptations to environment
   C. Temporal patterns

II. Behavioral ecology
   A. Habitat selection

B. Mating systems
C. Social systems
D. Resource acquisition

Good luck and best wishes in achieving all of your goals.

III. Population structure and function
A. Population dynamics/regulation
B. Demography and life history strategies

IV. Communities
A. Interspecific relationships
B. Community structure and diversity
C. Change and succession

V. Ecosystems
A. Productivity and energy flow
B. Chemical cycling

For Evolution, you should know about these topics:

I. Genetic variability
A. Origins (mutations, linkage, recombination, and chromosomal alterations)
B. Levels (including polymorphism and heritability)
C. Spatial patterns (including clines and ecotypes)
D. Hardy-Weinberg equilibrium

II. Evolutionary processes
A. Gene flow and genetic drift
B. Natural selection
C. Levels of selection (including individual and group)

III. Evolutionary consequences
A. Fitness and adaptation
B. Speciation
C. Systemics and phylogeny
D. Convergence, divergence, and extinction

## Why Are We Giving You ETS's Checklists?

Because these are the topics ETS will ask you about on the Biology GRE! Use the checklist to mark off the topics you know well, the topics you could use some brushing up on, and the topics you're going to guess aggressively on. Keep in mind that theoretically you can leave up to 32 questions blank and still hit the 99th percentile.

# PART II

# Cell and Molecular Biology

# 1

# Remember Organic Chemistry?

Organic chemistry is the chemistry of organic molecules, which are molecules that contain carbon and hydrogen atoms. In this chapter, we'll talk about some biologically important organic compounds that you should know for the test. We'll discuss sugars and carbohydrates and we'll talk about a variety of lipids and their significance to biological systems. What about proteins, you may ask? We wouldn't dream of leaving them out. We'll refresh your memory on generic amino acid structure, the significance of side chains, and peptide bonds.

Let's begin with sugars and carbohydrates.

## MONOSACCHARIDES—THE SUGAR UNIT

It's best not to talk of sugars but, rather, of *sugar units*. A single sugar unit is called a *monosaccharide*, and monosaccharides have the generic formula $C_nH_{2n}O_n$. Glucose, for example, is a monosaccharide and its formula is $C_6H_{12}O_6$.

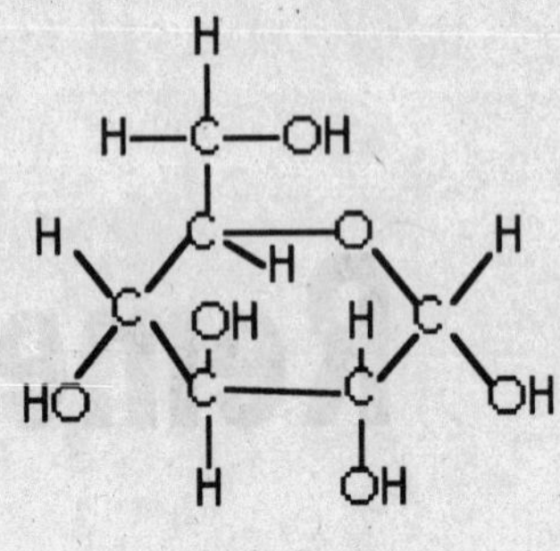

Glucose

Fructose and galactose are monosaccharides as well, and they also have the formula $C_6H_{12}O_6$. This means that fructose, glucose, and galactose are isomers.

### Remember Isomers?

The word *isomers* refers to two or more molecules that have the same molecular formula but differ in the geometric arrangement of their constituent atoms. For example, although fructose, galactose, and glucose have identical molecular formulas, they differ in the ways that their carbon, hydrogen, and oxygen atoms are situated within the molecule.

**Our bodies are programmed to break down right-handed sugar molecules. Left-handed sugars, on the other hand, throw our physiology a curve ball: because our bodies are not used to this isomer, they're unable to process them through the usual channels. As a result, calories from left-handed sugars are not absorbed.**

## WE'VE TALKED ABOUT MONOSACCHARIDES: LET'S TALK ABOUT DISACCHARIDES AND POLYSACCHARIDES

*Disaccharides* arise when two monosaccharides are joined by a glycosidic bond. When two monosaccharide units (sometimes called subunits) join to form a glycosidic bond, one water molecule is given off. This means that two hydrogen atoms and one oxygen atom have been lost, which makes the general formula for a disaccharide $C_nH_{2n-2}O_{n-1}$. Maltose, lactose, and sucrose are all examples of disaccharides.

- Maltose is formed from two glucose subunits.
- Lactose is formed from one galactose subunit and one glucose subunit.
- Sucrose is made up of fructose and glucose.

*Polysaccharides* are molecules that are composed of three or more monosaccharides. Among the biologically important polysaccharides are starch, glycogen, and cellulose. All three represent long, branched chains of glucose, but they differ in the way in which their glucose subunits are linked and branched. Recall that starch is associated primarily with alpha-1,4 linkages, glycogen is associated with poly-alpha-1,4 glucoside linkages, and cellulose is associated with 1,4 linked beta-glucoside chains.

## Now, What's a Carbohydrate?

The monosaccharides, disaccharides, and polysaccharides just discussed sometimes carry the generic name of *sugars*, which is a relatively nonspecific term. This inspires the following questions: (1) What's a carbohydrate? and (2) What's the difference between a carbohydrate and a sugar?

A *carbohydrate* is composed only of carbon, hydrogen, oxygen. So you can probably guess that all of the molecules we have discussed so far (glucose, fructose, galactose, lactose, maltose, and sucrose) are carbohydrates. By convention, the relatively small carbohydrate molecules are called sugars and the relatively large ones are called carbohydrates. There are some exceptions that that you should be aware of; for example, although glucose is a carbohydrate, it is popularly called a sugar. At this point, this is the only bizarre convention that you need to know, but you are mostly likely already aware that in biology and chemistry there are *always* exceptions.

## How Are Polysaccharides Made and Broken Down? By Dehydration Synthesis and Hydrolysis

Maltose is basically two glucose molecules joined by a glycosidic bond. Well, you have just learned that when the bond is formed, one glucose gives up an $OH^-$ group and the other loses an $H^+$ ion, and that the $OH^-$ and $H^+$ combine to form water. The disaccharide sucrose is also formed by dehydration synthesis; sucrose is just glucose and fructose joined by a glycosidic bond.

So you know how disaccharides are formed: Now let's talk now about how they're degraded. To break a glycosidic bond, a molecule of water must be added to the system in a process that's called *hydrolysis*. An $OH^-$ group is added to one subunit of the disaccharide and an $H^+$ ion is added to the other subunit, which yields two separate monosaccharide subunits.

# WHAT, EXACTLY, IS A LIPID?

*Lipids*, like carbohydrates, are molecules that are composed of carbon, hydrogen, and oxygen. One thing that makes lipids and carbohydrates different, however, is that in carbohydrates, the hydrogen to oxygen ratio is 2:1 while in lipids there are more than two hydrogens for each constituent oxygen. One type of lipid, a triglyceride, is pictured below. A *triglyceride* is made up of three fatty acids and a glycerol molecule.

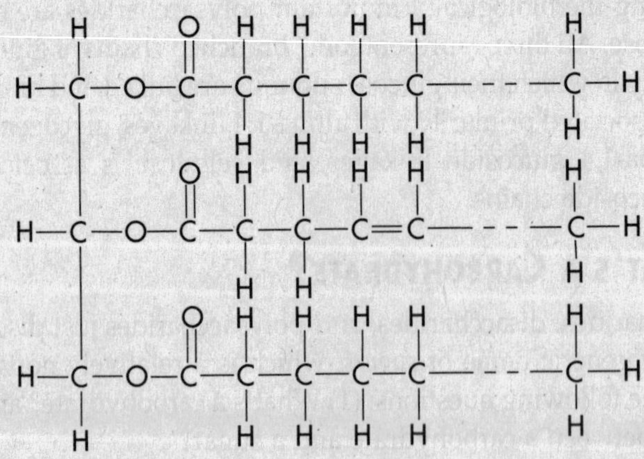

A Triglyceride

Like most things, cholesterol has its good and its bad side. Its good qualities are that it is an essential component of our plasma membranes, where it helps to regulate membrane fluidity. It's also a precursor structure for vitamin D, steroids, and bile acids. Its bad quality is what tends to get all the press, however: Too much of it clogs our arteries, impeding blood flow.

Lipids are a biologically important class of compounds that includes fats, oils, waxes, and cholesterol. Two important functions of lipids are (1) their roles as components of plasma membranes (discussed in chapter 2), and (2) their ability to store energy for cells.

## ABOUT AMINO ACIDS

So far, we've looked at molecules that are made up of only carbon, hydrogen, and oxygen. Now let's look at a compound that contains nitrogen as well. One class of compounds that contains C, H, O, and N is amino acids—as you may recall, amino acids are the building blocks of proteins.

### THERE'S SUCH A THING AS A PROTOTYPICAL AMINO ACID

The general form of an amino acid is depicted below. As you can see, all amino acids contain an amino group ($NH_2$), a carboxyl group (COOH), and a side chain which is represented below by the letter R. These groups are attached to a central carbon.

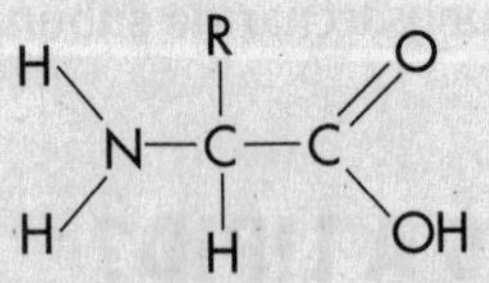

A Generic Amino Acid

### WHAT IS THE SIGNIFICANCE OF THE SIDE CHAINS?

Any one of twenty different R groups may be found on an amino acid. This means that twenty different types of amino acids exist; the structure of the side chain of each of the twenty amino acids is different. Some side chains are nonpolar (i.e., glutamine and serine) while others are polar (i.e., asparagine and threonine). Some amino acid side chains are acidic (i.e., aspartic acid and glutamic acid) while others are basic (i.e., histidine and lysine).

In many cases, the side chains of amino acids bear a charge; this charge is determined by the relative acidity or alkalinity of the amino acid's environment. Amino acids in acidic environments tend to retain and/or gain protons (hydrogens), while amino acids in basic environments tend to lose their protons. At physiologic pH (7.4—pretty close to neutral), the carboxyl group takes the form $COO^-$ and the amine group takes the form $NH_3^+$.

The amine and carboxyl groups do not interact with other charged atoms in molecules, which means that attractions and repulsions between the side groups of amino acids are what determine a protein's folding pattern.

## On Zwitterions and Isoelectric Points

When you think of amino acids, two important terms to know for the GRE are *zwitterion* and *isoelectric point*. A zwitterion is a dipolar molecule that has both a distinct negative and positive charge among its constituents. An amino acid that is in its isoelectric form, or is a zwitterion, is dipolar at that moment in time (it bears both a distinct positive and negative charge). A particular amino acid's isoelectric point is the pH (often determined by titration) at which it has both a positive and negative charge, which cancel each other out to make it electrically neutral.

## The Peptide Bond

"Get your facts first, and then you can distort them as much as you please."
—Mark Twain

Now that we know something about amino acid structure, let's see how individual amino acids are joined to one another to form a linear sequence. The bonds that join amino acids are called *peptide bonds*. Peptide bonds occur between the carboxyl group (–COOH) of one amino acid and the amine group ($-NH_2$) of another.

Peptide bonds are created via the same process that produces glycosidic bonds (dehydration synthesis). Here dehydration yields dipeptides, which are just two amino acids hooked together, and polypeptides, which are composed of many amino acids. And, just as we saw in the degradation of disaccharides and polysaccharides into monosaccharides, hydrolysis is the process that breaks peptide bonds.

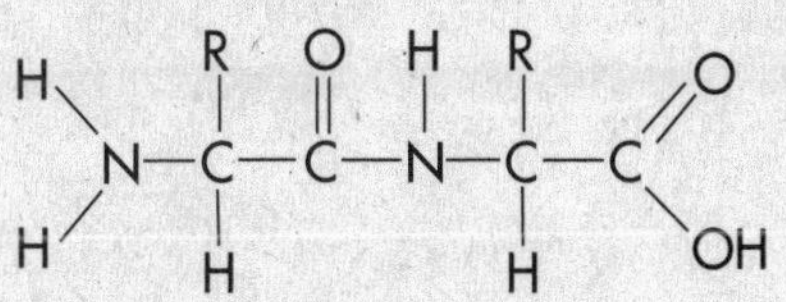

A Dipeptide

## UP TO FOUR SUBSTRUCTURES UNDERLIE A PROTEIN'S THREE-DIMENSIONAL SHAPE

Amino acids join to form polypeptides, which themselves fold to form protein. Each polypeptide has its own distinctive primary, secondary, and tertiary structure; if it interacts with one or more other polypeptides, it has a quaternary structure. The *primary structure* of a protein is just its sequence of amino acids (called residues). The *secondary structure* of a polypeptide refers to the pattern of its folds; two common types of folding patterns are alpha-helix and beta-pleated sheets, which describe the shape of the polypeptide backbone (the parts of the polypeptide that do not include the side chains). *Tertiary structure* refers to a protein's shape, which is determined by interactions between the side chains of the distinct amino acids that make up the polypeptide. Side chain interactions include hydrophobic and ionic interactions, hydrogen bonds, covalent cross-links, and disulfide bridges. Two common types of tertiary structure are globular (seen in hemoglobin) and fibrous (seen in collagen).

**What's the difference between cysteine and cystine? Cysteine is an amino acid containing the thiol group—SH. Cystine is the structure formed when two cysteine molecules form a disulfide bridge. The disulfide bridge is part of the tertiary structure of the protein.**

*Quaternary structures* exist in proteins that contain more than one polypeptide chain. A protein's quarternary structure depends on how the different polypeptide chains interact with one another to form the complete, three-dimensional structure of the protein.

# 2

# The Eukaryotic Cell

A *eukaryotic cell* has a nucleus that is bound by a membrane, and contains a number of organelles, for example the endoplasmic reticulum, the Golgi apparatus, mitochondria, and many others that you are already familiar with. Eukaryotic cells are different from *prokaryotic cells,* which are more primitive in design and lack specialized structures. In this chapter, we'll focus on the eukaryotic cell. We'll talk about the plasma membrane, which is actually a phospholipid bilayer, and how substances move across this membrane through endo- and exocytosis. We'll review the functions of specific organelles of eukaryotic cells in general, and then we'll take a look at some features that are unique to eukaryotic plant cells. We'll finish by reviewing the differences between eukaryotic and prokaryotic cells. So let's begin.

## REMEMBER THE PLASMA MEMBRANE?

In eukaryotes, the *plasma membrane* is made up of a *phospholipid bilayer* and embedded proteins. According to the *fluid mosaic model* of the plasma membrane, proteins are positioned within the bilayer in three different ways: (1) *peripheral proteins* are located at inner or outer surfaces of the phospholipid bilayer, (2) *transmembrane proteins* span the membrane, and (3) *integral proteins* are enclosed entirely within the membrane.

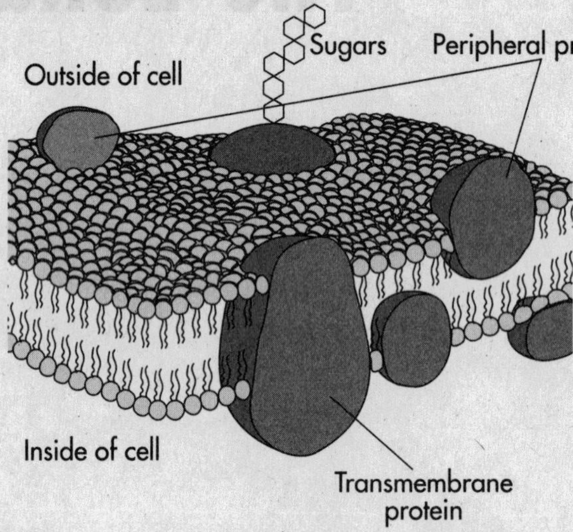


The two different properties of a phospholipid—hydrophobic and hydrophilic—make them amphipathic molecules [amphi = two-sided; pathic = feeling].

Let's take a closer look at the phospholipid bilayer. Phospholipids contain two fatty acid chains linked to two of the three carbons of a glycerol molecule. The glycerol heads of the phospholipids that make up the bilayer are *hydrophilic* (water-soluble), and the fatty acid chains (the tails) are *hydrophobic* (water-insoluble). Consequently, the phospholipids arrange themselves in such a way that in one of the layers of the bilayer their hydrophilic ends point toward the extracellular environment, and in the other layer these heads point toward the cytoplasm. This way, their hydrophobic tails point in, and are not forced to interact with an aqueous environment.

The phospholipid bilayer mediates movement of substances into and out of the cell. Let's talk about that.

## Transport Across the Cell Membrane

Materials pass through the cell membrane by either *passive* or *active transport.* Passive transport refers to the movement of a substance across the membrane in either direction according to a gradient of its concentration or according to its molecular charge. In this case, because net movement is determined by an existing electrochemical gradient, passive transport requires no energy. It does require, however, that the membrane be permeable to the molecule trying to cross it. Active transport, on the other hand, does require energy. It involves movement against an existing electrochemical gradient. Let's review passive and active transport in more detail.

### Forms of Passive Transport

To begin with, passive transport only takes place through *semi-permeable membranes* (also called selectively permeable membranes). A semi-permeable membrane is permeable to some substances and not to others. Passive transport can mean diffusion, osmosis, or facilitated transport.

**Simple diffusion, osmosis, and facilitated transport are all forms of passive transport.**

In *diffusion,* a small, lipid-soluble molecule passes directly through the lipid bilayer.

*Osmosis* is the diffusion of water (or another solvent) down its concentration gradient. The direction in which water will flow through a semi-permeable membrane depends on a cell's *tonicity.* A cell can be hypertonic, hypotonic, or isotonic. A cell is *hypertonic* if the solution inside it is more concentrated than its environment. A cell is *hypotonic* if the solution inside it is less concentrated than its environment. A cell is *isotonic* if the solution inside it is of equal concentration to that of its environment.

Hypertonicity and hypotonicity create something called *osmotic pressure.* If a cell is hypertonic, it tends to draw water inward in order to equalize the concentration on each side of the membrane. If a cell is hypotonic it tends to lose water, also in an effort to equalize concentrations across the membrane. When we refer to those tendencies, we use the phrase *osmotic pressure.* In a hypertonic cell, osmotic pressure draws water inward. In a hypotonic cell, osmotic pressure pushes water outward. In an isotonic cell, osmotic pressure is zero.

Both of the forms of passive transport that we've discussed thus far (diffusion and osmosis) move material through the cell membrane without any assistance. Now let's consider *facilitated diffusion,* which is a form of passive transport that involves proteins embedded in the cell membrane (remember, they're called transmembrane proteins). In facilitated diffusion, a *carrier molecule* (protein) assists a substance's movement across the plasma membrane. Here's how it works: A lipid-insoluble molecule seeking passage through the membrane hooks up with a carrier protein. The resulting complex—the carrier protein and the lipid-insoluble substance—is lipid-soluble. It crosses the lipid bilayer according to an existing electrochemical gradient. Once the complex traverses the membrane, the carrier protein disengages from the original lipid-insoluble molecule.

One thing to keep in mind here is that *facilitated diffusion can only occur down a concentration gradient.* Facilitated diffusion, like other forms of membrane transport, may occur in either direction; lipid-insoluble material may pass from the external environment into cell or from cell out to its environment.

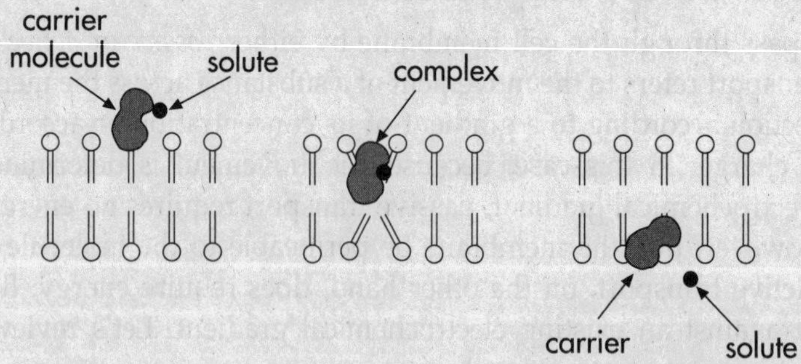


You might at first think that passive transport embodies the best of all possible worlds, because a substance moves through the cell membrane without the input of energy in a direction that's determined by the natural laws of the universe. But because the cell must perform special functions in order to exist and do its job, it oftentimes needs to incorporate atoms and molecules that are not provided through the process of diffusion. In other words, the cell requires another form of transport across its membrane; that process is not gradient-dependent and requires the input of energy.

## Active Transport

As we said earlier, active transport requires energy. That's because it moves substances against an electrochemical gradient. The cell obtains its energy for active transport by hydrolyzing adenosine triphosphate (ATP). The bond that connects the third phosphate group to adenosine diphosphate is a high-energy bond; when it is hydrolyzed (broken via the addition of a water molecule), the energy is released. The cell then uses that energy to transport a substance across the membrane against the substance's concentration gradient. Let's illustrate the point by examining the *sodium-potassium pump.*

The sodium-potassium pump is a transmembrane protein that sets up and maintains an artificial concentration gradient of sodium and potassium across the cell membrane. Its job is to move sodium outward and potassium inward. It moves three sodium ions out of the cell for every two potassium ions that it brings in. Because this arrangement runs counter to a natural tendency to equalize the ions' concentrations across the membrane, the pump requires energy. That energy, as we mentioned, is supplied by the hydrolysis of ATP.

**An ingenious example of cotransport occurs in the small intestine. Here, glucose and amino acids in the lumen get absorbed into cells by hitching a ride on the same carrier molecule that enables sodium to enter the cell. Because sodium is moving *down* its electrochemical gradient, the glucose may enter the cell *against* its concentration gradient without costing the cell any energy.**

The sodium-potassium pump is one example of a process called *coupled transport.* Coupled transport refers to processes in which the transmembrane movement of one substance, molecule, or ion is linked to the simultaneous movement of another. Coupled transport may take the forms of *uniport*, *symport*, and *antiport*. In antiport, one substance travels in one direction, and the substance that is moved concurrently travels in the opposite direction. Conversely, symport and uniport describe coupled transport processes where both substances proceed in the same direction. Which type of coupled transport is the sodium-potassium pump an example of? Antiport.

We've talked about passive and active transport across the plasma membrane. What these two forms have in common is the direct movement of molecules through the lipid bilayer. Now let's take a look at two more methods by which the cell transports material back and forth across its membrane.

## Endocytosis and Exocytosis

*Endocytosis* is the process by which a cell brings relatively large substances into the cell. A small section of the cell membrane begins to surround the target material, which is sitting on the surface of the membrane. The membrane continues to invaginate under and around the particle until it is completely surrounded. The particle is then located at the interior face of the cell, within a vesicle which is actually an old piece of the cell membrane. There are two types of endocytosis: *pinocytosis* and *phagocytosis*. Pinocytosis describes the process in which liquids and small particles are brought into the cell, while phagocytosis is what occurs when larger material, such as bacteria, must be accepted into the cell.

**Endosomes are intermediate vesicles involved in endocytosis. They appear to relay the endocytosed material from the original endocytic vesicles to lysosomes.**

### Focus on Clathrin-Coated Pits

There is also a transport process called *receptor-mediated endocytosis* that involves the use of protein receptors located on the surface of the plasma membrane. The substance to be brought into the cell (usually large complexes such as proteins) attaches to a receptor on the cell surface, which is located in what is called a coated pit. Coated pits are concave patches on the cell membrane that are coated with the protein *clathrin.* After a certain concentration of the substance has bound to the receptors in the pit, the membrane invaginates and then pinches off to become a coated vesicle. This is how, for example, a cell takes up cholesterol, which is complexed with LDL (low density lipoprotein).

So much for endocytosis. What about *exocytosis*? Suppose a cell wants to get rid of some material. The cell puts it in a vesicle and sends it to the plasma membrane. The vesicle fuses with the plasma membrane and its contents are expelled.

So far we've been talking only about movement in and out of a single cell. Now let's talk about how material moves from one cell to another. Specialized features of the cell membrane help to anchor a cell to its neighbors and regulate commerce across adjacent cell membranes.

## Cellular Adhesions

*Cellular adhesions* are points of attachment between abutting cell membranes. They allow adjoining cells to function as one cohesive unit. (Cellular adhesions are particularly valuable in epithelial cell sheets.) Three important animal cell adhesions to know about for the GRE are *tight junctions*, *gap junctions*, and *desmosomes*. Each type of adhesion has different characteristics and a different function. Tight junctions are regions in which there is absolutely no space in-between adjacent cells; they are basically connections between adjacent cells which molecules and ions can't pass through. Gap junctions are basically pores that connect adjacent cells; these pores are formed by a clusters of six molecules embedded in the membrane and arranged in circles, and the movement of these six molecules is what opens and closes the pores. Small molecules and ions can pass through gap junctions, and they permit electrical and molecular communication between adjacent cells. Desmosomes are spaces where adjacent cells are connected by thin filaments of glycoproteins. They are the most commonly seen type of cell junction, and they allow for some electrical and molecular communication between cells.

The cell membrane, with its specialized adhesions, constitutes one cellular organelle. Now it's time to review all of the other cellular organelles of eukaryotes.

## Eukaryotic Cell Organelles

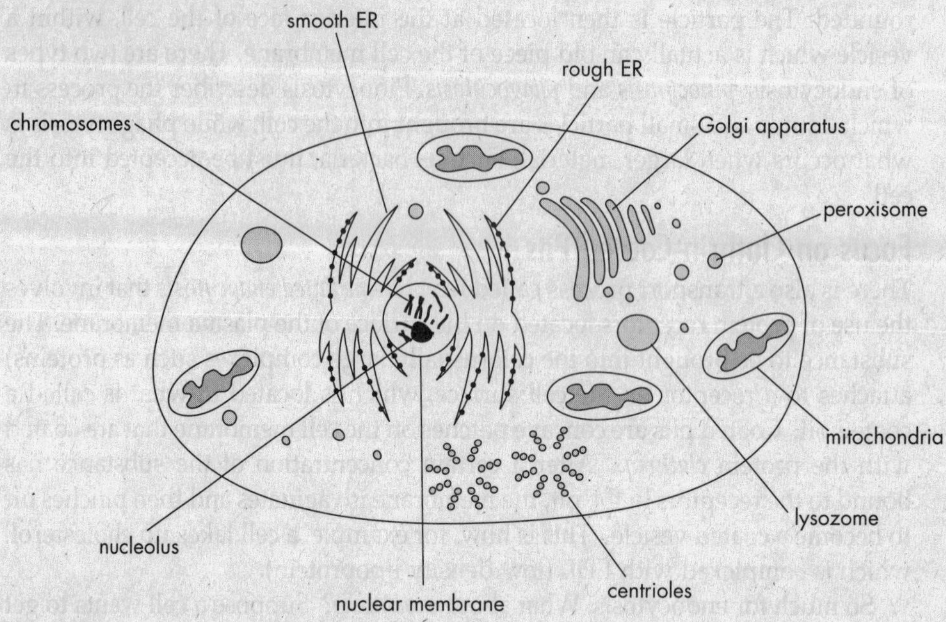


### The Nucleus and Its Contents

The nucleus of the eukaryotic cell is surrounded by a nuclear envelope and contains the cell's chromosomes as well as a large spherical structure called the nucleolus. *Chromosomes* are made up of *DNA (deoxyribonucleic acid)* and proteins, and you may recall that the full set of chromosomes is called the genome. The genomes of organisms vary widely in breadth (and complexity!) for example, the human genome is parceled out into 23 sets of chromosomes, while a prokaryote's entire genome is represented by a single chromosome. The other important structure in the nucleus, the nucleolus, plays a role in the manufacturing of ribosomal RNA (ribonucleic acid), which is integral in the synthesis of protein.

## The Membrane Systems

**In hepatocytes, or liver cells, smooth ER contains enzymes that act to detoxify drugs and harmful metabolic byproducts. One such enzyme is cytochrome P450.**

Membrane systems of the cell include *the plasma membrane, the endoplasmic reticulum, the nuclear membrane,* and the *Golgi apparatus*. The endoplasmic reticulum (ER) is a series of interconnected membranes found throughout the cytoplasm. *Rough ER* is endoplasmic reticulum that is covered in ribosomes, and since ribosomes are used as positioning elements in protein synthesis, rough ER serves as a site of protein synthesis. *Smooth ER* doesn't serve as a site of protein synthesis, since it does not have ribosomes associated with it.

Closely associated with the endoplasmic reticulum is the Golgi apparatus, which is made up of flattened membranes. Recall that the Golgi has a *cis* and a *trans* face to it. The *cis* side of the Golgi apparatus faces the ER; the *trans* side is oriented towards the plasma membrane. The Golgi apparatus processes the proteins that were produced on the rough ER and packages them into membrane vesicles either for storage or secretion. Once the proteins pass through the Golgi, they are enclosed in vesicles that bud off of the trans face of the Golgi. The vesicles fuse with the plasma membrane and are released into the extracellular space.

## Some Other Organelles

*Peroxisomes* are small, membrane-enclosed structures that contain catalases, which are enzymes that break down hydrogen peroxide into oxygen and water. *Lysosomes* are also membrane bound structures, they possess hydrolytic enzymes that digest foreign particles and worn-out organelles that are no longer needed by the cell. *Vacuoles* are spaces in the cytoplasm; they store fluid and wastes. (The vacuoles in plant cells are generally much larger than the ones in animal cells and are primarily used for the maintenance of water balance.) *Mitochondria* are double-membraned organelles present only in eukaryotic cells. They have an outer membrane that is relatively smooth and an inner membrane that is extensively folded. The folds in the inner membrane are called cristae, and the synthesis of ATP (adenosine triphosphate) occurs within the folds of the cristae. The space inside the inner membrane is called the matrix of the mitochondria, and the space between the inner and outer membranes is, not surprisingly, called the intermembrane space. Also, when you think of the mitochondria, there are two important biochemical process that should immediately come to mind. They are the citric acid cycle and oxidative phosphorylation.

### Focus on Cilia and Flagella

*Cilia* and *flagella* are both thin, hairlike structures that extend from the cell membrane of some eukaryotic cells and produce movement. Cilia and flagella have two general functions. For cells that are not mobile, meaning that they're anchored in one place for their whole lives, ciliary motion is used to push fluids across their membranes. Cells that are mobile use cilia and flagella to propel them throughout their fluid medium.

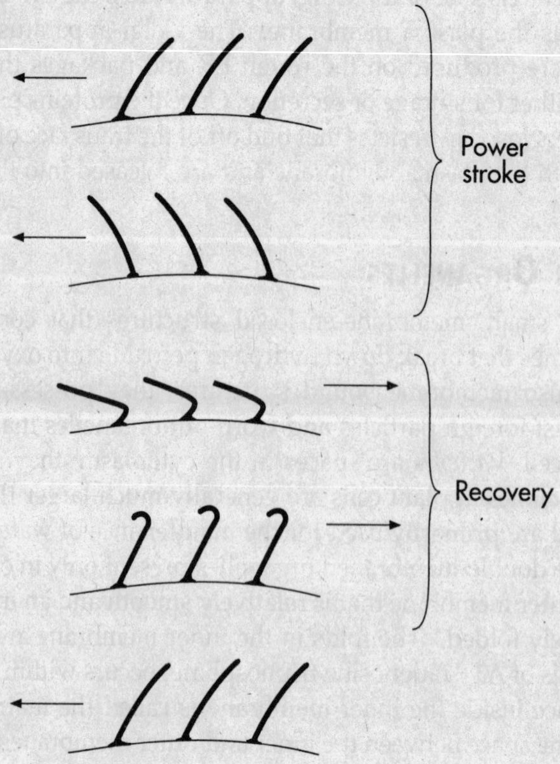


Unlike cilia, which occur in large numbers when they are present, flagella occur singly as long, hair-like structures. Flagella move in whiplike patterns which propel a cell or organism forward. Sperm cells, for instance, each contain a single flagella which enables them to propel themselves through the fluid towards the ovum.

Microtubules spontaneously self-assemble (polymerize) from tubulin subunits. The GRE Biology test writers also like to test you on this: If you add some colchicine, the microtubules quickly depolymerize. If you then remove the colchicine, they'll repolymerize.

Cilia and flagella both contain a regular backbone of linked microfilaments called an axoneme. The linked microtubules that make up the axoneme are arranged in what is commonly called the *9 + 2 arrangement.* This 9 + 2 arrangement is a pattern of nine doublet microtubules arranged in a circle around a pair of central microtubules. A cross-section of the axoneme serves to elucidate this. The two central microtubules each contain 13 globular subunits, while the doublets can each be thought of as two microtubules joined together; one of these microtubules has the complete set of 13 globular subunits while the other has only 10 or 11, because it shares a length of the first microtubule. The central microtubules are surrounded by a central sheath, and the 9 doublets are connected to each other by what are called nexin links—the protein that is most important in holding the microtubules together is called dyenin. *How does a cell grow a flagellum or cilia spontaneously?* you might ask at this point. Well, at the base of each cilia and flagellum is what's called a basal body, which is a cylindrical structure made up of nine sets of triplet microtubules that are arranged in a circle. (It has no central microtubules!) The basal body is what the cilia and flagellum arise from. We won't get into this rather complicated process here, but if you're curious about it, go back to your textbook.

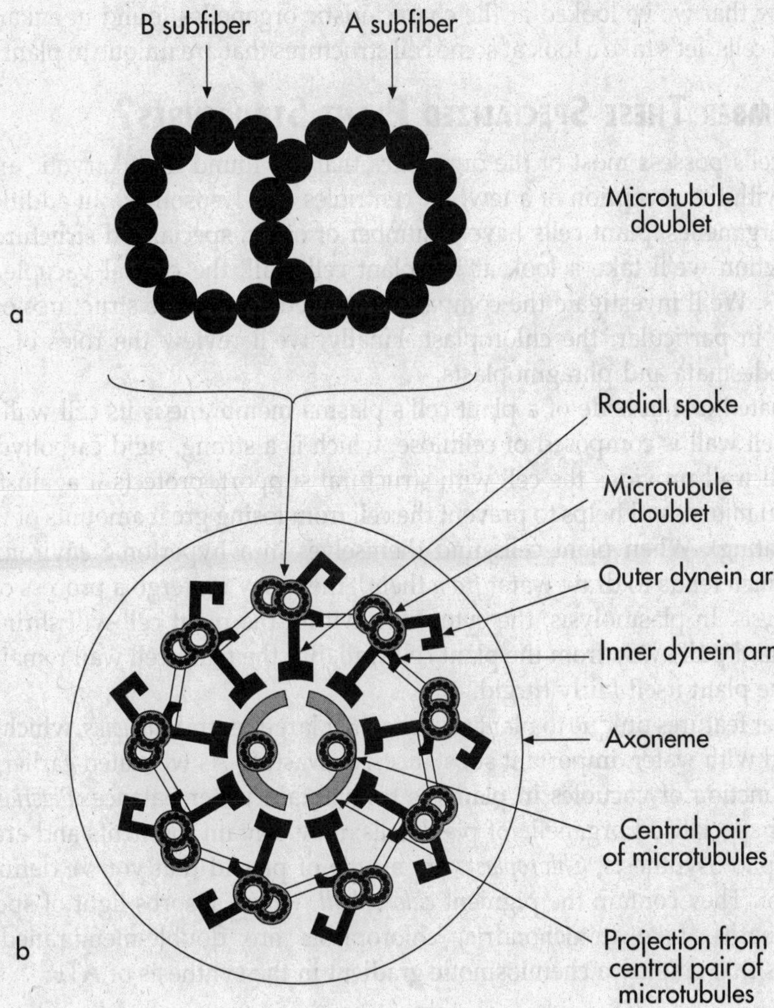


Now that we've tackled the role of microtubules in cilia and flagella, let's consider where else they show up in a cell. For starters, they form the centrioles, which help to create the mitotic spindle during cell division. They also show up as components of the cell's cytoskeleton.

## Cytoskeletal Components

The cell's cytoskeleton serves as its framework. This framework has two primary functions, the first is to act as the skeleton and primary organizer of the cell, and the second is to make the movement of substances inside the cell possible, as well as make it possible for the cell itself to move. The cytoskeleton is composed mainly of microtubules, microfilaments, and intermediate filaments. Microtubules help to confer some structure and rigidity to the cell, and as you saw, are important in cell locomotion. Microfilaments, which are composed of actin subunits, play an important role in muscle contraction. Intermediate filaments are often found in areas of mechanical stress in a cell, they are more involved in internal scaffolding than the other two cytoskeletal components.

(1) Skeleton

(2) Movement Substances

Now that we've looked at the characteristic organelles found in eukaryotic animal cells, let's take a look at some cell structures that are unique to plant cells.

## Remember These Specialized Plant Structures?

Plant cells possess most of the organelles that are found in eukaryotic animal cells (with the exception of a few, i.e. centrioles and lysosomes). In addition to these organelles, plant cells have a number of other, specialized structures. In this section we'll take a look at the plant cell wall, the central vacuole, and plastids. We'll investigate the compartmentalized membrane structures of one plastid in particular: the chloroplast. Finally, we'll review the roles of plant plasmodesmata and phragmoplasts.

**The plant cell wall helps to create turgor in a plant cell. Turgor is internal hydrostatic pressure that a plant cell exerts outwards against its rigid cell wall.**

Situated just outside of a plant cell's plasma membrane is its cell wall. The plant cell wall is composed of cellulose, which is a strong, rigid carbohydrate. The cell wall provides the cell with structural support, protects it against mechanical injury, and helps to prevent the cell from losing great amounts of water (dessicating). When plant cells find themselves in a hypertonic environment (one which tends to draw water *from* them), they may undergo a process called *plasmolysis*. In plasmolysis, the cytoplasm within the plant cell will shrink inwards and pull away from the plant cell wall. But the plant cell wall remains to keep the plant itself fairly turgid.

Other features unique to plant cells are their large central *vacuoles*, which may be filled with water, important substances, or wastes. As we stated earlier, one main function of vacuoles in plants is to maintain water balance. *Plastids* are another specialized organelle of plant cells; they contain pigments and are the site of photosynthesis. *Chloroplasts* are a type of plastid that you've definitely heard of. They contain the pigment *chlorophyll*, which absorbs light of specific wavelengths. Like mitochondria, chloroplasts are double-membraned organelles that employ a chemiosmotic gradient in the synthesis of ATP.

### Let's Take a Look at a Single Chloroplast

The chloroplast is full of membranes, and you'll need to keep in mind which membrane belongs to which compartment of the organelle. If we were to examine a chloroplast starting from its exterior and progressing to its interior, we could recognize three distinct membrane systems: the *outer membrane*, the *inner membrane*, and the *thylakoid membranes*. As with the mitochondria, the space between the outer and inner membrane of a chloroplast is called the intermembrane space. Inside the inner membrane of the chloroplast is a space called the *stroma*, which is roughly equivalent to the matrix of the mitochondria. Throughout the chloroplast's stroma are stacks of membranes that are connected to one another by thin membranous extensions. The membrane stacks are called *grana*. The membranes that make up these stacks and their connective extensions are called thylakoid membranes. It is on the thylakoid membrane that light energy gets converted into ATP and NADH. (The ATP and NADH are then used to fuel the synthesis of carbohydrates.) Inside the thylakoid membranes is the thylakoid space.

Just as animal cells possess cellular adhesions to allow or prevent communication with neighboring cells, the cells of higher plants possess *plasmodesmata* (the singular is plasmodesma). These are small cytoplasmic channels that cut through the plant cell wall and are continuous with adjacent cell walls. As a result, the cytoplasm of one plant cell is continuous with the cytoplasm of the next plant cell.

**When you see the word "Plasmodesmata," think: "Plant cellular adhesions that permit communication."**

Another term that specifically relates to plant cells is *phragmoplast*. What the heck is that? Well, it so happens that during cytokinesis (cytoplasmic division), a cell plate usually forms between the two daughter cells. The cell plate forms from sections of microtubules called phragmoplasts.

Now that we've highlighted the prominent features of eukaryotic animal and plant cells, let's review the ways in which eukaryotic cells differ from prokaryotic cells. The following box lists some comparisons to keep in mind for the GRE.

**Focus on Eukaryotes vs. Prokaryotes**

Eukaryotes have a "true nucleus," which is surrounded by a nuclear envelope. Prokaryotes don't have a separation of nucleus and cytoplasm. They don't have a nucleolus, either, although of course they do have genetic material.

Eukaryotes have comparatively larger genomes, which are parceled out into more than one linear chromosome. Prokaryotes have a comparatively smaller genome, which is contained in a single, circular chromosome. What's more, prokaryotes' genes usually don't feature introns (which are noncoding regions of DNA within a strand).

Eukaryotes have chromosomes that are made of DNA and proteins (including histones). Prokaryotes' single chromosome is composed of DNA only and has no associated proteins.

Eukaryotes have numerous membrane-bound organelles situated within their cytoplasm, such as the ER, Golgi, mitochondria, plastids, vacuoles, lysosomes, and peroxisomes. They also contain other specialized organelles, for example, centrioles, microtubules, and microfilaments. Prokaryotes do not have any of these organelles.

Of the eukaryotes, only plant cells have cell walls, and these are made of cellulose. Most prokaryotes, on the other hand, have cell walls, and these are made not of cellulose but of peptidoglycan.

# 3

# Cellular Energetics

Hundreds of metabolic reactions are continually taking place in living cells. These reactions are catalyzed by a special class of proteins called enzymes. In this chapter, we will review the important characteristics of enzymes and discuss the conditions under which they function. We'll explore an enzyme-related phenomenon called saturation kinetics and review the relationship between the Michaelis-Menten equation and saturation kinetics. We'll then tackle some methods by which enzymes themselves are regulated. Our discussion will include feedback inhibition as well as reversible and irreversible inhibition.

Next we will discuss the ways in which the cell obtains the energy it needs to carry out all of its activities. To this effect, we'll review aerobic and anaerobic respiration. We'll begin with glycolysis, then move on to the citric acid cycle, the electron transport chain, and oxidative phosphorylation. We'll wrap up this chapter with a review of fermentation; a strictly anaerobic form of cellular respiration.

## About Enzymatic Reactions

*Enzymes* are catalysts: they speed up reactions but aren't consumed by them. This means that enzymes can be recycled. Enzymes can only influence the speed with which a reaction can occur; they can't initiate a reaction that would not normally occur.

**"Time is nature's way of keeping everything from happening at once." —Unknown**

The names of enzymes usually end in "-ase" (as in phosphofructokinase, an enzyme which is integral to the process of glycolysis). Some enzymes work with cofactors, which are inorganic substances like metal ions. Others work with coenzymes, which are organic substances; vitamins are one example of a group of coenzymes.

### Keep These Important Enzyme Characteristics in Mind:

Enzymes DO:

- increase the rate of a reaction by lowering the reaction's activation energy
- provide an alternate reaction pathway
- remain unaffected by the reaction

Enzymes DON'T:

- alter the direction of a reaction
- alter the final concentrations of the products
- allow a reaction to happen that otherwise would never have happened

Enzymes are of extreme importance to cells, which rely on them for metabolic, anabolic, and other processes. The first step in the function of enzymes is the formation of the enzyme-substrate complex.

## The Enzyme-Substrate Complex

The name says it all. The *enzyme-substrate complex* is a temporary structure formed by the enzyme and the reactants of the reaction, which are called substrates.

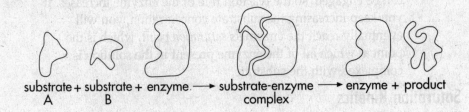

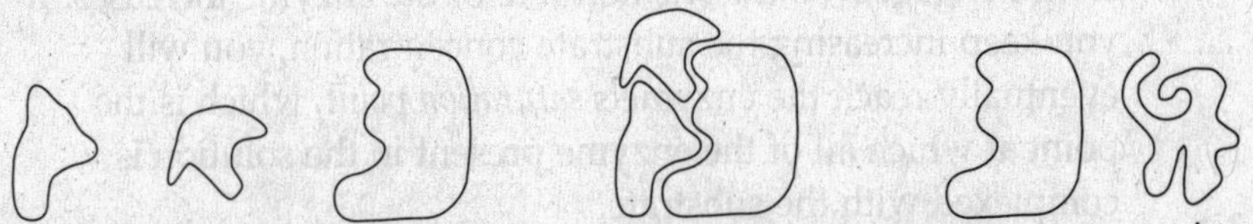


An enzyme binds with a substrate at what's known as the enzyme's active site. Enzymes are highly specific in their function; the three-dimensional shape of an enzyme's active site is customized for a specific substrate. This prevents other substrates which are associated with other reactions from binding to the enzyme. The specificity of structure and function of enzymes with relation to substrate is called the *lock and key theory*. In some cases, instead of simply binding to the active site in the enzyme, the substrate induces a structural change in the enzyme which then encases the substrate in its new shape; this is called *induced fit*. In both cases, the close proximity of the substrate and enzyme initiates the reaction between them, and when the enzyme-substrate complex dissociates, the reaction has taken place; the original substrates no longer exist and a product has formed. The equation for an enzyme-catalyzed reaction looks like this:

$$E + S \leftrightarrow E{:::}S \rightarrow E + P$$

where E = enzyme, S = substrate, E:::S = the enzyme-substrate complex, and P = product.

**Keep in mind that a denatured enzyme still retains its primary structure, that is, its original sequence of amino acids residues connected by peptide bonds.**

When an enzyme is broken down, or denatured (this can occur through chemical means or because of a temperature increase), it can no longer fit with its substrate because of its altered shape.

Not only are enzymes very particular about substrate fit, they're also very particular about their working conditions.

## Enzymatic Working Conditions Must Range from Good to Very Good

Enzymes are only able to function effectively under certain cellular conditions. Factors that affect enzymatic activity include:

- **pH**–Enzymes operate only at their optimal pH. (That's usually at the body's pH.) A pH that is too high or too low alters charges on the enzyme's active site and can ultimately cause the enzyme to denature.
- **temperature**–An increase in temperature increases the rate of enzymatic reactions to a critical point, which is called the maximal rate ($V_m$); however, a temperature that is too high denatures bonds in the active site.

- **substrate concentration**–Obviously, the fewer substrate molecules present in the reaction medium, the more slowly the reaction will proceed because there will be fewer substrate molecules present to react with the enzyme. An increase in substrate concentration increases the number of enzymes that can be engaged, so the reaction rate of the enzyme increases. If you keep increasing the substrate concentration, you will eventually reach the enzyme's *saturation point*, which is the point at which all of the enzyme present in the solution is complexed with the substrate.

## Saturation Kinetics

Enzymes exhibit *saturation kinetics*. That means that when all available enzymes are engaged, the enzymes are functioning at maximal velocity ($V_m$). Adding more substrate at this point has no effect on the rate of a reaction. A graph of the relationship between reaction velocity and increasing substrate shows a characteristic hyperbolic curve. The point at which the graph levels off is the saturation point of the enzyme.

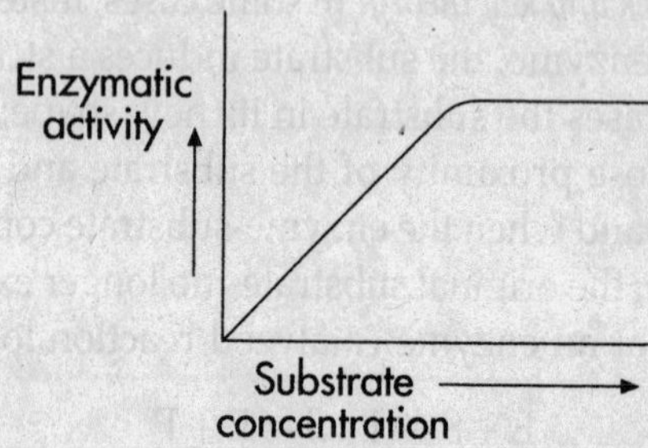


An Enzyme Shows Saturation Kinetics

## The Michaelis-Menten Equation of Saturation Kinetics

The *Michaelis-Menten equation* is closely affiliated with the concept of saturation kinetics, and applies only to *nonallosteric* enzymes (enzymes without a second binding site).

For the enzymatic reaction equation:

$k_1$, $k_2$, and $k_3$ are called *rate constants*

$$E + S \underset{k_2}{\overset{k_1}{\rightleftharpoons}} E{:::}S \xrightarrow{k_3} E + P$$

$E + S \rightarrow E{:::}S$ has rate constant $k_1$ ($k_1$ relates to the formation of the enzyme-substrate complex).

$E{:::}S \rightarrow E + S$ has rate constant $k_2$ ($k_2$ relates to the dissociation of the enzyme-substrate complex into enzyme and substrate).

$E{:::}S \rightarrow E + P$ has rate constant $k_3$ ($k_3$ relates to the turnover number of the enzyme, from E-S complex into P).

The Michaelis-Menten equation assumes that S is larger than E. The equation looks like this:

$$V_o = \frac{[V_m][S]}{K_m + [S]}$$

where $V_o$ is the initial velocity of the enzymatic equation, $V_m$ is the maximal velocity, and $K_m$ is the Michaelis constant, which is equal to $k_2 + k_3/k_1$.

The $K_m$ value reflects the enzyme's binding affinity for a substrate; a low $K_m$ indicates high affinity and a high $K_m$ indicates low affinity. $K_m$ is also the concentration of substrate at which half of the active sites are filled. That means that when [S] is equal to $K_m$, the enzyme's velocity is equal to 1/2 V.

## Enzyme Regulation

So far we've looked at how enzymes are able to control the rates of cellular reactions. What, in turn, controls the activity of the enzymes? Well, the cell employs a number of mechanisms to regulate enzyme activity. These include *feedback inhibition, reversible inhibition*, and *irreversible inhibition.*

### Feedback Inhibition

In feedback inhibition, the build-up of a product of the reaction catalyzed by an enzyme has the effect of shutting off or reducing the rate of the enzyme's activity. This allows a cell to regulate the rate of product formation. For example, in the reaction shown below,

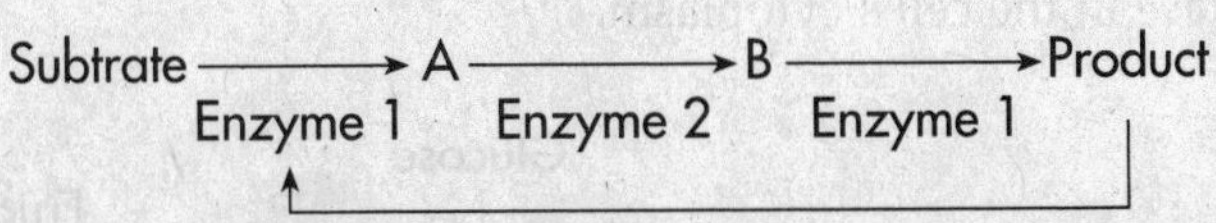


too much of the product will shut off Enzyme 1; this is an example of feedback inhibition.

### Reversible and Irreversible Inhibition

There are a number of other molecules that are capable of inhibiting the action of enzymes, and they're involved in the other types of enzymatic inhibition. Depending on whether the inhibitor molecule forms noncovalent or covalent bonds with enzymes, inhibition may be reversible or irreversible. Two types of reversible inhibition are *competitive* and *noncompetitive inhibition.*

In competitive inhibition, the inhibitor competes with the substrate for the enzyme's active site. When a competitive inhibitor reversibly binds to the active site of an enzyme, it prevents the enzyme from binding with the substrate and catalyzing the reaction that it's meant to catalyze. As you can imagine, increasing the substrate concentration relative to the inhibitor will result in an increase in the rate of the enzyme-catalyzed reaction despite the presence of the inhibitor. In noncompetitive inhibition, an inhibitor molecule binds to an enzyme, but not at the enzyme's active site. It binds to another region of the enzyme, and this binding causes a change in the enzyme's shape (called an allosteric change) that renders the active site of the substrate inaccessible to the catalytic enzyme. For obvious reasons, adding more substrate in the face of noncompetitive inhibition won't make the reaction go any faster.

**Noncompetitive inhibitors reduce the turnover number of an enzyme, and competitive inhibitors reduce the relative numbers of enzymes that are bound to substrate.**

Now let's consider *irreversible inhibition*. Irreversible inhibitors bind enzymes covalently. An irreversible inhibitor alters amino acid residues of an enzyme's active site, rendering it inaccessible to the substrate.

Just as cells require enzymes to regulate the rates of their reactions, cells require energy to carry out all of those reactions. They derive that energy through *cellular respiration*.

## CELLULAR RESPIRATION

ATP (adenosine triphosphate) is the predominant source of energy in a cell. Hydrolysis of the third phosphate group of the ATP molecule releases the energy needed to fuel cellular activities.

The synthesis of ATP is accomplished via *aerobic respiration* (specifically, the citric acid cycle, the electron transport chain, and oxidative phosphorylation) and *anaerobic respiration* (specifically, glycolysis and fermentation). Aerobic respiration is a process that requires oxygen, while anaerobic respiration does not require oxygen. Now we'll see how the cell derives the energy it needs in order to produce ATP.

### Glycolysis: Getting Energy out of Glucose

**Remember this about glycolysis, it happens in the cytoplasm and its anaerobic.**

Cellular respiration begins with the process of glycolysis. Glycolysis is the precursor of both aerobic and anaerobic respiration. It is itself an anaerobic process, meaning that it doesn't require oxygen. In glycolysis, one glucose molecule is broken down into two pyruvic acid molecules; this series of reactions takes place in the cell's cytoplasm.

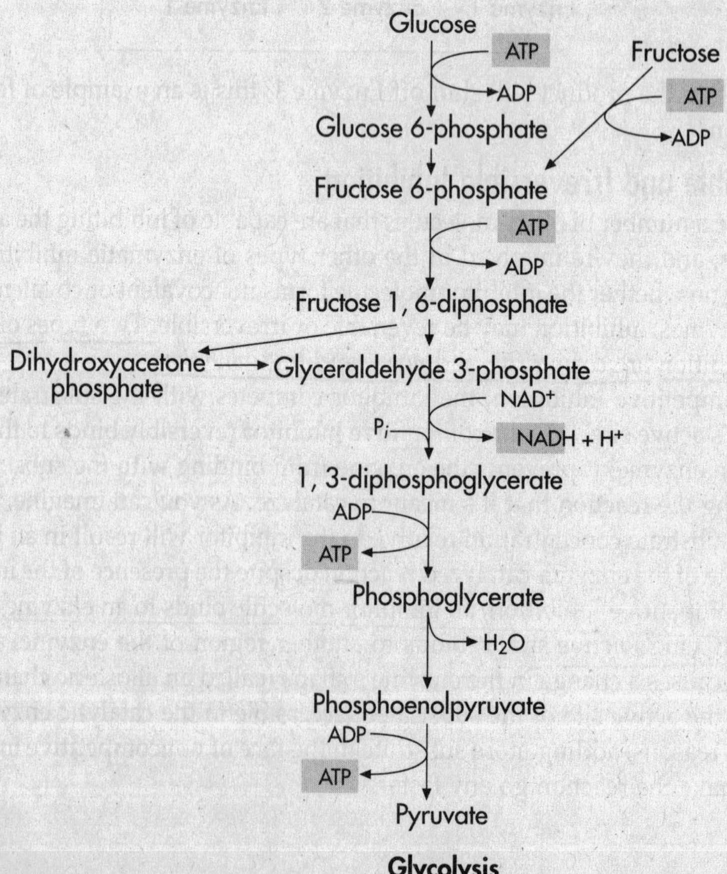


Glycolysis

Notice that the cell has to input 2 ATP molecules in the course of this reaction. Its total dividend from glycolysis is 4 ATP. It also gains 2 NADH molecules (NADH is a coenzyme that acts as a hydrogen acceptor), which contain energy that can either be used by the cell as is, or transferred to ATP.

1 glucose + 2 ATP $\rightarrow$ 2 pyruvic acid + 4 ATP + 2 NADH

## Aerobic Respiration

Aerobic respiration requires oxygen and is far more efficient than anaerobic respiration. During aerobic respiration, glucose is oxidized and broken down into carbon dioxide and water. Here's a summary of the aerobic processes, which occur in the cell's mitochondria: First, pyruvate (derived from glycolysis) is converted into acetyl CoA in the mitochondrial matrix. Then acetyl CoA enters the *citric acid cycle* (a.k.a. the Krebs cycle), which also takes place in the mitochondrial matrix. The products of the citric acid cycle simultaneously undergo oxidative phosphorylation and pass through the electron transport chain across the inner mitochondrial membrane.

Let's take a closer look at each process. If an organism is aerobic, the step following glycolysis is the conversion of pyruvic acid into *acetyl CoA*, a 2-carbon molecule. Now acetyl CoA can enter the citric acid cycle. The citric acid cycle consists of a series of eight oxidation reactions. The reactions are depicted in a circular progression because oxaloacetate, a molecule that is essential for the initiation of the series of reactions, is regenerated at the end of the cycle.

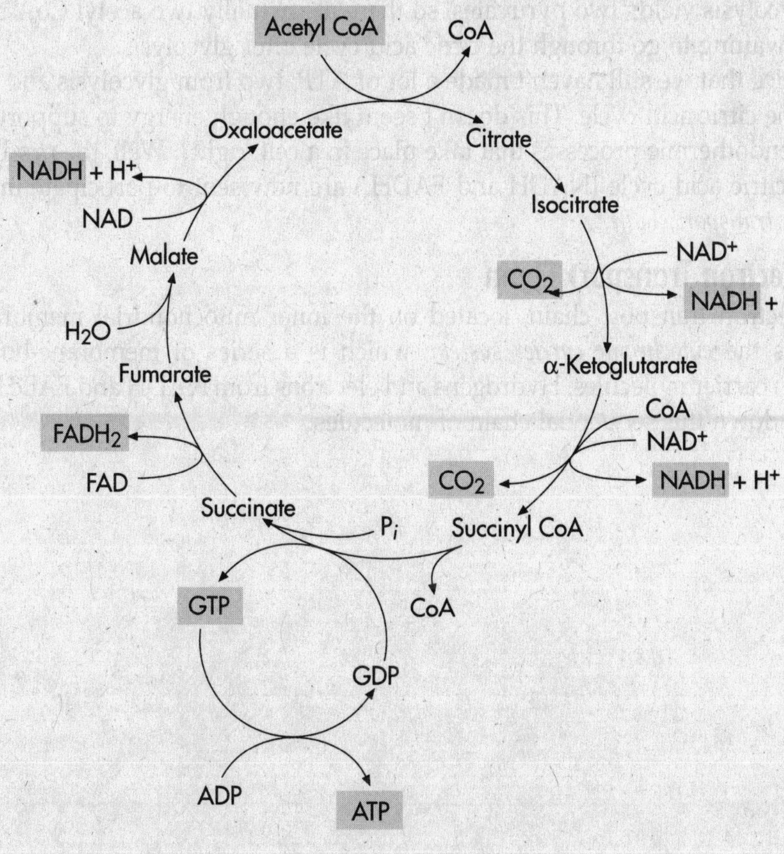


The Citric Acid Cycle

We said that acetyl CoA is a 2-carbon molecule. It hooks up with oxaloacetate, a 4-carbon molecule, and enters the citric acid cycle as a 6-carbon molecule called citrate. The citrate proceeds to lose two successive carbon molecules in the form of carbon dioxide.

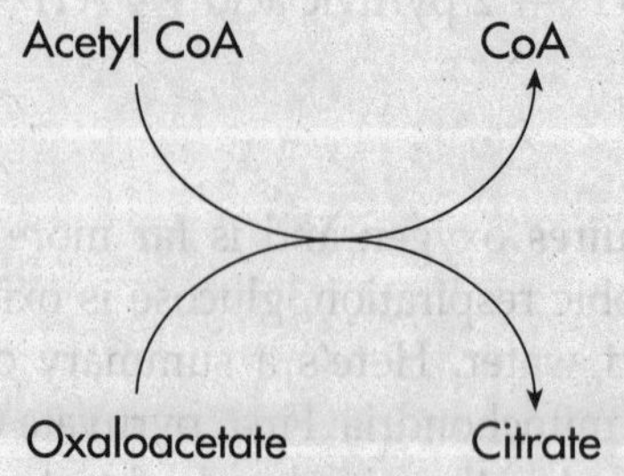


Jump-starting the Citric Acid Cycle

The citric acid cycle yields:

- Two $CO_2$ molecules
- A GTP molecule, which is converted to ATP
- Three NADH and one $FADH_2$ molecule

So what's the general order of the citric acid cycle, then? Acetyl CoA plus oxaloacetate form citrate ... ultimately oxaloacetate is regenerated.

By the end of the cycle, you're back to oxaloacetate, a 4-carbon molecule. One "turn" of the cycle consumes a molecule of acetyl CoA, created from pyruvate. But glycolysis yields two pyruvates, so there are actually two acetyl CoA molecules waiting to go through the citric acid cycle after glycolysis.

Notice that we still haven't made a lot of ATP; two from glycolysis and two from the citric acid cycle. This doesn't seem like enough energy to support the many endothermic processes that take place in a cell, right? Well, the products of the citric acid cycle (NADH and $FADH_2$) are now sent to participate in the *electron transport chain*.

## The Electron Transport Chain

The electron transport chain, located on the inner mitochondrial membrane, features the *cytochrome carrier system*, which is a series of membrane-bound electron carrier molecules. Hydrogens and electrons from NADH and FADH are passed down this sequential chain of molecules.

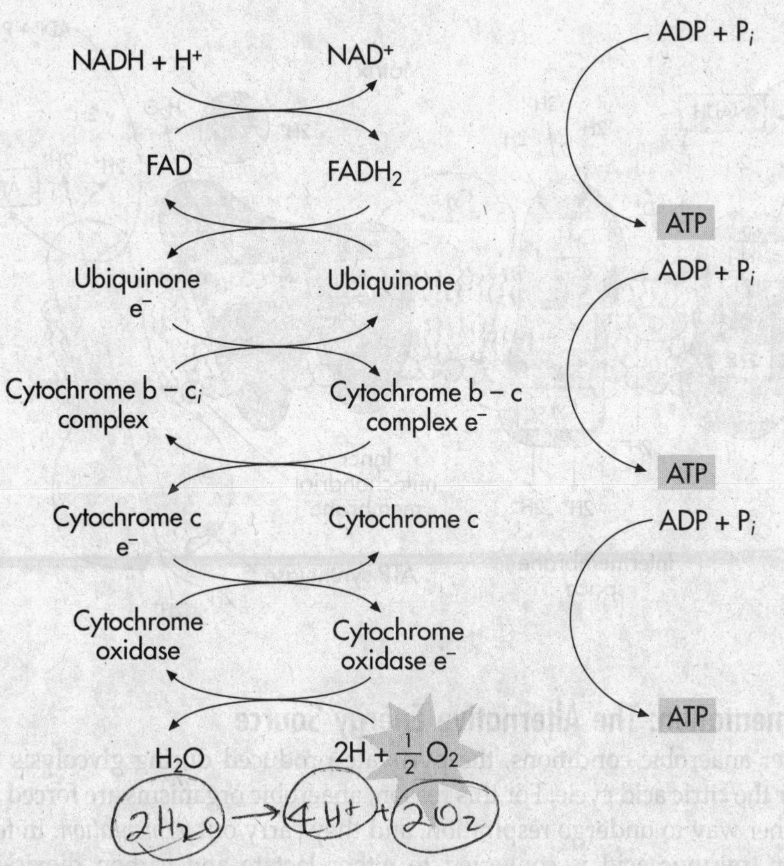


As you can see from the illustrations, starting with NADH, the electrons pass from carrier molecule to carrier molecule in a series of redox (reduction-oxidation) reactions. Each transferal of electrons liberates some energy. The final electron acceptor in the transport chain is molecular oxygen.

Now the final steps of cellular respiration can begin, in which ATP is generated.

**Remember that LEO says GER: Loss of Electrons equals Oxidation, and Gain of Electrons equals Reduction.**

## Oxidative Phosphorylation

The electron transport chain and oxidative phosphorylation are *coupled*. That means that as energy is liberated along the electron transport chain, some of it is used (shown on the right-hand side of the illustration) to phosphorylate ADP.

Here's how these two processes are coupled: The cell uses the energy that's released from the transport chain to pump protons across the inner mitochondrial membrane. Protons are pumped out of the matrix into the intermembrane space. This creates a proton gradient across the inner mitochondrial membrane; more protons are outside than inside the matrix, which creates potential energy across the mitochondrial membrane.

Protons pass back into the matrix through channels created by an enzyme complex called ATP synthetase. As the protons pass through the ATP synthetase and down their concentration gradient, the ATP synthetase uses the energy that is liberated to phosphorylate ADP. The total number of ATP molecules produced by aerobic respiration is 38. If you compare that to the number of ATP produced by anaerobic respiration you'll see why aerobic respiration is so much more efficient!

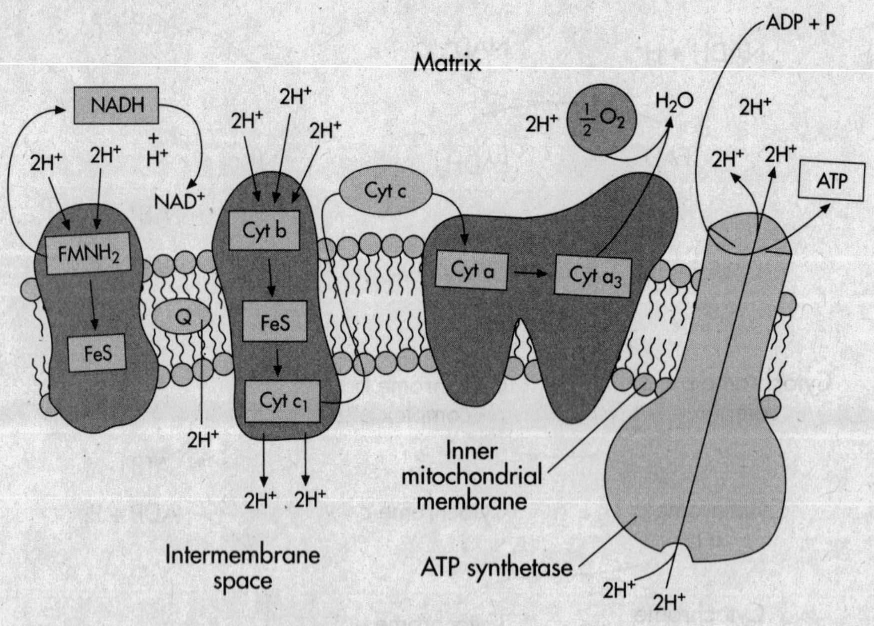


## Fermentation: The Alternative Energy Source

**Total tally:**
**Anaerobic respiration:**
**2 ATP net**
**Aerobic respiration:**
**36 ATP net**

Under anaerobic conditions, the pyruvate produced during glycolysis cannot enter the citric acid cycle. For this reason, anaerobic organisms are forced to find another way to undergo respiration, and they carry out *fermentation*. In fermentation, pyruvic acid is converted to either lactate and carbon dioxide or to alcohol. Fermentation yields no additional ATP.

What types of organisms undergo fermentation? Some bacteria undergo what's called lactic acid fermentation; this also occurs in human muscle cells that are experiencing oxygen debt. Other bacteria and fungi undergo a different type of fermentation called alcoholic fermentation.

What are the products of fermentation?

- **in yeast**—ethanol and carbon dioxide
- **in muscle cells**—lactic acid (lactate)
- **in bacteria**—either ethanol and carbon dioxide or lactic acid

A summary of anaerobic pathways looks like this:

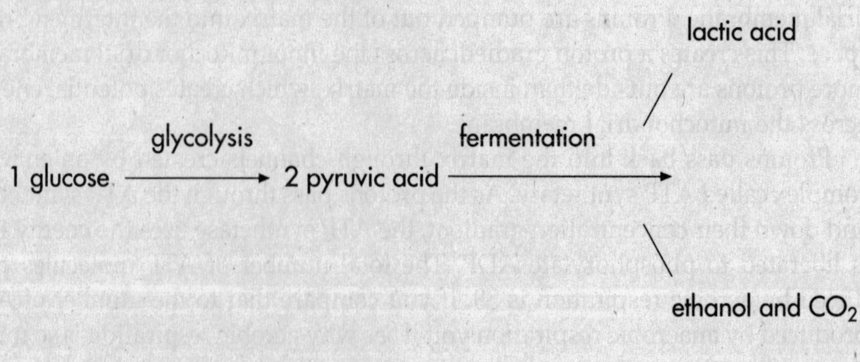

# 4

# DNA, RNA, Transcription, and Translation

Because deoxyribonucleic acid (DNA) constitutes the cell's genetic material, it is critical that you understand this compound's structure and the mechanisms by which it carries out its functions. The genes that are located on DNA dictate which proteins the cell will manufacture, and those protein products determine the cell's traits. A cell's traits may range from its capability to conduct a specific biochemical reaction to its possession of a specific structural property. In this chapter we investigate the structure and function of DNA. We'll talk first about the way in which DNA is packaged into a size small enough to fit into the minuscule space allotted to it in the nucleus. We'll study DNA's three-dimensional structure and consider its molecular subunits; its backbone and its base-pairs. We'll then take a look at how a molecule of DNA replicates. We'll also talk about another nucleic acid: ribonucleic acid, or RNA. We'll review how RNA is synthesized from DNA and how it is able to direct protein synthesis. We'll finish by taking a look at translation, the process by which proteins are made.

## REMEMBER CHROMOSOMES?

An ant has 1 haploid chromosome; a budding yeast has 17. A dog has 39, a human has 23, a chicken has 39, and an alga has 45. Go figure.

In chapter 2 we reminded you that chromosomes are located in the nucleus and are actually complexes made up of DNA and protein. The numbers and sizes of chromosomes differ in different organisms. Humans have 46 linear chromosomes that are arranged as 23 homologous pairs (homologous chromosomes are similar in structure and content). These homologous pairs do differ, however, in the sizes, shapes, and positions of their centromeres. (The centromere, you'll remember, connects the two chromosomal arms. It's reminiscent of a hinge.)

No review of chromosomes is complete without a discussion of *ploidy*. For any organism, ploidy refers to the number of copies of chromosomes an organism has. Organisms (or cells) that possess only a single copy of chromosomes are considered *haploid*. Organisms (or cells) possessing multiple copies of chromosomes are considered *polyploid*. Because the cells of humans generally contain *pairs* of chromosomes, humans are *diploid* organisms.

Let's see how a chromosome is actually created.

**Focus on Eukaryotic DNA Packaging**

The first step in packaging DNA into a chromosome occurs when DNA forms a complex with a core of positively charged *histone* proteins, which go by the names H2A, H2B, H3, and H4. Each section of DNA and its complexed protein core comprise an individual *nucleosome*. Each nucleosome is connected to the ones next to it by short segments of DNA called linker DNA and a fifth histone protein (H1). So what we have now is a linear thread composed of nucleosomes, linker DNA, and histones. The thread takes the form of a hollow helix called a *solonoid*. The solonoid interacts with other proteins to form the *chromatin*. Finally, chromatin condenses to form chromosomes.

Now that we've reviewed DNA's relationship to a chromosome, let's get a better handle on the DNA molecule itself.

## MOLECULAR STRUCTURE OF DNA

Eukaryotic DNA typically exists as a double-stranded, double-helix molecule. The subunits that make up each DNA strand are called nucleotides. Each nucleotide is made up of a nitrogenous base, the sugar deoxyribose, and a phosphate group. Consider a single strand of DNA, which is composed of (1) a nonvariable sugar-phosphate backbone, which is located on the outside of the structure, and (2) a series of nitrogenous bases, consisting of either adenine [A], thymine [T], cytosine [C], or guanine [G], positioned on the inside of the molecule. Unlike the components of the sugar-phosphate backbone, the nitrogenous bases of the DNA molecule vary. These variable bases located on the DNA are what define the genome. Let's take a closer look at them.

### The Nitrogenous Bases

Nitrogenous bases may be either *purines* or *pyrimidines*. The purines are *adenine [A]* and *guanine [G]*. The pyrimidines are *thymine [T]* and *cytosine [C]*. In the two strands of the DNA molecule, pyrimidines pair only with purines and purines pair only with pyrimidines. Here's how it works: One base from one strand of the double-stranded molecule pairs with a base opposite to it on the other strand. They pair by hydrogen bonding. According to the base-pairing rule, adenine [A] forms two hydrogen bonds with thymine [T] and cytosine [C] forms three hydrogen bonds with guanine [G]. The base-pairing rule ensures that the two strands of double-stranded DNA molecule are complementary to one another.

**Base-pairing rules: A = T; C = G; pyrimidines pair with purines; and purines pair with pyrimidines.**

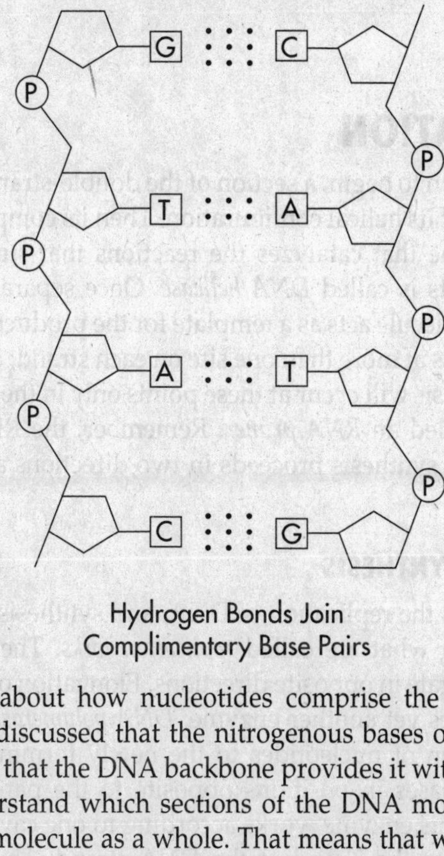


Hydrogen Bonds Join
Complimentary Base Pairs

We just talked about how nucleotides comprise the subunits of a DNA molecule. We also discussed that the nitrogenous bases of DNA comprise the actual genome, and that the DNA backbone provides it with structural support. Now that we understand which sections of the DNA molecule do what, let's consider the DNA molecule as a whole. That means that we should discuss the double-stranded DNA molecule's *antiparallel orientation*.

### Antiparallel Orientation

The two strands of a DNA molecule have antiparallel orientation: One strand is positioned in the 5' to 3' direction and the other in the 3' to 5' direction. By convention, DNA is read in the 5' to 3' direction. The 5' phosphate on one end of a DNA strand is exposed, while the 3' hydroxyl (OH) group is on the other end is exposed. On the sugar-phosphate backbone, the 5' phosphate of one sugar is linked to the 3' carbon of the next sugar by a 5', 3' phosphodiester bond. One strand has an unattached 5' carbon at one end and an unattached 3' carbon at the opposite end. The complementary strand, then, has the opposite orientation: an unattached 3' carbon atom opposite the unattached 5' C on the first strand, and an unattached 5' carbon atom opposite the 3' C on the first strand:

strand 1:
5'________________________________ 3'

strand 2:
3'________________________________ 5'

Now we have a pretty good idea of how our DNA molecule is assembled. Let's talk about how it replicates—that is, how it's able to reproduce its double-stranded structure.

## DNA REPLICATION

In order for replication to begin, a section of the double-stranded DNA molecule must first twist out of its helical configuration. Then its component strands must separate. The enzyme that catalyzes the reactions that summate to complete these two movements is called *DNA helicase*. Once separated from the other, each strand of the molecule acts as a template for the production of a new strand. DNA synthesis begins at more than one site on each strand; each site is an origin of replication. Synthesis will occur at these points only in the presence of another enzyme which is called an *RNA primer*. Remember, the RNA primer initiates DNA synthesis. This synthesis proceeds in two directions and is called *bidirectional synthesis*.

### Bidirectional Synthesis

**The replication fork leaves double-stranded DNA in its wake that's associated with one parental strand, and single-stranded DNA associated with the other parental strand.**

RNA primer initiates the replication of DNA, and synthesis continues from the sites of origin, along what are called *replication forks*. The two prongs of the replication fork elongate in opposite directions. Elongation of the newly forming DNA strands requires yet another enzyme: *DNA polymerase*. DNA polymerase catalyzes the addition of nucleotides to the newly forming DNA strand and aligns nitrogenous bases in positions opposite to the parent strand. Keep in mind, though, that this enzyme works according to one caveat: It will only add nucleotide subunits to the 3' end of the DNA strand. That means that DNA synthesis always occurs in the 5' to 3' direction.

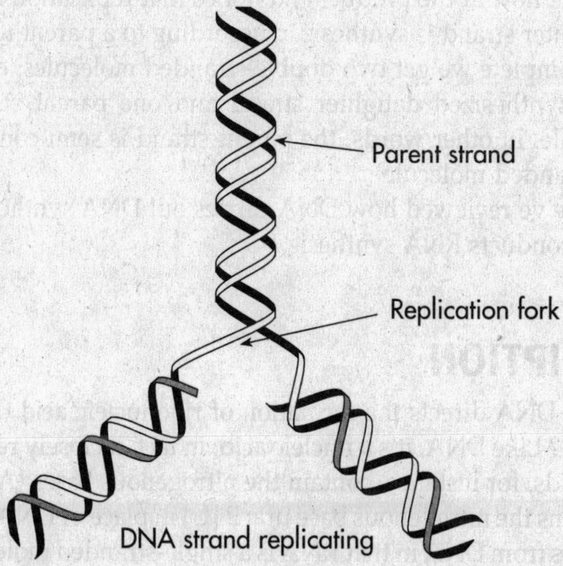


This leaves one big question: If synthesis always occurs in the 5' to 3' direction, and if DNA polymerase only catalyzes nucleotide addition in the 5' to 3' direction, then how does the cell undergo bidirectional synthesis during replication? Here's how:

> "Science is nothing but developed perception, integrated intent, common sense rounded out and minutely articulated."
> —George Santayana

## Okazaki Fragments

To circumvent the problem inherent in synthesizing in only the 3' to 5' direction (since DNA polymerase just won't do it), discontinuous small fragments of DNA called *Okazaki fragments* are employed on the strand which runs in the 3' to 5' direction. The Okazaki fragments are then connected to the parent, single-stranded DNA in the acceptable 5' to 3' direction. The growing strand of discontinuous DNA fragments is called the *lagging strand*; the uninterrupted strand that grows in the 5' to 3' direction is called the *leading strand*.

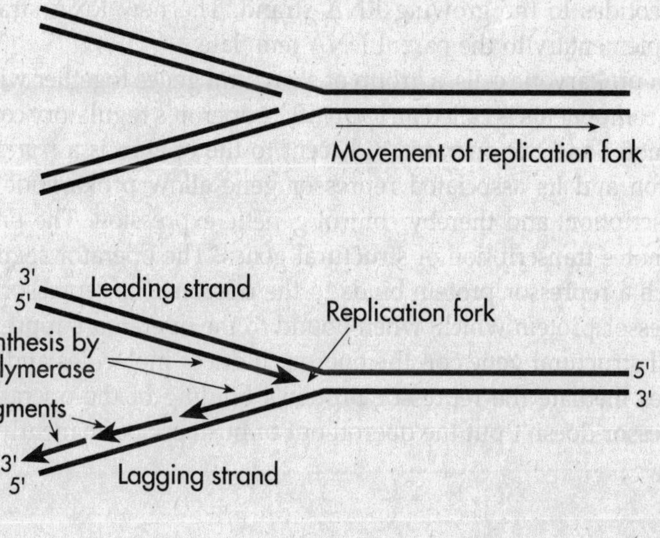

We've reminded you of how two new DNA strands arise from parent templates. Let's look now at the product and notice that replication is *semiconservative.* Each daughter strand is synthesized according to a parent template. When replication is complete we get two double-stranded molecules, each composed of one newly synthesized daughter strand and one parent strand from the original molecule. In other words, the parent strand is semi-conserved in each new double-stranded molecule.

Now that we've reviewed how DNA carries out DNA synthesis, let's take a look at how it conducts RNA synthesis.

## TRANSCRIPTION

**RNA is different from DNA in that it (1) is single-stranded, (2) contains uracil, and (3) contains ribose.**

In *transcription*, DNA directs the formation of ribonucleic acid (RNA). What is ribonucleic acid? Like DNA, it's a nucleic acid; in fact, it closely resembles DNA. Both nucleic acids, for instance, contain the nitrogenous bases [A], [C], and [G], but RNA contains the nitrogenous base uracil [U] in place of DNA's thymine [T]. RNA also differs from DNA in that RNA is a single-stranded molecule and DNA is a double-stranded molecule. Another difference is that RNA's constituent sugar is ribose while DNA's is deoxyribose.

Remember that there are three types of RNA: *messenger RNA* (mRNA), *ribosomal RNA* (rRNA), and *transfer RNA* (tRNA). All of the forms of RNA are involved in protein synthesis, which we'll talk about soon, and all three are produced in the nucleus and sent to the cytoplasm. They're produced through the process of transcription, in which DNA serves as the template.

### How Transcription Works: The DNA Template and the Operon

**Once messenger RNA is synthesized, it leaves the nucleus and enters the cytoplasm, where it associates with either a bound or free ribosome.**

RNA synthesis is similar to DNA synthesis, but there are a couple of important differences. First, RNA transcription proceeds from only one DNA template strand. It's called the *sense strand.* (The strand that is not transcribed is called the *missense strand.*) Second, RNA transcription doesn't require an RNA primer. RNA polymerase both initiates the synthesis and catalyzes the addition of nucleotides to the growing RNA strand. The new RNA strand's sequence is complementary to the parent DNA template.

In prokaryotic cells, a group of structural genes together with certain regulatory components is called an *operon.* The operon's regulatory components are the promoter and the operator. Adjacent to the operon is a *repressor gene*, and the operon and its associated repressor gene allow prokaryotic cells to regulate transcription, and thereby control genetic expression. The promoter sequence promotes transcription of structural genes. The operator segment is the site at which a repressor protein binds to the operon. The repressor gene produces a repressor protein which, when bound to the operator, suppresses transcription of all structural genes on the operon. Inducer molecules and corepressor molecules mediate the repressor protein's binding of the operator. That way the repressor doesn't put the operon out of business permanently.

A classic example of an operon is the *lac operon*, shown below.

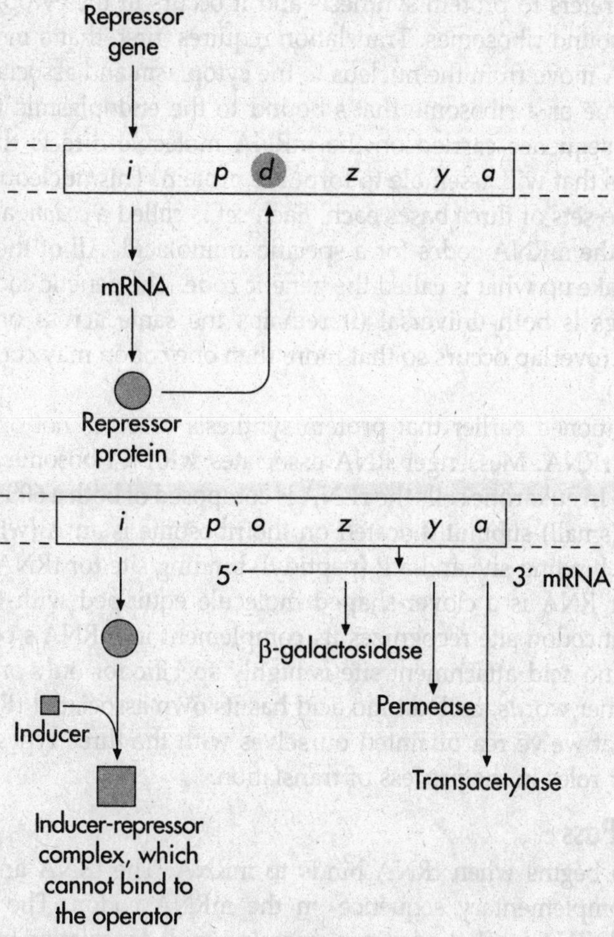


**Focus on Post-Transcriptional Modifications**

mRNA that has just been transcribed is called a *primary transcript*. It contains sequences of nucleotides that code for a polypeptide, and these sequences are called *exons*. However, primary transcript also has intervening sequences of noncoding sequences called *introns*. Introns are excised from primary transcript once the transcript is given a *cap* at its free 5' end and a poly(A) *tail* at its 3' end.

Having reviewed transcription, we're ready to discuss protein synthesis, which is also called *translation*.

**While eukaryotic primary transcript usually contains introns, prokaryotic primary transcript doesn't.**

## TRANSLATION

*Translation* refers to protein synthesis and it occurs in the cytoplasm at free or rough ER-bound ribosomes. Translation requires, first, that a molecule of messenger RNA move from the nucleus to the cytoplasm and associate itself with a free ribosome or a ribosome that's bound to the endoplasmic reticulum. The nucleotide sequence carried on the mRNA molecule directs the sequence of amino acids that will assemble to form the protein. This nucleotide sequence is divided into sets of three bases each. Each set is called a *codon*, and each codon carried by the mRNA codes for a specific amino acid. All of the codons taken together make up what is called the genetic code. The genetic code used among living things is both universal (it remains the same across organisms), and degenerate (overlap occurs so that more than one codon may code for the same amino acid).

We mentioned earlier that protein synthesis involves not only mRNA but tRNA and rRNA. Messenger RNA associates with a ribosome (rRNA) in the cytoplasm. In eukarotic cells the rRNA is composed of both a 60S (large) subunit and a 40S (small) subunit. Located on the ribosome is an A (which stands for aminoacyl) binding site and a P (peptidyl) binding site for tRNA.

Transfer RNA is a clover-shaped molecule equipped with two functional sites. Its anticodon site recognizes its complement in mRNA's codon. Transfer RNA's amino acid attachment site is highly specific for only one of 20 amino acids. In other words, each amino acid has its own associated tRNA.

Now that we've reacquainted ourselves with the three types of RNA, let's define their roles in the process of translation.

### The First Pass

Translation begins when tRNA binds to mRNA. The tRNA anticodon aligns with its complementary sequence on the mRNA codon. The association of mRNA and tRNA is what positions an amino acid. Association between mRNA and additional tRNA molecules positions the additional amino acids, causing them to "line up." The incoming amino acids join the growing polypeptide chain at its carboxyl end. Peptide bonds then join the individual amino acids to form a growing polypeptide, and the amino acids, released from their associated tRNA molecules, ultimately produce a full and free polypeptide.

## Let's Look at That in Some More Detail

Translation has three phases: an *initiation phase,* an *elongation phase,* and a *termination phase.* We'll start at the beginning, with the initiation phase. Initiation of protein synthesis requires a special tRNA called formylmethionyl-tRNA (f-methionyl tRNA; in eukaryotes the initiator tRNA carries methionine). Formylmethionyl-tRNA transports formylmethionyl to the 30S subunit of the ribosome. This tRNA recognizes the start codon AUG located on the strand of mRNA. The initiator methionyl-tRNA binds to the S ribosome subunit at the ribosome's peptidyl (P) site, forming a 40S initiation complex. Next the complex is joined by the 60S subunit; this creates the 80S initiation complex. In order to form this complex, the cell needs to supply energy; this energy is supplied in the form of GTP (guanosine triphosphate). Energy is also needed during the elongation process.

At this stage the P site is occupied with the f-methionyl tRNA and the A site is vacant. Formylmethionyl now binds the P site and tRNA's anticodon aligns with the codon of the mRNA.

Now the reading frame for translation is set up, and the elongation phase can begin.

Elongation begins with the addition of amino acids to methionine. During the elongation phase, incoming tRNAs that match successive codons bind the A site of the ribosome. This initiates the peptide bonding of adjacent amino acids. Formylmethionine (methionine in eukaryotes) breaks off from tRNA but remains bound to the new amino acid. The initiator tRNA moves off to be charged with another amino acid. Now the tRNA, carrying its two amino acids, shifts from the A site to the P site. At the same time, the ribosome moves one codon-length down the mRNA in the 5' to 3' direction. Transfer RNA has shifted from the A site to the P site which frees the A site for the next incoming tRNA. This is called translocation and it requires the hydrolysis of GTP. Elongation continues this way until all of the amino acids required for the primary structure are in place.

**Don't forget that peptide bonds are formed via dehydration synthesis.**

Once that's accomplished, the termination phase occurs and ends translation.

The termination phase requires a codon signal, which can be either UAG, UAA, or UGA. Stop codons don't have matching anticodons available on tRNAs. That means that a stop codon positioned at the A site of the ribosome, in effect, terminates translation, since no complementary tRNA anticodon exists to pair up with it. What happens next? The polypeptide gets released and the ribosome dissociates into its large and small subunits.

**The large and small subunits of a eukaryotic ribosome are called 60S and 40S, respectively. The whole ribosome is 80S. Why don't the numbers add up? Because the unit S is just a measure of the structures' respective rates of sedimentation in a centrifugal field.**

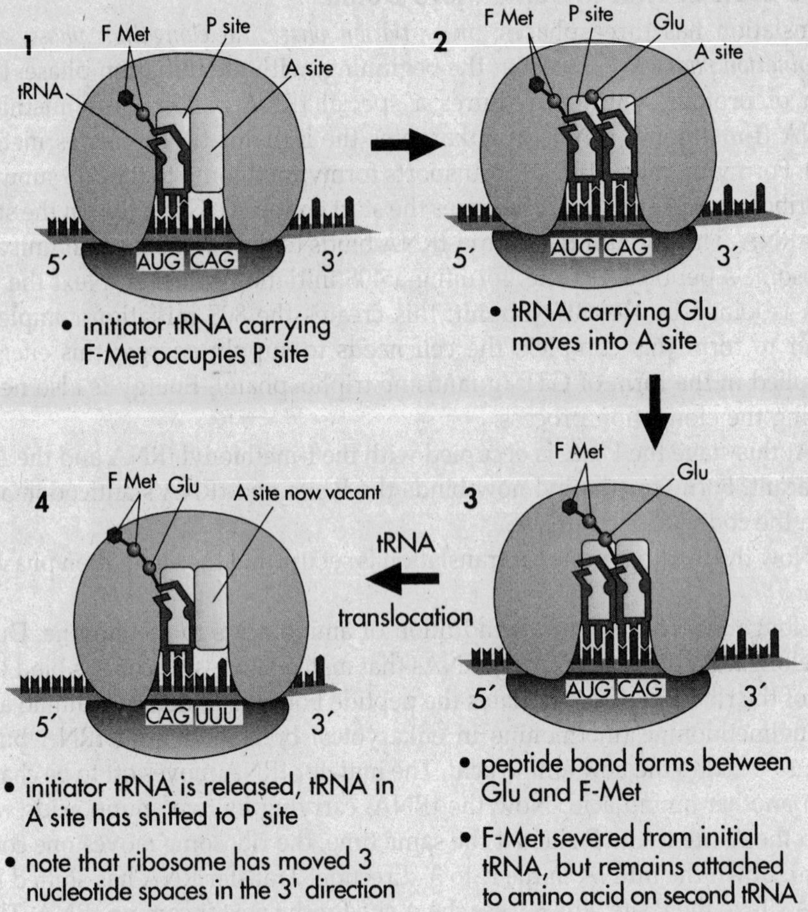
1
F Met
P site
tRNA
A site
AUG CAG
5′
3′
• initiator tRNA carrying F-Met occupies P site
2
F Met
P site
Glu
A site
AUG CAG
5′
3′
• tRNA carrying Glu moves into A site
3
F Met
Glu
AUG CAG
5′
3′
• peptide bond forms between Glu and F-Met
• F-Met severed from initial tRNA, but remains attached to amino acid on second tRNA
tRNA
translocation
4
F Met
Glu
A site now vacant
CAG UUU
5′
3′
• initiator tRNA is released, tRNA in A site has shifted to P site
• note that ribosome has moved 3 nucleotide spaces in the 3' direction

# 5

# Cell Division: Mitosis and Meiosis

Mitosis and cytokinesis are the processes by which individual cells replicate themselves. These processes allow single-celled species, such as bacteria, to perpetuate. They are also the processes by which worn-out cells are replaced, and they allow for the growth and development of multicellular organisms. We'll start this chapter with a discussion of the cell cycle. Next we'll consider the four stages of mitosis and review the important characteristics of each stage. We'll then tackle the other form of cell division which is called meiosis. We'll highlight the similarities and differences between meiosis and mitosis. Finally, since meiosis is the process by which the gametes form, we'll finish up the chapter by reviewing gametogenesis in both males and females. Let's get started.

## THE CELL CYCLE

The cell's life cycle is called the *cell cycle*. The cell cycle is usually depicted as a circular series which is made up of the following stages: interphase, mitosis, and cytokinesis. Let's review each portion. Interphase, the longest section of the cell cycle, encompasses the entire portion of the cell cycle excluding cell division. Interphase is also known as the "resting state" of the cell, but that characterization needs a qualifier. By "resting," we mean that the cell is not undergoing division. We do not mean that the cell isn't doing anything; in fact, it is during interphase that the cell performs most of its metabolic activities.

**Thymidine acts to synchronize cells at the same point in their cell cycles, which is useful during research on the cell cycle.**

### More About Interphase

Interphase may be broken up into three separate sections; the *G1 phase*, which is the first stage, and is also called the first gap phase, the second phrase, which is the *S phase* and is usually called the synthesis phase, and the final phase, the *G2 phase*, which is usually called the second gap phase. During the G1 phase, the cell carries out its day-to-day metabolic functions. During the synthesis phase, the cell replicates its DNA in preparation for cell division later in the cycle. It is at this stage that single-stranded chromosomes become double-stranded chromosomes. The identical individual strands of the double-stranded chromosomes are known as *chromatids* and they're attached to each other by a centromere. The centromere is a specific section of the chromosome; it's the section of chromosome where the two sister chromatids attach to one another. The double-stranded chromosomes exist in interphase in an uncondensed, extended form that is called chromatin. Once replication is finished, the cell enters the G2 phase. Recall that the G2 phase is the part of the cell cycle when the cell increases its rate of protein synthesis, again in preparation for cell division. By the end of the G2 phase, the cell is ready to enter into the M phase, also known as *mitosis*.

## Mitosis

We know that you've been hearing about mitosis since high school. Well, here we go again. The four phases of mitosis are *prophase*, *metaphase*, *anaphase*, and *telophase*. Take a look at the illustrations of each of the stages provided below, and then we'll go over the key aspects of each stage.

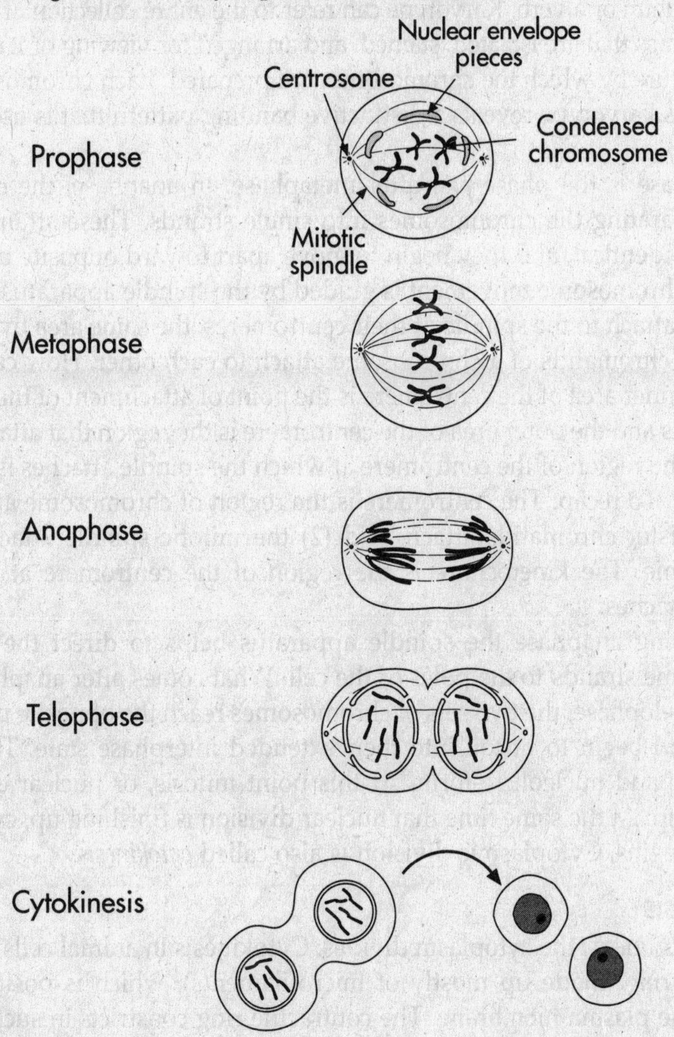


O.K. You've already heard it a thousand times, and we're going to make it one thousand and one. Prophase begins the process of mitosis. During prophase, the double-stranded chromosomes begin to condense and a spindle apparatus starts to appear. The spindle originates from the opposite poles of the cell and is formed from a mix of microtubules and proteins. The poles from which the spindles arise are called *centrosomes*. Inside the centrosome in animal cells are the centrioles. Interestingly, dividing plant cells have centrosomes, but their centrosomes lack centrioles. What else happens during prophase? The nuclear membrane begins to disappear.

In somatic cells (non-sex cells) chromosomes are aligned at the metaphase plate very briefly. In the sex cells, during meiosis, they can stay positioned in metaphase for months or years.

During the next phase of cell division, metaphase, the double-stranded chromosomes line up one by one along the equatorial plane of the cell. Metaphase chromosomes make valuable research subjects because at this stage they are highly condensed and easily visible. It is for this reason that chromosomes in metaphase are preferable for karyotyping. The word karyotype has two meanings because it can be used as a noun or a verb. Karyotype can refer to the entire collection of metaphase chromosomes that are isolated, stained, and arranged for viewing or it can refer to the procedure by which the chromosomes are prepared. Each chromosome of an organism's karyotype reveals a distinctive banding pattern that is used to identify it.

Anaphase is the phase just after metaphase. In anaphase, the centromere splits, separating the chromosomes into single strands. These strands, as you recall, are identical, and they begin to move apart toward opposite poles of the spindle. Chromosome movement is guided by the spindle apparatus. The chromosomes attach to the spindle at their centromeres, the same area by which the two sister chromatids of a chromosome attach to each other. How can that be? Well, the inner area of the centromere is the point of attachment of the two sister chromatids and the outer area of the centromere is the region that attaches to the spindle. The region of the centromere at which the spindle attaches is called the *kinetochore*. To recap: The centromere is the region of chromosome at which (1) the two sister chromatids attach, and (2) the mitotic spindle attaches to the chromosome. The kinetochore is the region of the centromere at which the spindle attaches.

Keep in mind that when it comes to cell division, mitosis refers only to nuclear division, and cytokinesis refers to cytoplasmic division. Both processes overlap slightly.

So during anaphase the spindle apparatus helps to direct the separated chromosome strands to the poles of the cell. What comes after anaphase? Telophase. In telophase, the two sets of chromosomes reach the opposite poles of the spindle and begin to uncoil into their extended interphase state. The nuclear membrane and nucleoli re-form. At this point mitosis, or nuclear division, is finishing up. At the same time that nuclear division is finishing up, cytoplasmic division begins. Cytoplasmic division is also called *cytokinesis*.

## Cytokinesis

During *cytokinesis*, the cytoplasm divides. Cytokinesis in animal cells involves a *contractile ring* (made up mostly of microfilaments), which is positioned just beneath the plasma membrane. The contractile ring constricts in such a way as to create a cleavage furrow that eventually divides the parent cell into two daughter cells. Plant cells differ from animal cells in that during cytokinesis they rely on a *cell plate* rather than a contractile ring to segregate daughter cells. The cell plate develops from numerous vesicles derived from the Golgi apparatus. The vesicles aggregate at the site of the former metaphase plate. At this stage, the collection of vesicles is called the *phragmoplast*. The vesicles then fuse to form the plasma membranes of the plant daughter cells.

So what is the end product of the processes of mitosis and cytokinesis? Two daughter cells that arose from one parent cell. And, just as the parent cell did, each daughter cell carries the diploid copy of chromosomes.

Now that we've reviewed mitosis, let's take a look at a similar process; meiosis.

## MEIOSIS

Meiosis—also called reduction division—is the process whereby a single diploid parent cell produces four haploid daughter cells. (Sperm and ova are produced in this way, during a process called gametogenesis, which we'll discuss shortly.) Meiosis is similar to mitosis in that it has the same stages: prophase, metaphase, anaphase, and telophase. How, then, does it act to (1) reduce the genome by half, and (2) generate four instead of two daughter cells? This is how: It is composed of two cycles of cell division, called meiosis I and meiosis II. Peruse the illustrations provided below to refresh your memory of meiosis, and then let's talk.

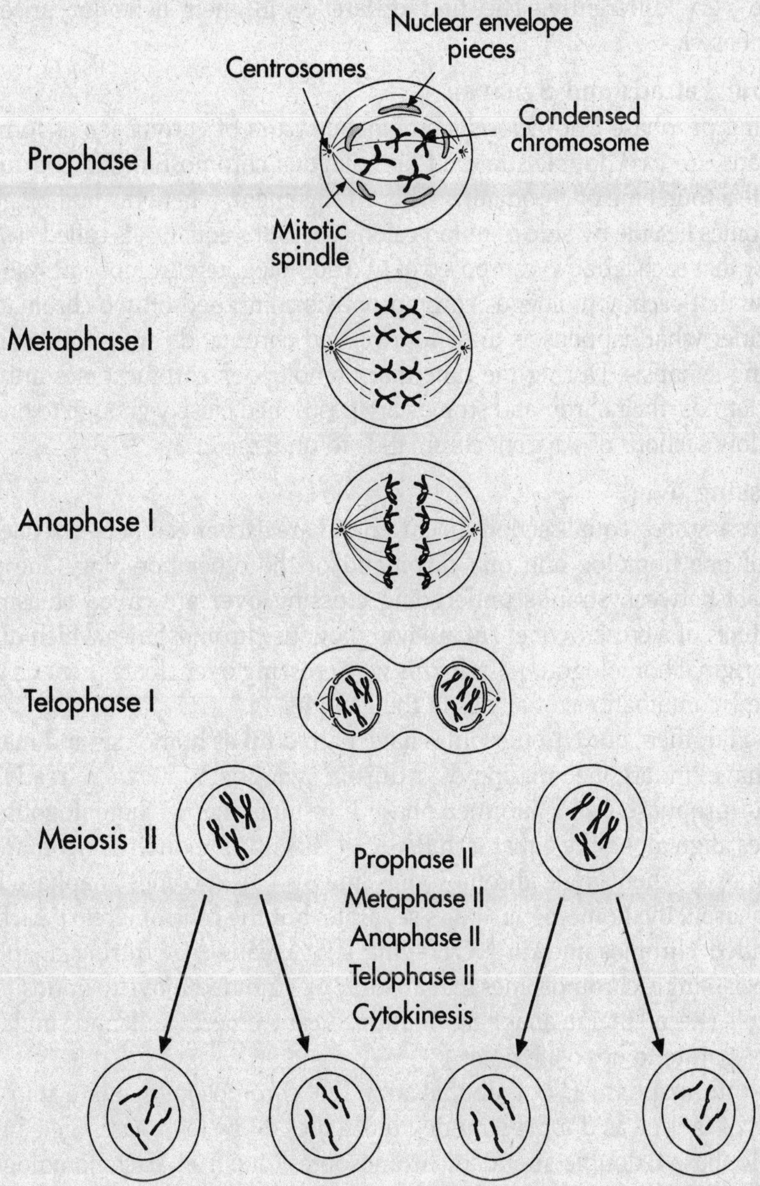


"Art is I; science is we."
—Claude Bernard

## Meiosis I

Just as in mitosis, the stages of meiosis I are called prophase, metaphase, anaphase, and telophase. The crucial difference, though, is this: During meiosis, the chromosomes arrange themselves very differently than they do during mitosis. That's why we have to talk now about *homologous chromosomes*. Homologous chromosomes are paired chromosomes that are similar, but not identical, to one another. In a diploid organism, one of the *homologs* came from one parent, and the other came from the other parent. Think back a minute to mitosis. During mitosis, the homologous chromosomes behaved singly and independently of each other. During meiosis, however, homologous chromosomes behave very differently. The first difference in their behavior arises during prophase I.

### About Tetrads and Synapsis

During prophase I of meiosis, homologous pairs of chromosomes form tetrads. Tetrads are two double-stranded homologous chromosomes joined together to create a foursome of chromatids. This arrangement, where the homologous chromosomes lie side by side as tetrads along the cell's equator, is called *synapsis*. We know that each tetrad is composed of two homologous chromosomes, and we also know that each homologous chromosome is composed of two chromatids. Let's consider what happens as these four related chromatids are positioned together during synapsis. During the time that homologous chromosomes are arranged into tetrads, their chromatid strands are positioned closely enough to one another to allow sections of adjacent chromatids to undergo . . .

### Crossing over

In *crossing over*, equal sections of chromatid are exchanged between one chromatid of one homolog and one chromatid of the other homolog. The points of contact between strands undergoing crossing over are called chiasmata. The products of a cross-over event are homologous chromosomes which differ from the original homologous pair. In this way crossing over creates genetic variation, or new combinations of alleles in the genome.

**What signal causes the centromeres to split during anaphase of mitosis and anaphase of meiosis II? No one really knows yet.**

So far, then, our chromosomes have paired up as homologs and may or may not have undergone crossing-over during synapsis. Now we're ready to move out of prophase I and into metaphase I. In metaphase I, homologous chromosomes align along the equator in PAIRS. (This is quite different from metaphase of mitosis, when single chromosomes line up.) Next comes anaphase I. During anaphase I, the homologous pairs separate, but the centromeres of each double-stranded chromosome do NOT split. That means that during anaphase I of meiosis, single chromosomes that are double-stranded move to opposite poles of the cell. (Recall that in anaphase of mitosis, centromeres split and single chromatids separate to opposite poles.)

So in anaphase I, our double-stranded chromosomes move into opposite poles of the cell as double-stranded molecules. Now telophase I gets underway. In telophase I, double-stranded chromosomes (one from each homologous pair) reach each of the cell's poles, and cytokinesis takes place. Thus at the end of the first meiotic division, two cells have been produced. The two daughter cells are monoploid (they contain a single copy of the genome) and each of their chromosomes is double-stranded.

We've just finished with meiosis I. During meiosis I, a single diploid cell generates two haploid cells. Now, without wasting any time, the cell proceeds with the second round of division, which is called . . .

**When the first round of meiosis ends, we're looking at haploid cells containing double-stranded chromosomes.**

## Meiosis II

The two daughter cells that arose from meiosis I divide again, right away in meiosis II. Meiosis II unfolds in essentially the same way as does mitosis. In meiosis II, each haploid cell undergoes prophase, metaphase, anaphase, and telophase. Each haploid cell's double-stranded chromosome lines up at the cell's equator and separates at its centromere, and single strands move to opposite poles of the cell. The nuclear membrane begins to regroup, the mitotic spindle begins to disassemble, and cytokinesis takes place. Now, while the mechanism of meiosis II may resemble that of mitosis, the results are drastically different. Mitosis yields two diploid daughter cells, but meiosis yields four haploid daughter cells.

In which cells is meiosis conducted and not mitosis? In mammals, meiosis takes place in cells of the *gonads*. The gonads are the sex organs—*testes* are the male gonads and *ovaries* are the female gonads. Cells within the gonads conduct meiosis in order to produce the sex cells. *Ova* (single is *ovum*, or egg) are the female sex cells and *sperm* are the male sex cells. Why is it necessary for the sex cells to be haploid? Because the process of fertilization will unite the nuclear contents of a sperm and an egg cell. If the sex cells were diploid, like all of the other somatic (non-sex) cells in the body, fertilization would create a zygote (fertilized egg) that is tetraploid—two times the correct number of chromosomes. The sex cells are haploid, then, so that the fusing of their nuclear contents during fertilization results in the regeneration of the appropriate diploid state in the zygote. Now we know why meiosis happens in cells of the gonads; to generate the sex cells, which are also called the gametes. The process whereby cells of the gonads undergo meiosis to generate the gametes is called . . .

## Gametogenesis

*Gametogenesis* in human males is called *spermatogenesis* and it takes place in the *seminiferous tubules* of the testes. Spermatogenesis results in four viable sperm cells. Gametogenesis in human females is called *oogenesis*, and it takes place in the *ovaries*. In oogenesis, instead of four daughter cells, only one viable egg results from a cycle of meiosis, and here's why. While four cells are generated, as we would expect from meiosis, three of the daughter cells are non-viable egg cells called *polar bodies*. They eventually degenerate.

So what happens to the single viable egg that gets produced during a cycle of oogenesis? It eventually gets released from the ovary in a process which is called ovulation.

## Ovulation

Within an ovary, a follicle that contains a layer of *granulosa cells* and a layer of *thecal cells* envelops a precursor cell called an oocyte. There, an oocyte matures into an ovum at a rate of approximately once a month. The follicle grows and matures in response to two hormones that are produced by the pituitary gland—*FSH*, or *follicle stimulating hormone*, and *LH*, or *luteinizing hormone*. The mature ovum then ruptures from the ovary in the process called ovulation. What's left of the follicle becomes the *corpus luteum*, which secretes a little bit of *estrogen* and a lot of *progesterone*. The progesterone helps to prepare the uterus for implantation of a fertilized egg. What's happening to the egg at this point? It's traveling through the *fallopian tube* toward the uterus. The fallopian tube is the most common site of fertilization by sperm. If the ovum is not fertilized, it passes out of the body through the vagina, along with the shed uterine lining, during menstruation.

**Ectopic pregnancies occur when the fertilized egg implants someplace where it shouldn't, like in the fallopian tube.**

# 6

# Fertilization and Development

Fertilization is the point at which two haploid cells unite to produce a single diploid cell, called the *zygote*. In this chapter, we'll review some of the specialized features of the sperm and egg cell that allow them to fuse. We'll also review the mechanisms by which the zygote blocks the entry of additional sperm in order to guard against fertilization by more than one sperm (known as polyspermy). We'll review the early developmental stages of the embryo, beginning with cleavage and ending with neurulation. Along the way, we'll define some important developmental biology terms.

## FERTILIZATION

*Fertilization* is the fusion of the haploid egg and haploid sperm. In order for fertilization to occur, an *acrosomal reaction* must first take place within the sperm cell. In the course of the acrosomal reaction, acrosomal enzymes are released from the head of the sperm cell. These proteolytic (degradative) enzymes digest their way through the many protective oocyte layers in order to reach the plasma membrane of the oocyte. Once the acrosomal enzymes clear a path to the plasma membrane, the sperm cell membrane and the oocyte plasma membrane can actually fuse. The fusion of both plasma membranes is the point at which fertilization takes place. Next, a fertilization cone develops around both plasma membranes at their point of fusion, helping to draw the nucleus of the sperm into the oocyte.

"The hen is an egg's way of producing another egg."
—Samuel Butler

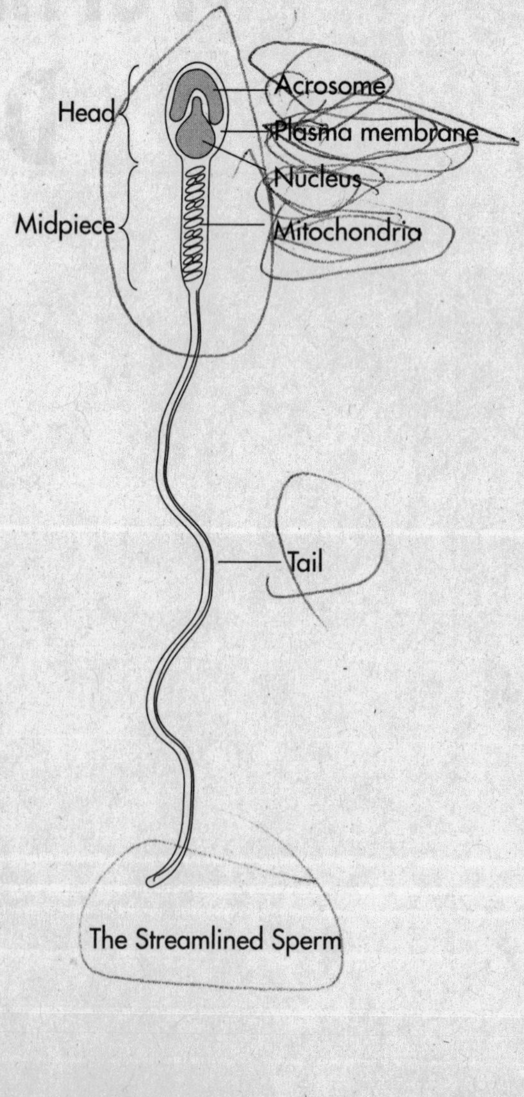


The Streamlined Sperm

If the fertilized egg, with its diploid state now restored, were not able to prevent other sperm cells from contributing additional sperm, it would create conditions such as triploidy or polyploidy in the zygote. To protect itself against that possibility, the fertilized egg exhibits two mechanisms, called the *fast* and *slow blocks* to polyspermy.

## Focus on The Fast and Slow Blocks to Polyspermy

Sea urchins are a classic example of fast and slow *blocks to polyspermy*. In the *fast block* to polyspermy, fertilization of a sea urchin oocyte causes a change in the oocyte's membrane potential (the charge across the membrane). Just prior to fertilization, the interior charge of the sea urchin egg measures –70 mV. Just after fertilization, it shoots up to approximately 0 mV. This change in membrane potential prevents sperm from entering the oocyte membrane.

In the *slow block* to polyspermy—also known as the *cortical reaction*—fertilization sets off a series of reactions in the oocyte, beginning with a rise in intracellular calcium. This causes a release of proteolytic enzymes from cortical granules just under the oocyte membrane surface. The enzymes act to separate the *vitelline membrane* from the *oocyte membrane*. Water enters the space and the elevated vitelline membrane is now called the fertilization membrane. Sperm receptors get stripped off the membrane, and the membrane hardens. Once again, the effect of the slow block to polyspermy is to keep additional sperm from penetrating the oocyte plasma membrane.

**To recap: The fast block to polyspermy entails a swift change in the oocyte membrane's electrical potential. The slow block involves a sort of domino effect unleashed by the release of proteolytic enzymes from oocyte cortical granules.**

We've talked about how fertilization takes place and we've looked at the mechanisms employed to ward off additional fertilization. Where, exactly, do these events occur in mammalian females? It happens that fertilization takes place in the fallopian tubes (oviduct) of female mammals. As soon as the oocyte is fertilized, the traveling zygote begins to undergo cleavage and enters and implants in the uterus.

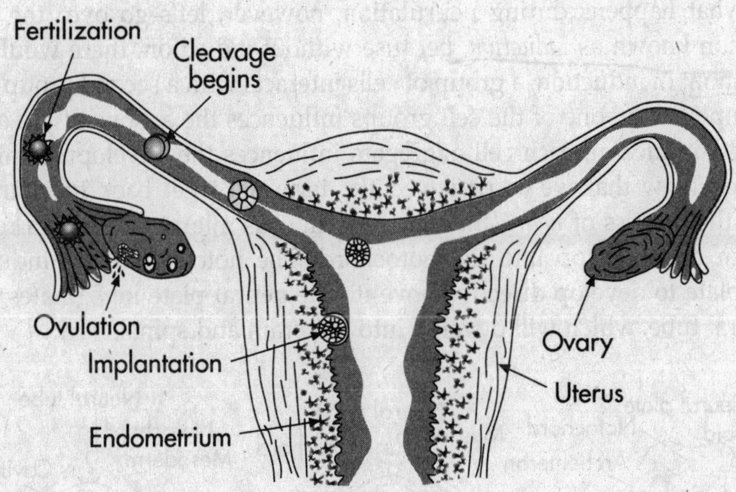

## Early Developmental Stages

> "One must show the greatest respect towards any thing that increases exponentially, no matter how small."
> —Garrett Hardin

*Zygotic cleavage* is a series of rapid-fire cell divisions marked by an absence of synthesis and growth periods in the cells. (This means instead of increasing in size, the cells just increase in number.) Cells produced during cleavage are called *blastomeres.* At approximately the 16-32-cell stage of cleavage, the embryo is called a *morula,* which resembles a berrylike cluster. Now the embryo begins to undergo morphogenesis. In morphogenesis, the embryo's shape changes as a result of cell migration. In rapid transition the blastomeres arrange themselves into a *blastula,* a *gastrula,* and then a *neurula.* The blastula is a ball of cells that has the blastocoel, which is a fluid-filled space at its center. Additional cell movement produces the gastrula, which retains the ball-like shape of the blastula but bears an indentation at one face.

**Focus on The Germ Layers**

During gastrulation, the three germ cell layers arise. These are the:

- *ectoderm* (the outer cell layer), which produces the epidermis, the eye, and the nervous system
- *mesoderm* (the middle cell layer), which produces the connective tissue, the heart, blood cells, the urogenital system, and sections of the internal organs
- *endoderm* (the inner cell layer), which produces the inner linings of the digestive tract and its accessory organs (pancreas, gall bladder, and liver) and the inner linings of the respiratory tract

Once the germ cell layers have formed, neurulation proceeds. Before we talk about what happens during neurulation, however, let's go over the cell-cell interaction known as *induction,* because without induction, there would be no neurulation. In induction, a group of cells interacts with a second group of cells; more importantly, one of the cell groups influences the actions of the other. In reciprocal induction, each cell aggregate influences the developmental fate of the other. Now that we've reviewed the term, let's get back to neurulation. During the process of *neurulation,* mesoderm cells migrate beneath a region of ectoderm and develop into the notochord. The notochord then induces the neural plate to develop directly above it. The neural plate invaginates to form the neural tube, which will develop into the brain and spinal cord:

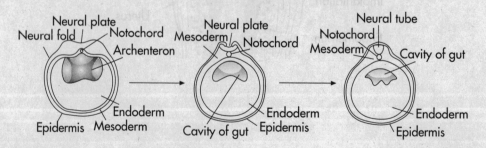

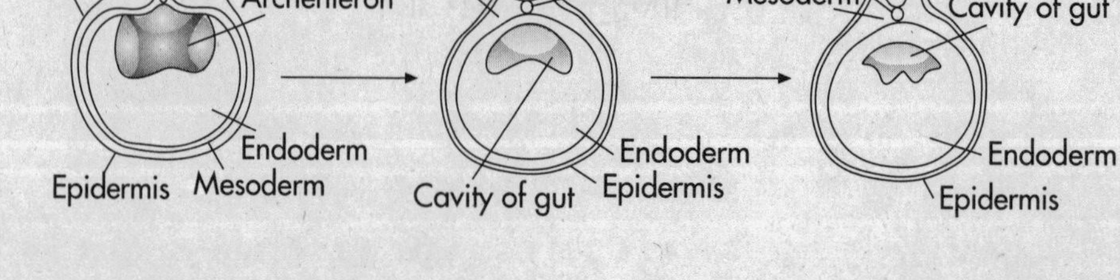

## Determination and Differentiation

Two other phenomena observed in developmental biology are *determination* and *differentiation*. Determined cells are genetically programmed to express some genes instead of others. They develop into a specific type of cell. Differentiation is the process that a determined cell goes through to become highly specialized. The developmental process always proceeds from the more generic type of cell to the more specific type of cell.

# 7

# Microorganisms: Bacteria, Fungi, and Viruses

Among the simplest organisms that grace the Earth are single-celled prokaryotes called bacteria. In this chapter we'll review the key characteristics of bacteria. We'll take into account their structures, how they are classified, how they reproduce, and their methods for obtaining nutrition. We'll also zero in on some specific types of bacteria, like chemosynthetic bacteria and nitrifying bacteria. After reviewing bacteria, we'll move on to eukaryotic fungi, which are more evolutionarily advanced. We'll review important characteristics of fungi, such as their structures and their methods of reproduction, which can be either asexual or sexual. Lastly, we'll turn our attention to viruses. We'll review what a virus is, and the process by which a virus infects its host cell. We'll wrap up the chapter with a look at two specific types of viruses: bacteriophages and retroviruses. Let's get started.

## BACTERIA

Peptidoglycan is primarily made up of sugars, with only a few amino acids.

Bacteria (singular: bacterium) were among the earliest forms of life. Bacteria are unicellular prokaryotes that belong to the kingdom Monera. They lack most of the organelles found in eukaryotes (see chapter 2). What they do have, though, is a single round chromosome, a cell membrane, and an outer cell wall that contains peptido-glycan.

This outer cell wall is a convenient tool for those interested in classifying bacteria. By applying a dye to the cell wall in a procedure called Gram-staining, a person can classify the bacteria as belonging to one of two types: Gram-positive bacteria have cell walls that absorb the dye and Gram-negative bacteria have cell walls that don't absorb the dye.

Another way in which bacteria may be classified is according to their shape. Rod-shaped bacteria are called *bacilli*, round bacteria are called *cocci*, and spiral-shaped bacteria are called *spirilla*.

### How Do Bacteria Reproduce?

Bacteria grow at exponential rates. Under ideal conditions, they divide every 20 minutes. Bacteria divide asexually by *binary fission* (an equal split of the duplicated chromosome and cytoplasm). Sounds simple. However, bacteria still manage to shuffle around their genomes by a number of different methods. Three processes produce genetic recombination in bacteria across successive generations: *transformation*, *conjugation*, and *transduction*. In transformation, chromosome sections from a cell are introduced into the bacterial genome. In conjugation, donor bacteria DNA is transferred into recipient bacteria DNA during bacterial "mating." The mating is accomplished by the F (fertility) factor, which is a plasmid. In transduction, DNA from one bacterium is virally transferred into the DNA of another bacterium.

Now that we've covered their sex life, there are a few other bacterial activities to review. One is their respiratory activity.

### Some Bacteria Are Aerobes While Others Are Anaerobes

Aerobic bacteria require oxygen for respiration, while anaerobes do not. Anaerobes can further be divided into two groups: *obligate anaerobes* and *facultative anaerobes*. To obligate anaerobes, oxygen is a killer. Obligate anaerobes conduct fermentation and will actually die in the presence of oxygen. Facultative anaerobes, on the other hand, can conduct either aerobic respiration or fermentation; for them the presence of oxygen is unimportant.

The fuel for bacterial respiration, of course, is the food that bacteria procure. Let's look at the different ways in which bacteria go about obtaining their nutrition.

## Some Bacteria Are Autotrophs While Others Are Heterotrophs

The many types of bacteria obtain their nutrition in different ways. Some bacteria are *autotrophs* (they synthesize their own food), while others are *heterotrophs* (they must ingest their nutrition). Heterotrophs fall into the following categories:

*herbivores* (plant-eaters)
*carnivores* (meat-eaters)
*omnivores* (both plant- and meat-eaters )
*saprophytes* (eat decaying matter)
*parasites*

Herbivores, carnivores, and omnivores possess digestive systems that are equipped to process ingested food. Parasites and saprophytes don't have digestive systems. Parasites absorb nutrients directly from their host organisms. Saprophytes and most fungi absorb nutrients directly from dead organisms. In this way they recycle carbon, nitrogen, and minerals.

One type of autotroph that the GRE writers expect you to know about is the chemosynthetic bacterium.

**Focus on Chemosynthetic Bacteria**

Chemosynthetic bacteria are autotrophs: they produce their own food. However, they don't possess photosynthesizing pigments so they can't photosynthesize. Instead, they oxidize inorganic compounds like ammonia, hydrogen gas, and sulfur. They use the energy they obtain from the oxidation process to synthesize organic food molecules.

Another type of bacteria that it's important to know about for the GRE Biology test are the ones that spend their lives hanging out on the root nodules of certain plants. Because these bacteria "fix" nitrogen, they're called *nitrifying bacteria*.

## Nitrifying Bacteria: The Good Guys

Nitrifying bacteria have a mutually beneficial relationship with legumes (plants). At the legume's root nodules, the nitrogen-fixing bacteria convert diatomic nitrogen in the soil into nitrate, a form of nitrogen that the plant can utilize. This is why the relationship between the bacteria and the root nodes is

**"The universe is full of magical things patiently waiting for our wits to grow sharper."**
**—Eden Phillpots**

mutually beneficial: Plants need nitrogen, since it's a nutrient that they must have in order to synthesize proteins. The hitch is that while nitrogen is present in the soil, it isn't present in a form that plants can utilize. This is where the nitrifying bacteria come in; they convert the nitrogen into a usable form for the plants. In return for this service, the bacteria gain access to sugars produced by the legume.

Now that we've reviewed a few things about bacteria, let's consider fungi. One curious thing about these eukaryotes is that...

## FUNGI HAVE BOTH TRADITIONALLY PLANT AND ANIMAL CHARACTERISTICS

**One parasitic fungus, when eaten by an ant, actually commandeers the ant via its nervous system to climb up to a leaf high up in a tree. The ant soon dies there and the fungus proceeds to lay down reproductive structures throughout the ant's carcass. The nonmotile fungus is thus able to distribute itself across a wide area.**

Fungi are eukaryotic, haploid organisms that belong to the kingdom Fungi. (That's the animal-like characteristic.) Their rigid cell walls contain a polysaccharide called *chitin*. (That's the plant-like characteristic.) Fungi may be unicellular (like yeast) or multicellular (like molds and mushrooms). Multicellular fungi are multinucleated and unicellular because they lack partitions between cells.

### So How Do Fungi Reproduce?

First off, recall that fungi can reproduce either asexually or sexually. They can reproduce asexually in one of three ways: (1) In *budding*, part of a fungus splits off of the parent fungus and develops into a full-sized organism. (2) In *binary fission*, a fungus cell divides equally into two daughter cells. (3) In *sporulation* (spore formation), a fungus produces spores in its hyphae (long arm-like extensions). The spores are then dispersed by wind or other organisms and can develop into full-grown fungi themselves.

So much for fungi's asexual means of reproduction. How do they reproduce sexually?

Fungi reproduce sexually via a process called *conjugation*, which works like this: Fungi spend most of their time in a haploid state. In conjugation, the hyphae of each mating partner (called *plus* and *minus haploid types*) fuse to produce a diploid zygote. The zygote then undergoes meiosis to produce haploid spores, which can germinate and develop into fully grown fungi progeny.

We've now covered all of the ways by which fungi may reproduce. Let's quickly review them by considering an example. Take a look at the figure below, which shows asexual and sexual reproduction in a bread mold.

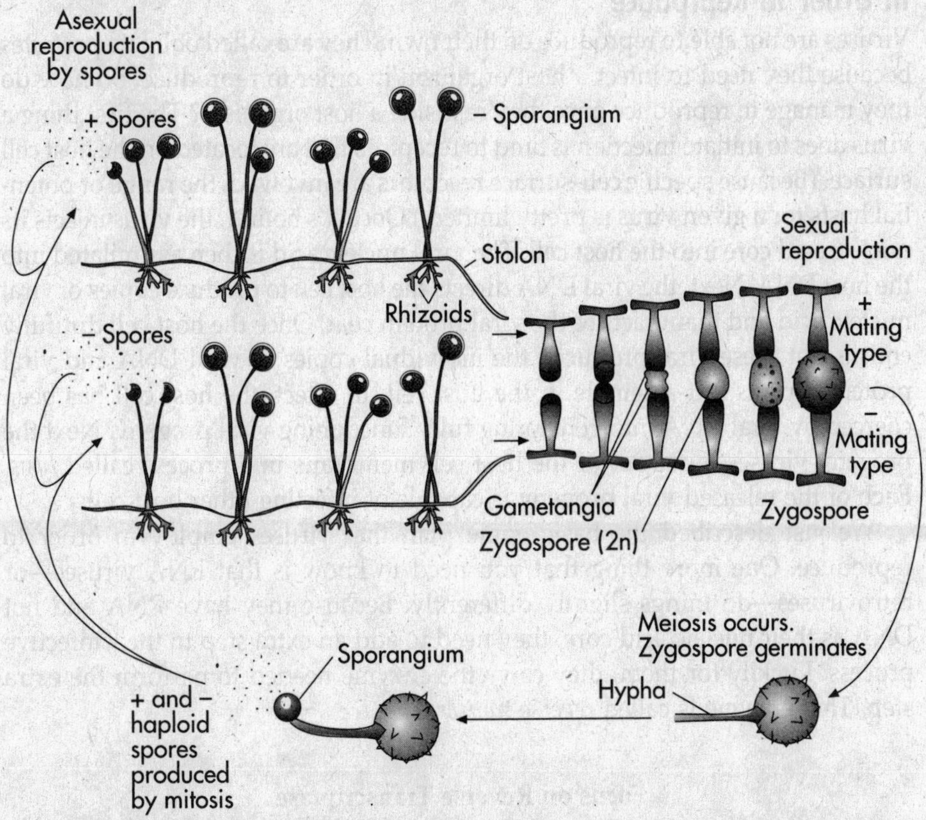


So, we said that bacteria are prokaryotes and that fungi are eukaryotes. Both are composed of one or more cells and both are living organisms. The next group of microorganisms that we'll look at are extremely different from bacteria and fungi, for instance, they are not multicellular, and they are not strictly living. They're called viruses.

## Viruses

What, exactly, are *viruses*? Viruses are small particles that possess two component structures: an outer protein coat (the *capsid*) and a nucleic acid core. The core can be composed of either DNA or RNA. For example, retroviruses by definition contain RNA cores. On the other hand, a class of viruses called *bacteriophages* include some viruses which contain DNA cores and others which contain RNA cores.

**Similar to, but even stranger than viruses, are prions. They are presumably nothing but a bit of infective protein. However, they can have devastating effects on their host, producing diseases such as Jakob-Creutzfeldt and the related "mad-cow" disease.**

### About Bacteriophages

*Bacteriophages* are viruses that infect only bacteria. Unlike other viruses, bacteriophages are equipped with a tail and attached tail fibers. The tail fibers enable the bacteriophages to latch on to the surface of a host bacterium, which they must do in order to be able to infect them.

Now consider this: Why would a virus want to infect a host organism? The usual reason in such cases—to obtain nutrition—doesn't apply here, because we said that a virus is not a living thing. So why does a virus infect a host?

## In Order To Reproduce

Viruses are not able to reproduce on their own. They are called obligate parasites because they need to infect a host organism in order to reproduce. So how do they manage to reproduce once they're inside a host organism? The first thing a virus does to initiate infection is bind to receptors that are located on the host cell surface. (Because specific cell-surface receptors are involved, the range of potential hosts for a given virus is pretty limited.) Once it's bound, the virus injects its nucleic acid core into the host cell. The viral nucleic acid is then assimilated into the host DNA. Next, the viral DNA directs the host cell to produce copies of viral nucleic acid and manufacture the viral protein coat. Once the host cell dutifully churns out these viral products, the individual copies of viral DNA and viral protein capsids self-assemble in the host cell. In effect, the host cell has been coerced by viral DNA into generating fully functioning viral progeny. Next the progeny viruses burst out of the host cell membrane in a process called *lysis*. Each of the released viral progeny is capable of infecting other host cells.

"Well is it known that ambition can creep as well as soar."
—Edmund Burke

We just described the basic game plan that viruses employ in order to reproduce. One more thing that you need to know is that RNA viruses—or retroviruses—do things slightly differently. Because they have RNA and not DNA as their nucleic acid core, they need to add an extra step to their infective process. Luckily for them, they carry the enzyme needed to perform the extra step. That enzyme is called *reverse transcriptase*.

**Focus on Reverse Transcriptase**

RNA viruses reproduce by nearly the same process as DNA viruses, except that they utilize the enzyme reverse transcriptase during the infection process. The RNA viruses rely on reverse transcriptase to synthesize DNA from RNA.

# PART III

# Human Physiology

# 8

# The Circulatory System

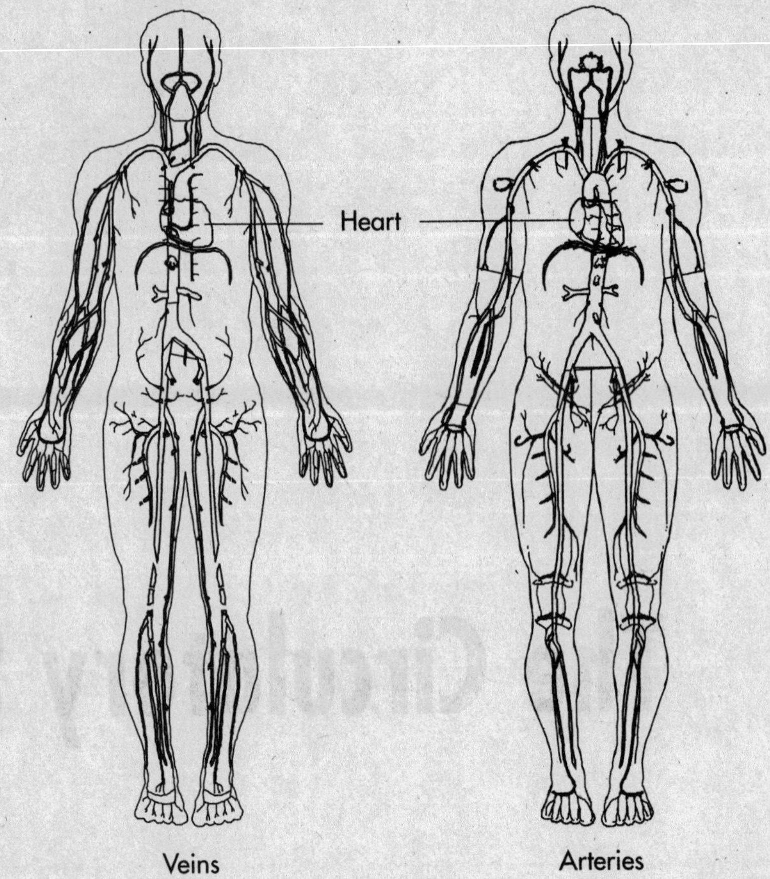


The circulatory system transports gases and nutrients throughout the body. It's also responsible for many other activities, such as transporting heat and supporting the immune system. In this chapter, first we're going to tell you what blood is composed of, trace its flow throughout the body, review how nutrients and wastes get exchanged at the tissues, and investigate the pattern of electrical conduction through the heart. Next we'll tackle the structure and composition of the lymphatic system. Finally, we'll review what antigens and antibodies are, and which types of antibodies do what.

The best place to begin our discussion of the circulatory system is with the heart.

## ABOUT THE HEART

**Malfunctioning heart valves can cause blood to leak back into the heart chamber, creating heart murmurs. These can be detected through a stethoscope.**

The key organ in the circulatory system is the heart. The heart acts as a pump to circulate blood throughout the body. It has two upper chambers, the left and right atria, and two lower chambers, the left and right ventricles. The left atrium and left ventricle are connected by a valve, as are the right atrium and right ventricle. There's no connection between the left and right sides of the heart.

# SYSTEMIC CIRCULATION

Blood leaves the heart and travels throughout the body via *systemic circulation.*

The term "systemic" refers to the route blood takes when it travels to the body. How does the blood get around the body? Let's trace the flow of blood starting with the left atrium. Blood enters the left atrium through the pulmonary veins, moves to the left ventricle and into the aorta, which transports the blood throughout the body. Arteries carry blood away from the heart and veins carry blood back to the heart.

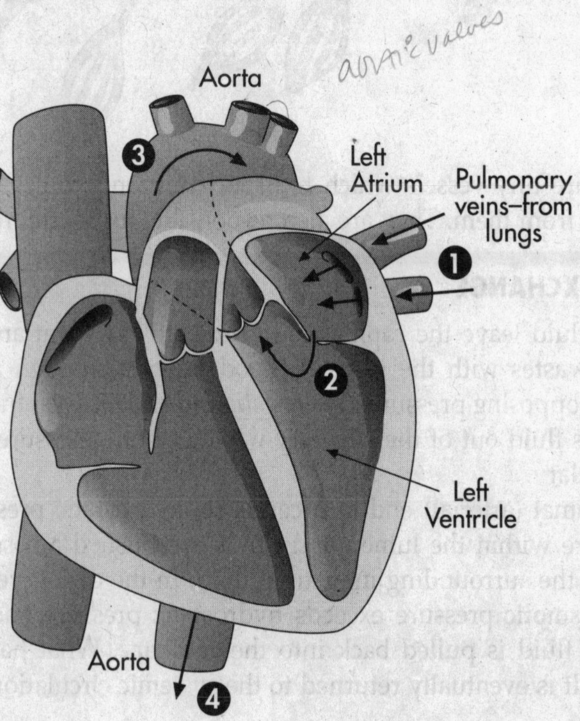


❶ blood from lungs enters left atrium through pulmonary veins
❷ blood from left atrium moves to left ventricle
❸ from left ventricle blood moves into aorta
❹ blood leaves aorta

"Aristotle was famous for knowing everything. He taught that the brain exists merely to cool the blood and is not involved in the process of thinking. This is true only of certain persons."
—Will Cuppy

The aorta branches into successively smaller vessels called arteries. Arteries further branch off into smaller vessels called arterioles, which branch into microscopic capillaries.

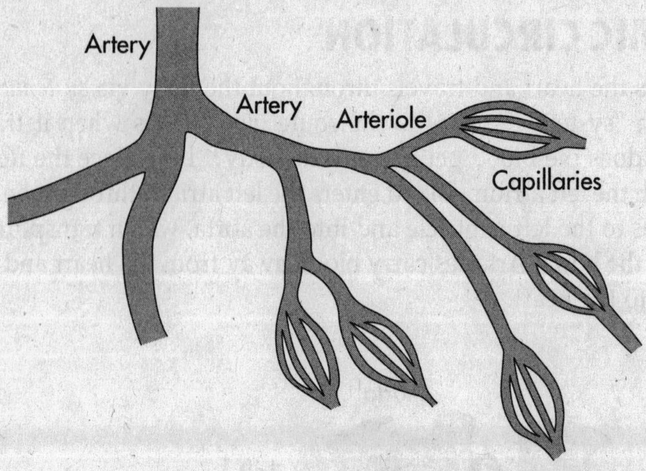


Capillaries are tiny vessels which transport nutrients to cells and remove waste products from them. They are also responsible for thermoregulation.

## Capillary Exchange

But how does fluid leave the capillaries in order to carry out an exchange of nutrients and wastes with the tissues? Blood flowing through a capillary is exposed to two opposing pressures: *hydrostatic* and *osmotic pressure*. Hydrostatic pressure pushes fluid out of the capillary while osmotic pressures keeps fluid within the capillary.

At the proximal (arterial) end of a capillary, hydrostatic pressure exceeds osmotic pressure within the lumen and fluids are pushed across the vessel's membrane into the surrounding interstitial fluid. In the distal (venous) half of the capillary, osmotic pressure exceeds hydrostatic pressure and 99% of the previously lost fluid is pulled back into the capillary. What happens to the remaining 1%? It is eventually returned to the systemic circulation by the lymphatic system.

Capillaries are one-cell thick. They are so narrow that red blood cells must line up single file to pass through them.

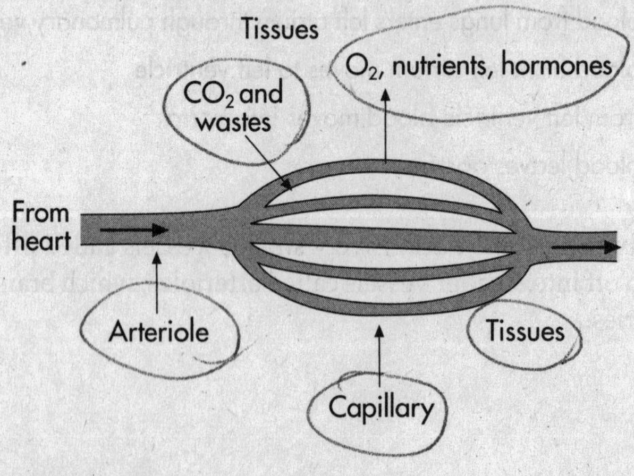


Once nutrient exchange takes place, blood is ready to flow back to the heart: Blood leaves the capillaries via *venules*. From the capillary bed, the vessels join together into larger venules, which after some distance join together to form larger veins. Veins continue to join as they return to the heart until finally only two large vessels, the *superior* and *inferior venae cava*, directly connect to the heart.

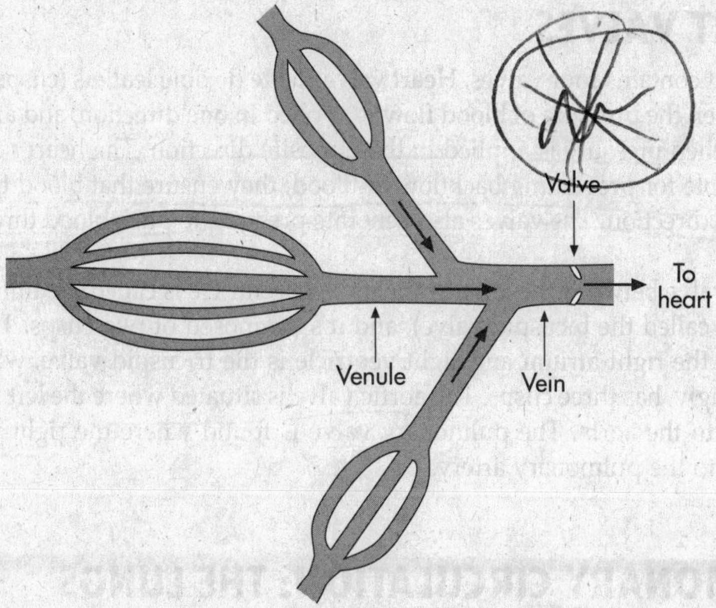


Blood then enters the right atrium through the superior and inferior venae cava. The right atrium contracts, squeezing the blood in the right ventricle. Immediately after that, the right ventricle contracts, squeezing blood through the pulmonary artery.

"The art of medicine consists of amusing the patient while nature cures the disease."
–Voltaire

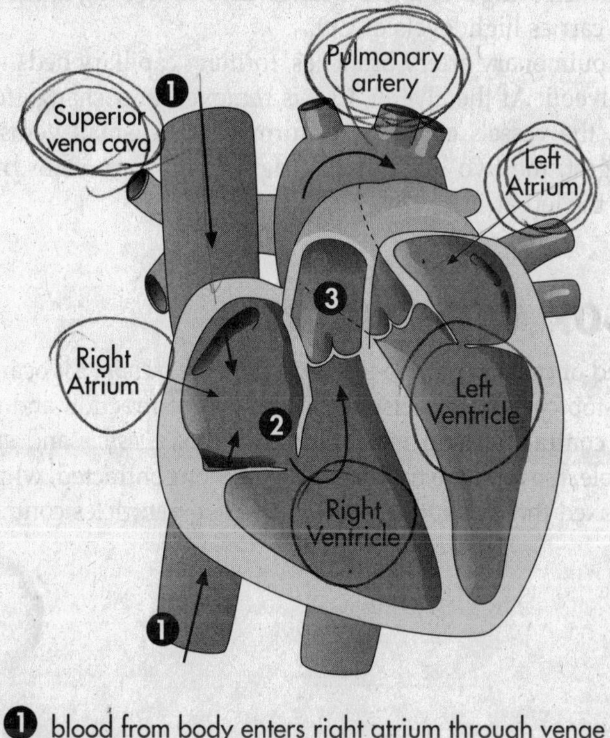


1. blood from body enters right atrium through venae cava
2. the right atrium contracts, squeezing blood into right ventricle
3. the right ventricle contracts, squeezing blood through pulmonary artery

## HEART VALVES

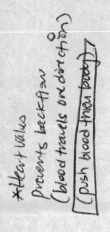

The heart contains four valves. Heart valves have flexible leaflets (cusps), which open when the pressure of blood flow is applied in one direction, and are forced closed when pressure is applied in the opposite direction. The heart valves are responsible for preventing backflow of blood; they ensure that blood travels in only one direction. The valves also generate pressure to push blood through the body.

The valve between the left atrium and left ventricle is called the mitral valve (it's also called the bicuspid valve), and it's composed of two cusps. The valve between the right atrium and right ventricle is the tricuspid valve, which, not surprisingly, has three cusps. The aortic valve is situated where the left ventricle opens into the aorta. The pulmonary valve is found where the right ventricle opens into the pulmonary artery.

## PULMONARY CIRCULATION: THE LUNGS

When we say "pulmonary" we are referring to the route blood takes when it travels through the lungs and is oxygenated. Blood entering the heart via the superior and inferior venae cavae travels through the right atrium to the right ventricle. The right ventricle contracts, propelling blood through the pulmonary valve into the pulmonary trunk. The trunk branches into the left and right pulmonary arteries, which bring blood to the lungs. Blood traveling to the lungs is deoxygenated and carries high levels of $CO_2$.

**Veins provide a large volume with low pressure, making them ideal storage reservoirs of blood.**

At each lung, the pulmonary artery branches, forming capillary beds which surround all of the alveoli. At the alveoli, $CO_2$ is removed in exchange for $O_2$. From the capillaries, the vessels converge to form venules, small veins, and larger veins. The largest, the two left and two right pulmonary veins, return oxygenated blood to the left atrium.

## A CLOSER LOOK AT THE HEART

The heart is composed of cardiac muscle fibers called *myocardium*. Myocardium is designed for non-stop cycles of precisely coordinated contraction and relaxation. The stages of contraction and relaxation are called *diastole* and *systole*, respectively. In diastole, the atria are first relaxed and then contracted, while the ventricles remain relaxed throughout. In systole, the two ventricles contract.

## ELECTRICAL CONDUCTION

*Electrical conduction* refers to the signals which stimulate the heart to contract. In a healthy adult at rest, the heart automatically contracts and relaxes at an average rate of 72 beats per minute. This rhythm is maintained by an electrical signal generated by the sinoatrial node (S-A node), which is in the right atrium at the junction with the superior vena cava. Tracing the signal's pathway, we find that the signal from the S-A node travels along specialized fibers to the *atrioventricular node* (A-V node), which is located near the intersection of the four heart chambers. From the A-V node, the signal passes along the septum between the ventricles, by way of the *bundle of His*. From the distal end of the bundle of His, myocardial fibers called Purkinje fibers spread out to the two ventricles.

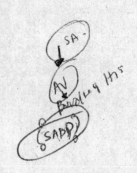

The whole pattern of electrical excitation just described can be abbreviated with the letters *SABP* (S-A node, A-V node, bundle of His, Perkinje fibers).

We've traced the flow of blood through the vessels of the body and the chambers of the heart. Now let's look at the blood itself.

## COMPONENTS OF THE BLOOD

Blood has two components: plasma and formed elements, which include red blood cells (*erythrocytes*), white blood cells (*leukocytes*), and platelets (cell fragments of *megakaryocytes*). The erythrocytes carry $O_2$ and $CO_2$ between the lungs and all other body tissues. Leukocytes compose the cellular immune system, and include lymphocytes. They're the ones that fight infections. Platelets, which arise from precursors in bone marrow, are required in order for blood to clot. Blood also contains ions and proteins, including *albumin* and *immunoglobulins*.

**Plasma is the clear fluid component of blood, minus the blood cells.**
**Hematocrit is the volume of RBCs per unit volume of blood.**
**Serum is the fluid portion of blood minus its fibrin clot and its blood cells.**

## THE LYMPHATIC SYSTEM

The lymphatic system circulates lymph, which is composed of a clear liquid, white blood cells, and a few red blood cells. It is also made up of a series of vessels that run throughout the body. These vessels are not continuous; instead, they begin as thin, blind-ended vessels that coalesce to form larger lymph vessels. The vessels ultimately converge as two large lymphatic ducts, which return lymph fluid to the venous circulation near the beginning of the superior vena cava. The lymphatic system also contains the *lymph nodes*, the *spleen*, and the *thymus*.

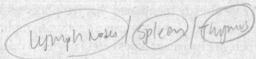

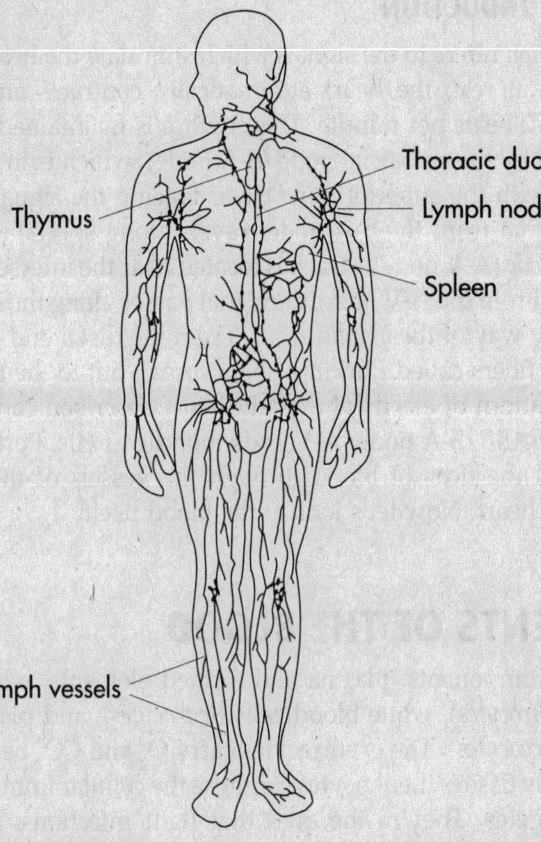


Remember the fluid and proteins that get filtered across the capillaries into the tissues? Well, the lymphatic system returns the overflow back to the blood stream.

Numerous lymph nodes lie at intervals along every lymph vessel. They contain many of the same lymphocytes that circulate in the blood stream. When an infection occurs in the body, lymphocytes in the lymph nodes multiply to fight the infection. The spleen is located on the left side of the body under the stomach and it functions much like a large lymph node, except that it acts as a filter and lymphatic organ for the blood. The spleen also filters out and destroys old, damaged, or malformed red blood cells. The thymus is a small lymphoid organ in the mediastinum, and is especially active in embryonic development through the prepubertal years. It is the site of development of the T lymphocytes.

## LYMPHOCYTES

We've already mentioned that lymphocytes are an integral part of the circulatory system. Now we can add this: lymphocytes are circulating leukocytes. There are two main types of leukocytes: T cells and B cells. T cells originate in the bone marrow and mature in the thymus and are the major players in cellular immunity. There are several types of T cells, including *helper*, *suppressor*, and *killer T cells.* B cells also originate in the marrow, but they're responsible for humoral (fluid-based) immunity, through the production of immunoglobulins (also called antibodies).

## ANTIBODY PRODUCTION

When a circulating lymphocyte encounters an antigen (in other words, a foreign particle or molecule), cell surface receptors on the lymphocyte bind to the antigen. This stimulates the lymphocyte to differentiate into B plasma cells. What do B plasma cells do? They synthesize and churn out antibodies created to destroy that antigen. (Keep in mind that antibody production involves an actual reshuffling of genes in cells.) A typical antibody looks like this:

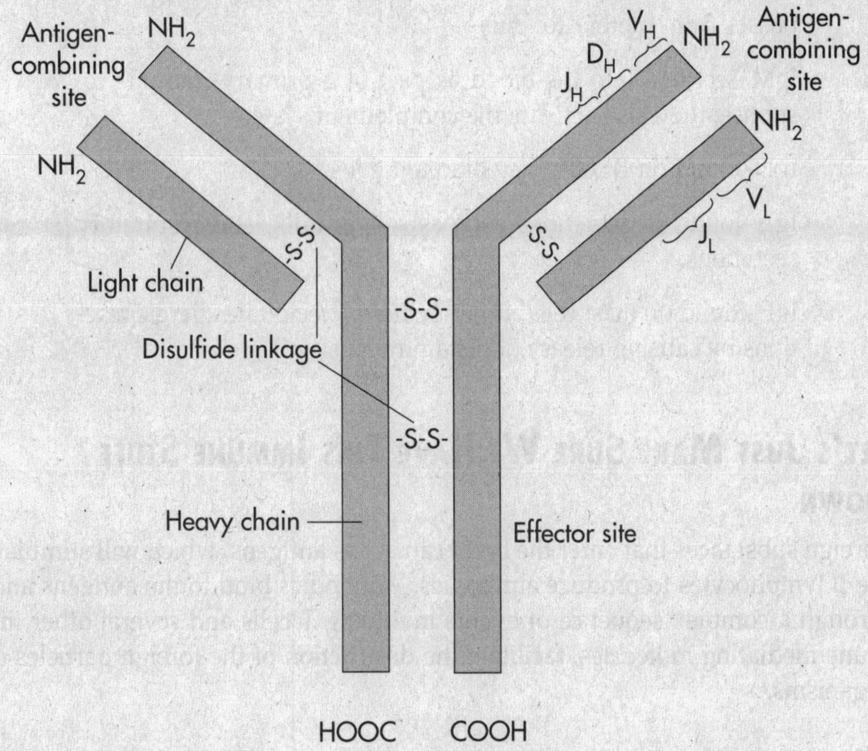


All antibodies are composed of four polypeptide chains. Two of those chains are long polypeptides called *heavy chains* (H chains), and two are shorter polypeptides called *light chains* (L chains). The heavy chains make up the tail of the antibody (the Fc region). It is the tail that dictates the actual duties of the antibody; see the immunoglobulin types listed below. The light chains are made of either lambda or kappa chains.

At first biologists thought that antibodies were generated in response to specific antigens (i.e., the antigens instructed what antibody would form). Now we know that's not true; astoundingly, all of the body's antibodies already exist, BEFORE they ever encounter their matching antigen.

## Antigen-Binding Sites

The upper regions of both the light chains and heavy chains (at the variable regions) make up the antigen-binding sites. The antigen-binding sites form cross-links with antigens in the early stages of immunological defense.

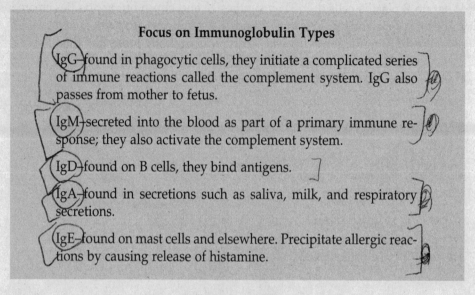

**Focus on Immunoglobulin Types**

IgG–found in phagocytic cells, they initiate a complicated series of immune reactions called the complement system. IgG also passes from mother to fetus.

IgM–secreted into the blood as part of a primary immune response; they also activate the complement system.

IgD–found on B cells, they bind antigens.

IgA–found in secretions such as saliva, milk, and respiratory secretions.

IgE–found on mast cells and elsewhere. Precipitate allergic reactions by causing release of histamine.

## Let's Just Make Sure We Have This Immune Stuff Down

Foreign substances that enter the body can act as antigens, which will stimulate the B lymphocytes to produce antibodies. Antibodies bind to the antigens and, through a complex sequence of events involving T cells and several other immune-mediating molecules, facilitate the destruction of the foreign particles or organisms.

# 9

# The Digestive System

Digestion is the process by which food molecules are broken down and eventually absorbed by the blood stream. What's so important about food? HA! It provides us with the nutrients needed to build and repair the body as well as the energy needed for chemical reactions. The human digestive system includes the mouth, esophagus, stomach, small intestine, large intestine, and accessory organs.

## MOUTH AND ESOPHAGUS

"There is no love sincerer than the love of food."
—George Bernard Shaw

The digestion of food begins in the mouth. The salivary enzyme amylase, also called ptyalin, begins chemical digestion by breaking starches down into sugars. Digestion is also assisted by mechanical action. The teeth and powerful muscles of the jaw contribute to mechanical digestion by increasing the surface area of food. In the process of chewing (called mastication), food is also lubricated to facilitate the process of peristalsis. In peristalsis, smooth muscle contractions move food through the esophagus. From the esophagus, food enters the stomach.

## THE STOMACH

The muscular organ known as the stomach serves as temporary storage area for food. It is characterized by its extremely low pH (about 1). This acidic environment is caused by hydrochloric acid secreted by the parietal cells in glands of the gastric mucosa. Production and secretion of the acid is stimulated by the vagal nerve. Why is an acid environment important? There are several reasons:

- acid kills the bacteria in the stomach.
- low pH is required for the gastric enzyme pepsin to work. Pepsin begins the process of the chemical digestion of proteins. It's produced and secreted by the chief cells of the gastric mucosa.
- hydrochloric acid stimulates the flow of bile and pancreatic enzymes.

At the same time that some chemical digestion is taking place in the stomach, mechanical digestion is underway. Mechanical digestion is accomplished through the churning action created by the stomach muscles. Eventually, through coordinated muscle activity, the watery, acidic food mixture—called chyme—passes through the pyloric sphincter into the small intestine.

## ABOUT THE SMALL INTESTINE

The first part of the small intestine is called the *duodenum*. This is where chemical digestion is completed. The pancreas, an accessory organ, produces lots of enzymes essential for digestion and secretes them into the duodenum through the pancreatic duct. Let's take a look at these enzymes.

## Pancreatic Enzymes

You'll need to know the enzymes responsible for the breakdown of the three food groups: proteins, carbohydrates, and fats. *Pancreatic amylase* is identical to salivary amylase and continues the digestion of carbohydrates. *Pancreatic lipase* is involved in the process of fat digestion.

*Trypsin* and the *chymotrypsins* do the major work of enzymatic protein digestion. They digest large protein molecules into short chains of only a few amino acids by breaking specific peptide bonds.

**Focus on Zymogens**

Other pancreatic enzymes, known as zymogens, are secreted into the duodenum in their inactive forms. Zymogens require activation by another enzyme. Trypsinogen is a pancreatic zymogen which is cleaved by the duodenal enzyme enterokinase to produce trypsin, which then serves as both a digestive enzyme itself and as the activating enzyme for several other pancreatic zymogens, as shown below:

$$\text{chymotrypsinogens} \xrightarrow{\text{trypsin}} \text{chymotrypsins}$$

$$\text{proelastase} \xrightarrow{\text{trypsin}} \text{elastase}$$

$$\text{procarboxypeptidases} \xrightarrow{\text{trypsin}} \text{carboxypeptidases}$$

## What About Bile?

Another important substance is bile. Bile is a complex mixture secreted by the liver, stored in the gall bladder, and dumped into the duodenum via the bile duct. Bile contains bile pigments and bile salts that act as detergents. What is the significance of bile? Bile salts play an important role in the digestion of fats through several mechanisms. They reduce surface tension, help to emulsify fats, and activate lipases. Since bile mechanically breaks down fats, it's *not* an enzyme. It combines with lipids to produce water-soluble complexes called micelles.

# MORE ABOUT THE SMALL INTESTINE

Now that we've discussed the action of pancreatic enzymes, let's talk about the absorption of food. Enzymatic digestion continues as peristaltic action pushes food forward through the rest of the small intestine, beginning with the jejunum. As food is broken down into sufficiently small particles, it is absorbed through the small intestinal wall directly into the blood stream. In the blood stream it is carried to the liver, where certain toxins are removed.

**The small intestine is loaded up with extra levels of absorptive surface area. It twists and turns. Then, on its surface are finger-like extensions called villi, and on THOSE are even smaller extensions called microvilli.**

Feces is composed of water, bacteria, cellulose, salts, dead cells, and bile pigments.

## THE LARGE INTESTINE, THE RECTUM, AND THE ANUS

If all digested food is absorbed in the small intestine then what does the large intestine do? The large intestine, or colon, receives the bulky, watery mass of indigestible and non-absorbable material left over from the small intestine. The colon transforms that mass into a more compact material known as feces. How? By resorbing a large amount of water from the colonic lumen (interior space). (If too little water is resorbed by the large intestine, diarrhea results. Frequent diarrhea can cause dehydration and electrolyte imbalance.) The compact feces is stored in the rectum and passes out of the body through the anus.

# 10

# The Excretory System

During metabolism, a lot of nitrogenous wastes are produced in the form of urea. Two important processes that must be continually regulated in the body are the excretion of wastes and the retention of water. The excretory system is responsible for these two actions.

The excretory system is made up of the kidneys, ureter, urinary bladder, and urethra. The primary organs of excretion are the kidneys. Structurally, the kidneys consist of an outer portion (the renal cortex), a middle region (the renal medulla), and an inner region (comprised of the renal pyramids and a renal pelvis).

Fish don't excrete urea. They excrete ammonia, which is quite toxic and water-soluble.

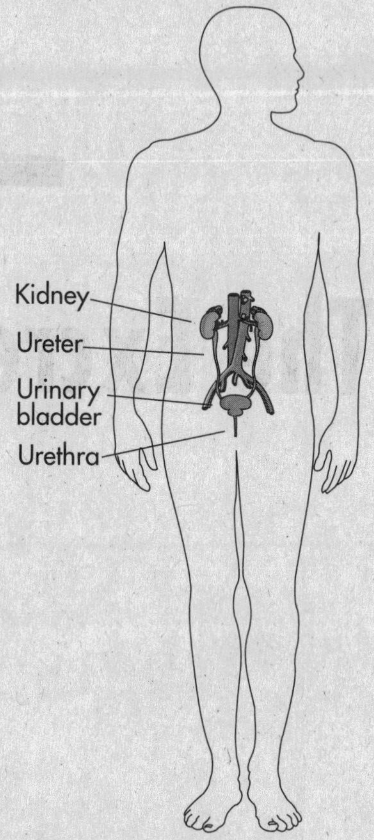


Each kidney is composed of over a million *nephrons.* The nephron is the basic functional and structural unit of the kidney. Each nephron has a renal corpuscle continuous with a renal tubule. The renal corpuscle is comprised of the glomerulus (a tuft of capillaries) and its surrounding Bowman's capsule, which is a double-walled, hollow cup of cells. Fluid filtered from blood in the glomerulus enters the renal tubule at the Bowman's capsule.

Right next to the Bowman's capsule is the proximal convoluted tubule. Let's look at the sections of the renal tubule, from proximal to distal. There's the proximal convoluted tubule, the loop of Henle (including the descending limb and the ascending limb), and the distal convoluted tubule. Each distal convoluted tubule delivers its contents into a collecting duct.

A single collecting duct carries away fluid from several individual collecting ducts. Collecting ducts then empty into one of about six spaces called the *renal pyramids*. These pyramids open into a single renal pelvis. From the renal pelvis the ureter carries the now-formed urine away from the kidney to the urinary bladder, where it's stored until it passes from the body (micturition) through the urethra.

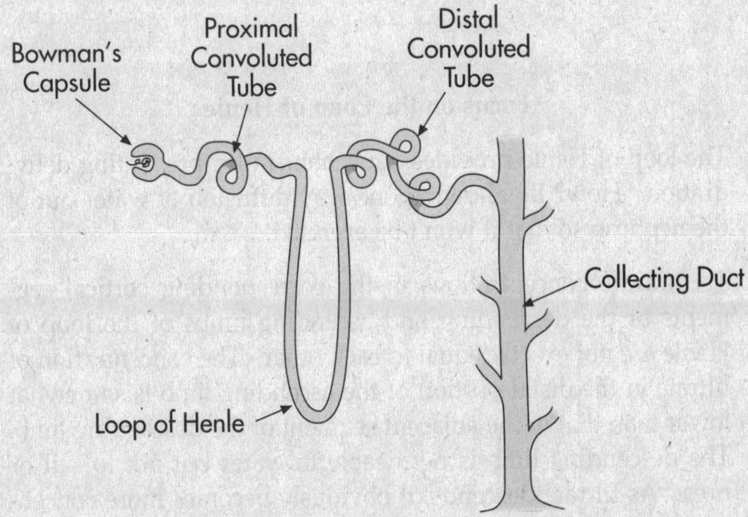


**The more concentrated the urine needs to be, the longer the loop of Henle is, in order to perform that job. For instance, the desert-dwelling kangaroo rat must conserve all the water it can; its loop of Henle is far longer than ours.**

How does the kidney actually produce urine? By employing a combination of filtration, reabsorption, and tubular secretion.

## About Filtration

Blood that is to be filtered by the kidneys arrives at the kidneys via the renal arteries. The arteries branch into afferent arterioles, which themselves branch to form the glomerular capillaries inside the Bowman's capsule. The capillaries then join together to form the efferent arterioles.

Now let's take a look at how fluid is filtered across the glomerular capillary walls and into the Bowman's capsule. The efferent arteriole constricts, producing high hydrostatic pressure in the glomerulus. This forces fluid to leave the capillaries. The cell membranes of the capillaries allow everything but cells, platelets, and macromolecules (i.e., large proteins) to pass through into the glomerular space.

The fluid that filters out of the capillaries has the same composition as the blood entering the glomerulus—it contains sugars, amino acids, ions, and water. The fluid that enters the urinary space of the Bowman's capsule is called glomerular filtrate.

## Remembering Reabsorption and Secretion

About 99% of the fluid filtered by the kidneys is reabsorbed into the blood, leaving about 1.5 liters to be excreted as urine. Some reabsorption occurs along the length of the nephron, but most (65%) occurs when the filtrate passes through the proximal convoluted tubule. Keep in mind that reabsorption is a selective process; it returns needed materials to the blood and adjusts the composition of the filtrate. Meanwhile, potassium ions, hydrogen ions, ammonia, and certain drugs are secreted from the blood into the renal tubule.

A countercurrent exchange establishes a very hypertonic interstitial fluid, which draws water osmotically from the filtrate in the collecting ducts and allows the urine to become more concentrated. Just how the countercurrent mechanism at the loop of Henle accomplishes this is explained in the focus box below.

**What is the difference between *secretion* and *excretion*? In secretion, something is sent into an internal space in the organism. In excretion, something is sent out of the body.**

**Focus on the Loop of Henle**

The loop of Henle provides a mechanism for preventing dehydration. How? By allowing one-way diffusion of water out of the nephron so that it won't be excreted.

The filtrate concentrations in the corresponding cortical segments of the descending and ascending limbs of the loop of Henle are not exactly equal to each other. The concentration of filtrate in the distal portion of the ascending limb is somewhat lower than that in the adjacent segment of the descending limb. The descending limb is permeable to water but not to salt or urea. As filtrate descends, it obviously becomes more concentrated as water leaves. At the point where the loop of Henle turns and becomes the ascending limb, the filtrate becomes more dilute as salt leaves. This contributes to the hypertonic interstitial fluid of the renal medulla.

What if urine volume needs to be adjusted? Does any regulatory mechanism exist to maintain fluid balance? You bet.

## Hormonal Regulation

Urine volume is regulated by a hormone called antidiuretic hormone (ADH), which increases the permeability of the collecting tubule to water. Earlier we mentioned that ADH was a hormone released by the posterior lobe of the pituitary. When dehydration stimulates the release of ADH, more water is resorbed, producing a small amount of concentrated urine. On the other hand, when the body is adequately hydrated, less ADH is secreted.

Another way the body regulates water and ions is through the largest organ in the body:

## THE SKIN

The skin maintains body temperature, registers cues from the environment—like pressure, temperature, and pain—through sensory receptors, and provides a barrier against infection.

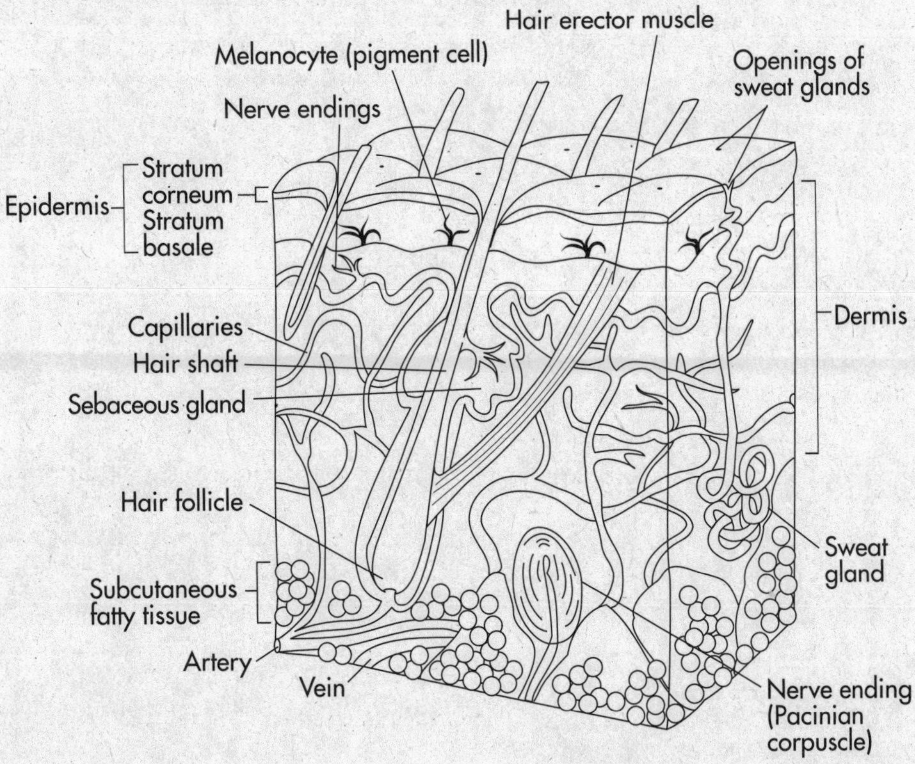


The goose bumps we humans display on cold days are produced by pilomotor muscles in our skin. This response hearkens back to the days when our ancestors had fur on their epidermis to erect, which trapped air for warmth

The skin is composed of three layers: the *epidermis,* the *dermis,* and the *subcutaneous tissue.*

The epidermis is called stratified squamous epithelium because it is a layered, flat structure. The external layer of the epidermis is the stratus corneum, which is composed of a layer of dead cells filled with the protein keratin. The stratus corneum provides resistance to invading microorganisms. Dead cells at the surface of the epidermis slough off and are replaced by new epithelial cells.

The dermis lies directly below the epidermis and contains the blood vessels, nerve endings, sebaceous glands (which secrete oils), and the sweat glands. The sweat glands secrete water and ions in response to high temperatures and sympathetic stimulation. They help to maintain a constant temperature and optimal balance of sodium and chloride ions in the body.

Subcutaneous tissue contains, among other structures, adipose tissue (fat).

# 11

# The Endocrine System

The endocrine system is responsible for many complex activities in the body, including metabolism, growth, and reproduction. How does the endocrine system work? It releases hormones which provide communication between various parts of an organism. These hormones, which travel in the blood, have a wide range of effects on their target cells.

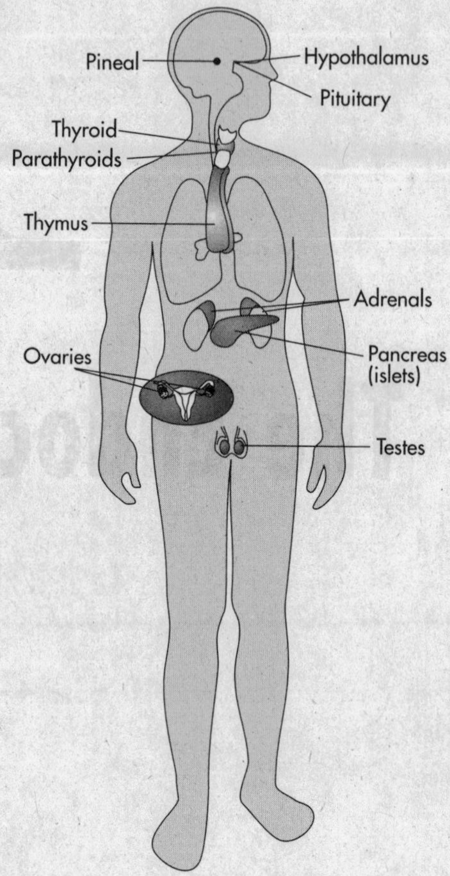


Before we discuss hormones in detail, let's compare the action of hormones to that of neurotransmitters. Hormones differ from neurotransmitters in two ways: (1) Hormones can act at targets locations far from where they are produced. (Neurotransmitters act locally.) Endocrine hormones are secreted by ductless glands and carried to their target organs by the bloodstream. (2) Hormones tend to be secreted and act in a slow and chronic manner. (Neurotransmitters tend to have rapid and short-lived effects.)

An endocrine hormone can produce many different effects, depending on the functions of its target cells (cells that are susceptible to the hormone) and the organs it reaches. Although a given hormone can be brought into contact with practically any cell in the body via the bloodstream, it will only stimulate a response in cells that have receptors for that hormone. Cells and organs may be the targets of few or many different hormones.

# ENDOCRINE ORGANS

The endocrine glands associated with the endocrine system include the pancreas, adrenals, thyroid, parathyroids, ovaries, and testes. Two glands that exert a regulatory effect over the endocrine system are the hypothalamus and the pituitary gland. The regulatory effects may be direct or transmitted through other, intermediate, endocrine glands.

## ABOUT THE HYPOTHALAMUS

The hypothalamus, which is a part of the brain, exerts the highest-level control of all the endocrine organs. It integrates information received from the nervous center, processing signals from the autonomic nervous system as well as the limbic system. The hypothalamus exerts a regulatory influence on many other functions through its effects on the pituitary gland. It also influences processes as varied as thirst and hunger, temperature regulation, and circadian (24-hour cycles) time-keeping.

**Alternatively**
"Night is the other half of life, and the better half."
—Goethe

The hypothalamus synthesizes and releases seven regulatory hormones. They are corticotropin-releasing hormone (CRH), thyrotropin-releasing hormone (TRH), growth-hormone-releasing hormone (GRH), growth hormone-inhibiting hormone (GIH, also called somatostatin), luteinizing hormone-releasing hormone (LHRH), prolactin-releasing hormone (PRH), and prolactin-inhibiting hormone (PIH).

## THE PITUITARY GLAND

Located just below the hypothalamus are two small lobes that make up the anterior and posterior pituitary gland. This tiny organ (pea-sized, in fact) secretes no fewer than eight major hormones between its posterior and anterior parts. What's more, the anterior and posterior sections of this small organ derive from different embryologic tissue and carry out very different functions. We'll show you what this means.

## THE ANTERIOR PITUITARY

The six hormones secreted by the anterior pituitary are:

1. Corticotropin, or ACTH (adrenocorticotropic hormone), whose release is stimulated by CRH from the hypothalamus. This hormone stimulates aldosterone and steroid hormone secretion from the adrenals.
2. Growth hormone (GH), regulated by GRH and GIH.
3. Thyroid-stimulating hormone, stimulated by TRH.
4. Follicle-stimulating hormone (FSH), which stimulates follicle growth and ovulation in females, and stimulates secretion of testosterone in males.

5. Luteinizing hormone (LH), which stimulates formation of the corpus luteum and progesterone secretion in females, and stimulates spermatogenesis in males. LH secretion is regulated by LHRH.
6. Prolactin, which stimulates milk secretion and is regulated by PRH and PIH.

## The Posterior Pituitary

The pineal gland is a small endocrine organ that is located near the pituitary; it secretes the hormone melatonin, which is believed to influence sleep-wake cycles.

The posterior pituitary secretes two hormones: *vasopressin* and *oxytocin*. These hormones are actually synthesized in the hypothalamus. Once they're made, however, they travel down the associated axons and are stored in the posterior pituitary, ready for their eventual release into the circulation. Vasopressin, also known as antidiuretic hormone (ADH), increases water retention in the kidney by increasing the permeability of the collecting ducts.

The other hormone of the posterior pituitary, oxytocin, is responsible for the uterine muscle contractions during labor and delivery.

## The Pancreas

The endocrine portion of the pancreas is called the *islets of Langerhans* and regulates many aspects of an organism's metabolism. Two principle hormones arising from the pancreas are *insulin,* which is secreted by the beta cells, and *glucagon,* which is secreted by alpha cells. Insulin and glucagon work together to regulate carbohydrate, protein, and fat metabolism.

Insulin is responsible for the storage of glucose, fatty acids, and amino acids in various tissues of the body. The primary stimulus for insulin secretion is an increase in the blood glucose level, which is detected by the pancreas. Target cells of the body possess insulin receptors on their cell membranes. Insulin receptors are transmembrane glycoproteins made up of four subunits. Insulin can bind at either of two receptor sites on the receptor. What happens when insulin binds at the receptors? This increases membrane permeability, so that more glucose enters target cells. The increase in membrane permeability results from an increase in the number of glucose transporters available on the cell's membrane. The resulting influx of glucose into cells rapidly lowers blood glucose levels.

Once inside the cell, glucose is transformed into glycogen by *glycogenesis*. The glycogen gets stored in muscle and liver tissue until it's needed. Insulin also promotes *lipogenesis* (transformation of fatty acids into triglycerides) for storage in adipose tissue, and promotes amino acid storage in tissues by increasing the rate of amino acid incorporation into proteins.

## Glucagon

By regulating glycogenolysis, glucagon stimulates an increase in blood glucose levels. This hormone also prompts glucose synthesis (gluconeogenesis), catabolism of stored fats (lipolysis), and ketone production. In the liver, glucagon exerts its effect by stimulating a cyclic AMP-protein kinase cascade, causing glycogen to break down. Glucagon is released from the pancreatic islet alpha cells in response to starvation, exercise, and increased blood levels of specific amino acids.

# ABOUT THE ADRENALS

The adrenal glands are located above the kidneys. Each adrenal gland is basically composed of two glands: The outer portion, the cortex, secretes steroid hormones, while the inner portion, the medulla, produces catecholamines (e.g., epinephrine and norepinephrine).

## The Adrenal Cortex

The steroid hormones synthesized by the adrenal cortex fall into two categories; the *mineralocorticoids* and *glucocorticoids*. The mineralocorticoid aldosterone plays an important role in the kidneys' regulation of potassium and sodium ion concentrations. Aldosterone acts to increase sodium retention at the distal tubule and collecting duct of the kidney. As a consequence of its effect on sodium and potassium concentrations, aldosterone tends to promote water retention.

Aldosterone also promotes sodium reabsorption from various body fluids, which results in increased extracellular sodium concentration. The primary stimulants of aldosterone secretion are decreased blood volume, decreased serum sodium levels, and elevated extracellular potassium concentrations.

Glucocorticoids, which include cortisol and corticosterone, predominantly affect glucose and protein metabolism. They elevate blood glucose concentrations, increase the force of cardiac muscle contractions, and increase water retention. In addition, they have important anti-inflammatory and anti-allergic activities.

## The Adrenal Medulla

The adrenal medulla secretes the catacholamines, epinephrine and norepinephrine. These compounds are responsible for an organism's "flight or fight" response in the face of stressful conditions. Among the effects of epinephrine and norepinephrine are increases in heart rate, blood pressure, free fatty acid release, blood sugar concentration, and alertness.

**The catacholamines are secreted in response to sympathetic nervous system enervation. In other words, when the world is being unsympathetic, your sympathetic nervous system kicks in.**

## The Thyroid Gland

The thyroid gland is located just below the larynx and secretes thyroid hormone. Thyroid hormone produces a wide range of effects throughout the body, but is principally involved in regulating the body's basal metabolic rate. The thyroid gland is stimulated by thyroid-stimulating hormone, which is secreted by the anterior pituitary gland. The binding of thyroid hormone to its cellular receptors results in increased cellular oxygen consumption and heat production, and serves to regulate growth and development.

Overstimulation of the thyroid gland is called hyperthyroidism. The condition may arise from a variety of causes and is characterized by weight loss, increased appetite, tremor, and heat intolerance. One indication of the presence of this condition is a dramatic increase in metabolic rate. The most common form of hyperthyroidism is Graves disease, which is characterized by the presence of goiter and exophthalmos (protrusion of the eyeballs).

## The Parathyroid Glands

The four pea-sized parathyroid glands, which are located behind the thyroid gland, secrete parathyroid hormone, or parathormone. This hormone increases calcium concentration in the blood and acts as an antagonist to calcitonin. How, exactly, does parathyroid hormone increase calcium concentration? It stimulates bone resorption, which frees up calcium. It also causes the intestine to increase its uptake of calcium, and the kidney to increase its reuptake of calcium.

The last set of endocrine organs that we need to recall here are the gonadal organs.

Female secondary sex characteristics include:

- breast development
- widening pelvis
- fat storage on specific areas of the body

Male secondary sex characteristics include:

- muscle development
- deepening voice
- growth of facial and body hair

## The Testes and Ovaries

The testes and ovaries are the location of the production of the sex hormones. Estrogen is synthesized in the ovaries and is responsible for secondary sex characteristics in the female. (It also plays a role in the menstrual cycle.) Testosterone, which is primarily synthesized by the testes, is necessary for the normal development of male secondary sex characteristics and sperm formation.

# 12

# The Musculoskeletal System

The musculoskeletal system is an integral part of the body. The endoskeleton is made up of bone, the more flexible cartilage (found, for instance, at the tip of the nose and the external ear), collagen, and other forms of connective tissue. The endoskeleton gives support to the body and provides a framework for muscle attachment. What else does it do? It produces blood cells. The muscles, of course, provide motility. Let's begin our review with the skeletal system.

## THE SKELETAL SYSTEM

The human skeleton provides a lever against which muscles contract. This allows bodily movements, such as ambulation. Bones also provide structural support and protection for the organs of the cranium, thorax, abdomen and pelvis.

Bones are also responsible for the blood supply; red blood cells and platelets are created in the marrow of bone. What's more, bone serves as a storage depot for calcium, phosphate and other ions. It takes up or releases these ions in response to changing conditions and signals.

"Critics?—I love every bone in their heads."
—Eugene O'Neill

What, exactly, is bone made of? If you look closely at it, you'll notice that its tissue is composed of two substances; bone matrix and bone cells.

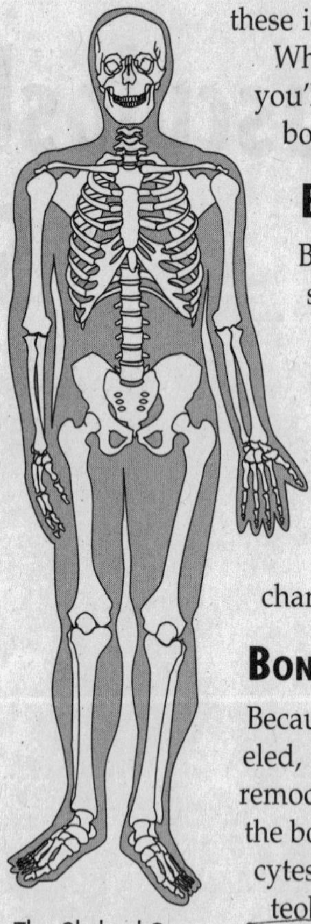

The Skeletal System

### BONE MATRIX

Bone matrix is a mixture of inorganic and organic substances. The primary inorganic substances are calcium and phosphorous, which form hydroxyapatite. Also present are noncrystalline calcium phosphate, bicarbonate, citrate, magnesium, potassium, and sodium. The organic substances are type I collagen and amorphous ground substance, which consists of glycosaminoglycans and proteins. It's the mixture of hydroxyapatite and collagen that causes the characteristic hardness and resistance of bone.

### BONE CELLS

Because bone is a living tissue that is continually remodeled, bone cells hang out in the matrix to carry out the remodeling jobs. There are three types of bone cells within the bone matrix: *osteocytes*, *osteoblasts*, and *osteoclasts*. Osteocytes are responsible for maintaining the bony matrix; osteoblasts are the "bone builders" and osteoclasts are the "bone breakers."

### COMPACT BONE AND SPONGY BONE

Bone has two distinct morphologies. Compact bone is the dense outer portion of the bone, and spongy bone is the inner, spongy-looking area. Interestingly, these two types of bone, while having a different outward appearance, have the same composition. The difference between the two is this: Spongy bone has many small cavities which contain bone marrow.

## About Bone Marrow: It May Be Red Or Yellow

In a mature adult, red marrow is found in flat bones (ribs, clavicles, pelvic bones, and skull bones). The red marrow is the site of red blood cell and platelet production, as well as being the site of some immune cell development and maturation. The yellow marrow is filled with adipocytes (fat cells). Are these two types of marrow mutually exclusive? No, it turns out. Under stress, or when exposed to a poor oxygen supply, yellow marrow can transform into red marrow to increase red blood cell production.

Now we know something about spongy bone. Is there anything to know about compact bone? Yes, as a matter of fact. Compact bone contains . . .

## Haversian Systems

Microscopic sections of compact bone show a set of concentric lamellae called haversian systems, which run parallel to the long axis of bones. Many of these haversian systems together give compact bone its bulk and strength. The central canal within each haversian system is called the *haversian canal* and carries blood vessels and nerves. The canal also is filled with loose connective tissue. Haversian systems distribute nutrients throughout compact bone.

Spongy bone, on the other hand, does not require haversian systems for its nutrient supply because the spicules (thin segments of bone) that surround the marrow spaces are able to absorb nutrients directly from the marrow.

## What About Ligaments, Tendons, and Joints?

Ligaments are tough, elastic connective tissue. Their job? To keep bones attached across joints, like at the elbow or knee. Tendons, on the other hand, are a tough and inelastic fiber made up mostly of collagen; they attach muscle to bones. Joints are important too; they represent discontinuities in bone throughout the skeleton and allow for motion and flexibility. There are three types of joints: *fibrous*, *synovial*, and *cartilaginous*.

**Bursa fluid protects and cushions areas of friction, like where a tendon passes over a bone. Inflammation of the bursa is called bursitis.**

1. Fibrous joints are joined by fibrous tissue and allow for almost no motion.
2. In synovial joints the opposing bony surfaces are covered with a layer of hyaline cartilage. There is a joint cavity containing synovial fluid that is lined with synovial membrane and reinforced by a fibrous capsule and ligaments. These joints allow for the wide range of body movement. Examples of these joints are the knee, hip, shoulder, and fingers.
3. Cartilaginous joints are joints in which the opposed bony surfaces are united by cartilage.

We've talked about bone and the ways in which muscle is connected to bone. Now let's look at muscles.

## THE MUSCULAR SYSTEM

There are three types of muscle: *skeletal*, *cardiac*, and *smooth*. Both skeletal and cardiac muscle have striated (striped) appearances and so they're called striated muscle. The striations are produced by thin and thick filaments that are made up of the proteins actin and myosin, respectively.

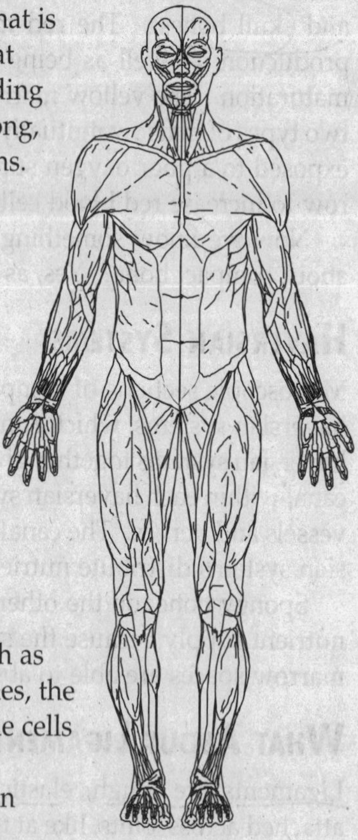

- Skeletal muscle is the type of muscle that is under voluntary control. A muscle that traverses a joint is responsible for bending that joint. A skeletal muscle cell is a long, multinucleated cell with many striations.
- Cardiac muscle is also striated, and its cells branch and bind to adjacent cells, giving it an interwoven appearance. Cardiac muscle contains intercalated discs (darkly-staining transverse lines), which anchor actin filaments at the end of a cell. Cardiac muscles resemble and work much like skeletal muscles, except that cardiac muscle contraction is not under voluntary control.
- Smooth muscle is not under voluntary control, either; it's found in organs such as blood vessels, the stomach and intestines, the skin, glands, and ducts. Smooth muscle cells are mononucleated, elongated, and nonstriated. Here, the actin and myosin filaments are arranged in an irregular pattern that crisscrosses to form a lattice. The contraction process, however, is similar to that found in striated muscle.

"Running is an unnatural act, except from enemies and to the bathroom."
—Unknown

That said, let's take a closer look at how skeletal muscle contracts. To do that, we need to examine the basic unit of contraction.

### THE SARCOMERE

The functional unit of contraction in muscle cells is the *sarcomere*, which is a segment of a myofibril between two adjacent *Z lines* (see diagram). A sarcomere is made up of a series of *thick* and *thin filaments* that are parallel to the length of the muscle fiber. Each thin filament is composed of the protein *actin* and is anchored at one end to a Z line. The thick filaments, composed of the protein *myosin*, have no connection to the Z lines. Regularly spaced cross-bridges which extend from myosin filaments connect the actin and myosin filaments, thus allowing muscle contraction to occur. When the actin and myosin filaments connect and then slide relative to each other, they bring the Z lines closer together and cause the muscle fiber to contract.

The length of the myosin (thick) filament corresponds to the sector called the *A band*. Because the filament itself does not contract, the A band has a fixed length, equal to that of the myosin strands. The *I band* is the space between one end of a group of thick filaments and the Z line, and contains only actin (thin) filaments. The *H band* is the space in the middle of the sarcomere that contains only myosin filaments with no overlapping actin filaments.

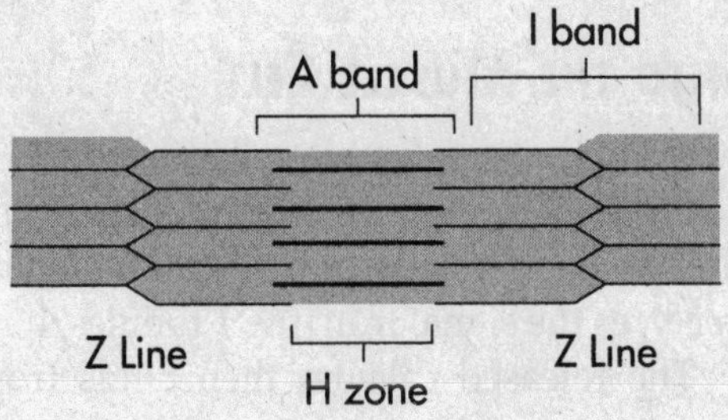


A Sarcomere is Bounded by Z Lines on Either Side

## WHAT CAUSES A MUSCLE TO CONTRACT?

To understand the answer, we have to look at how muscles are prevented from contracting during rest. Two regulatory proteins perform this job; their names are troponin and tropomyosin.

**The two pairs of proteins you need to keep straight when it comes to muscle contraction are (1) actin and myosin, and (2) troponin and tropomyosin.**

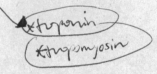

## MUSCLE CELLS AT REST

Actin (thin) filaments have, at regular intervals, myosin-binding sites which allow myosin to form cross-bridges with actin and initiate contraction. When the muscle cell is at rest, these sites contain *troponin*, which is a three-subunit molecule that also has a binding site for calcium. Associated with each troponin complex is a long, thin tropomyosin molecule. The *tropomyosin* wraps itself in a long helix around the actin filaments, covering actin's binding sites and preventing myosin from binding to actin.

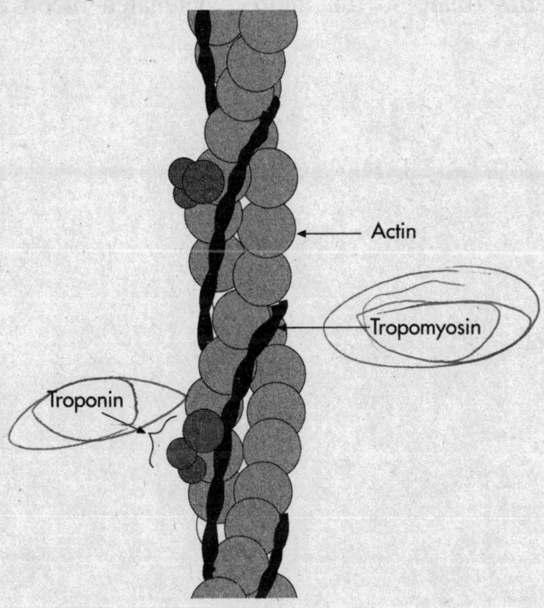


Now let's see what happens when a muscle cell receives a signal to contract.

## The Neuromuscular Junction

Special types of nerve cells called motor neurons stimulate muscle fibers. When the motor neuron fires (see The Nervous System), it releases the neurotransmitter acetylcholine across the neuromuscular junction. The acetylcholine binds to the muscle cell membrane (which is called a sarcolemma), causing the membrane to depolarize.

## Transmission into the Muscle Cell

A series of invaginations of the sarcolemma called T tubules then carry the nerve impulse further inside the cell to the muscle's endoplasmic reticulum (called the sarcoplasmic reticulum). The sarcoplasmic reticulum's job is to sequester $Ca^{2+}$ ions. When the SR receives the signal from the T tubules, it releases $Ca^{2+}$ into the intracellular space. The released calcium then binds troponin at troponin's calcium-binding sites.

## This Has A Big Effect on Tropomyosin

When calcium binds to troponin, it causes a conformational change in the position of tropomyosin on actin. The conformational change shifts tropomyosin out of the way of the actin's myosin-binding site. Now myosin can bind to actin at actin's binding sites and contraction ensues.

## Contraction Requires Energy

You'll need to remember that ATP is required in order for myosin and actin to form cross-bridges. That's why there is an ATPase site on myosin's cross-bridge. Hydrolysis of this ATP is normally slow, but when actin is its cofactor, myosin quickly breaks down ATP, releasing the energy required to detach actin from myosin. New ATP molecules quickly replace the hydrolyzed ones. To meet the energy needs of muscle contraction, muscle fibers contain large numbers of mitochondria. Actively contracting muscle also requires lots of oxygen, which makes the arteries dilate so that more oxygenated blood can arrive at the muscles.

The wing cells of insects are chock full of mitochondria to keep those wings beating.

# 13

# The Nervous System

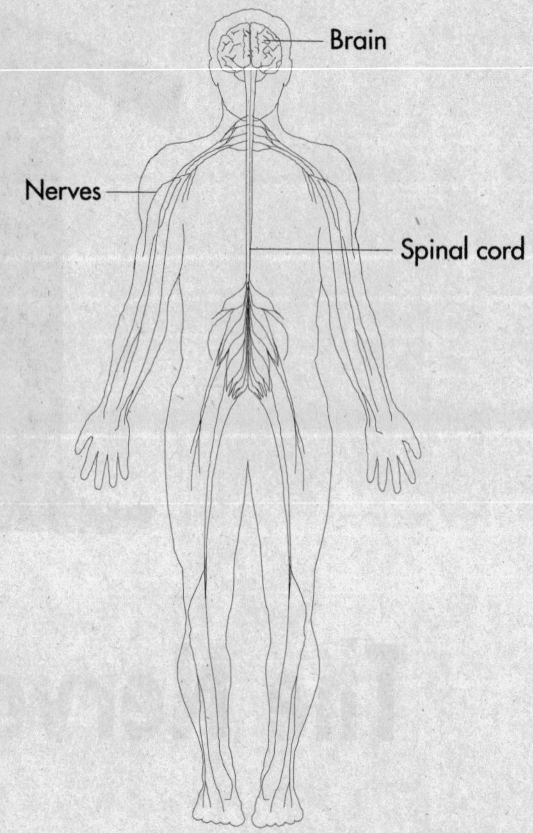


The Nervous System

Organisms' ability to respond to stimuli is made possible by the nervous system. Let's take a global view of the nervous system; it consists of two major parts: The central nervous system and the peripheral nervous system.

## THE CENTRAL NERVOUS SYSTEM

The central nervous system is composed of the brain and the spinal cord. The vertebrate brain consists of three regions: The forebrain, the midbrain, and the hindbrain. Let's review the structures and functions of the parts of the brain.

### PARTS OF THE BRAIN

"I must have a prodigious quantity of mind; it takes me as much as a week sometimes to make it up."
—Mark Twain

The *cerebral cortex* (cerebrum) is the largest part of the brain. It integrates sensory impulses, controls voluntary motor function, and is responsible for language, cognition and other higher functions. The *hypothalamus* maintains homeostasis of the organism through hormonal regulation. Information is relayed between the spinal cord and the cerebrum by the thalamus. The cerebellum is responsible for posture, muscle tone, and equilibrium. In other words, the *cerebellum* is the part of the brain that we use to maintain our balance. Involuntary processes (i.e., respiration, heart rate, blood pressure, and reflex reactions, like coughing) are regulated by the medulla.

### The Spinal Cord

The spinal cord regulates simple motor reflexes and transmits information from the rest of the body to the brain (and vice versa). Inside the spinal cord are the cell bodies of spinal cord neurons (called the gray matter). The outside contains myelinated spinal cord axons (called the white matter).

## THE PERIPHERAL NERVOUS SYSTEM

The peripheral nervous system includes all of the nerves that lie outside of the central nervous system. The peripheral nervous system is made up of the sensory receptors and the cranial and spinal nerves. The PNS is divided into the somatic nervous system and the autonomic nervous system. The somatic nervous system handles voluntary activities, sending motor fibers to skeletal muscle. The autonomic nervous system handles involuntary actions, like those involved in the digestive, circulatory, and excretory systems.

"The most decisive actions of our life...are most often unconsidered actions."
—Andre Gide

### Autonomic Nervous System

The autonomic nervous system itself also has two subdivisions: The *sympathetic* and *parasympathetic* systems. Many organs are enervated by both of these systems, which have opposing effects. Cardiac muscle, smooth muscle, and the glands of the body are all enervated by the autonomic nervous system.

The sympathetic nervous system is active during emergency conditions. It produces the fight or flight response to stress. During the fight or flight response heart rate and blood pressure rises and gastrointestinal motility and digestive secretion slow. The parasympathetic nervous system is antagonistic to the sympathetic system and brings the body back to homeostasis. It causes the heart rate to slow down and digestive activity to increase. Parasympathetic fibers reach the thoracic and abdominal regions via the vagus nerve.

## A CLOSER LOOK AT THE NERVOUS SYSTEM

The nervous system is made up of individual cells called neurons (nerve cells). Neurons contain specialized features designed to receive and transmit nerve impulses. There are two cytoplasmic extensions of the cells: *dendrites* and *axons*. Dendrites receive stimuli and transport signals toward the cell body. Axons transmit signals away from the cell body.

At the terminal end of the axon are *synaptic knobs,* which are filled with vesicles that contain neurotransmitters. Each neuron has its own distinctive neurotransmitter (chemicals which transmit messages between two neurons). Some neurotransmitters have excitatory effects on neurons while others have an inhibitory effects. The space between two neurons is called a synapse.

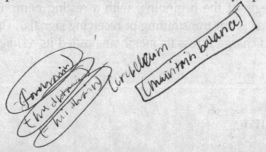

forebrain
thindbrain
hindbrain
cerebellum
(maintain balance)

## Classification of Nerve Cell Types

A neuron has a resting potential of approximately —70 millivolts.

Nerve cells can be categorized based on their position and role in the nervous system. Receptor cells register a given stimulus, such as a smell or sight. Sensory neurons (also called *afferent* neurons) receive information from the sensory receptors and send it to the central nervous system, where one or more interneurons receive and process the information. In some cases (i.e., in olfactory transduction) the receptor is a modified part of the sensory neuron itself. Motor neurons (also called *effector* or *efferent* neurons), convey signals from the central nervous system to the target muscle or gland. Interneurons (also called associative neurons) relay signals to other neurons, but do not directly communicate with either sensory or motor neurons.

## The Simple Reflex Arc

What is a *simple reflex arc*? A simple reflex arc, such as the Achilles reflex or a patellar reflex (knee-jerk response), involves only two neurons which complete a circuit of nerve impulse transmission. The route of the impulse is:

stimulus site → CNS → target organ

In the Achilles simple reflex arc, a tap on the tendon produces a stretch in the muscle fiber. The stretch is registered by stretch receptors (these are specialized endings of sensory neurons) on the muscle fiber. The sensory neuron then signals the central nervous system and the signal is processed. Next, the CNS sends a signal to the motor neuron, and the motor neuron transmits the signal to the muscle. The muscle responds by contracting.

We've gone over the ways in which neurons are assembled to transmit information. Now let's look at exactly how they send and receive signals. Before we go any further, though, we need to review a few terms.

## Terms You Need to Know About The Axonal Membrane's Potential

*Polarization*–a separation of charge across a membrane

*Depolarization*–a reduction in the separation of charge across a membrane

*Repolarization*–re-establishment of a separation of charge across a membrane

*Hyperpolarization*–an increase in the separation of charge across a membrane

We begin at the beginning, with a resting neuron. A resting neuron is a neuron that is not transmitting or receiving signals. The resting neuron has an associated charge across its membrane called its *resting potential*.

## THE RESTING POTENTIAL

A resting neuron is said to be polarized, which we just said means that there is a difference in charge across its membrane. It has an electrical potential (a difference) across its membrane of approximately –70 mV. The resting potential is created by large anions and a concentration gradient of potassium ions inside the neuron. Let's review what you'll need to know about the concentration gradient across the axonal membrane:

Recall that the sodium-potassium pump is a form of cotransport. More specifically, it operates as an antiport system.

Outside the neuron, there is:

- a high sodium concentration
- a low potassium concentration

Inside the neuron, there is:

- a low sodium concentration
- a high potassium concentration

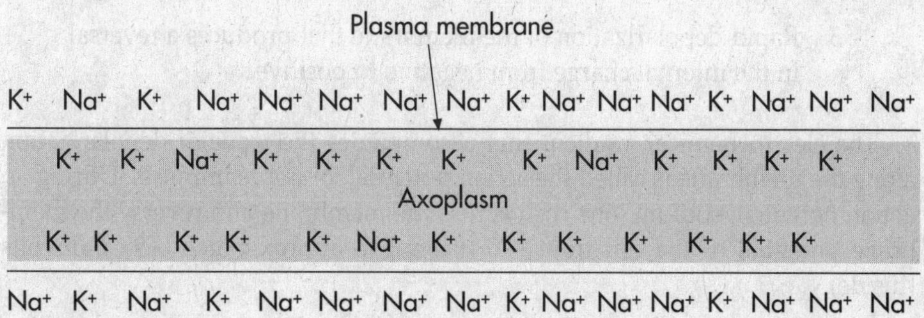


Overall, this means that the inside of a resting neuron is more negative than the outside.

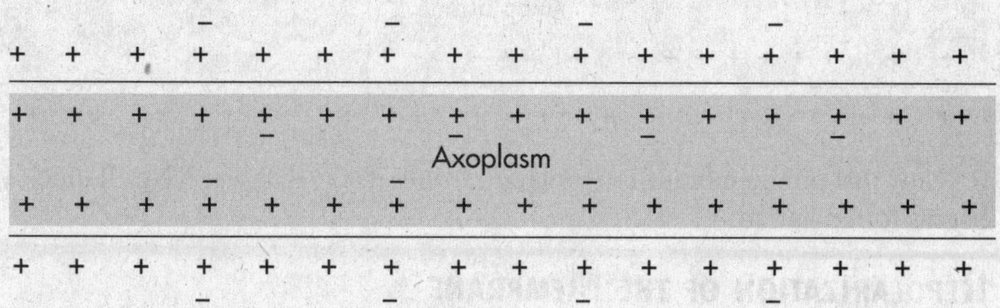

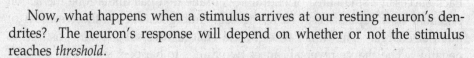

Now, what happens when a stimulus arrives at our resting neuron's dendrites? The neuron's response will depend on whether or not the stimulus reaches *threshold*.

## THRESHOLD

A stimulus to the dendrites causes a small area of the membrane to depolarize. The slight change in electrical charge opens up voltage-gated sodium channels on the membrane. Sodium enters the cell (down its concentration gradient), bringing in positive charges. This depolarizes the cell some more. In order to initiate a coordinated and sustained neuronal response, however, the signal must carry a certain strength. That strength is called the threshold level. The neuronal response initiated by a threshold-level stimulus is called *all or nothing*. What does that mean? It means that a minor stimulus only causes a local polarization that quickly dissipates, and a threshold-level stimulus causes the neuron to respond at the axon hillock with a highly regular sequence of reactions. What's more, those reactions are carried out in their entirety.

> "A great man represents a great ganglion in the nerves of society..."
> – John Marshall

## An Action Potential

Let's trace the events that occur during an action potential, beginning with a threshold-level stimulus. These events occur in the order shown below, along successive segments of the neural membrane. In response to a stimulus that reaches threshold, the neuron undergoes:

1. Sudden permeability of the membrane to sodium ions via the voltage-gated opening of sodium channels.
2. Rapid influx of sodium ions.
3. Rapid depolarization of the membrane that produces a reversal in the internal charge from negative to positive.

The electrochemical gradient that accompanies the wave of depolarization along the membrane is called the action potential, or nerve impulse. During an action potential, sodium ions rush across the membrane and reverse the membrane potential of the cell from –70 (inside) to approximately +50 millivolts (inside).

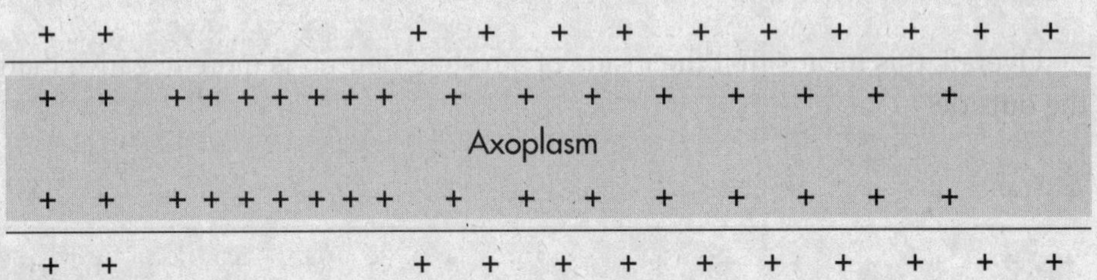


Now that our membrane is depolarized, does it stay that way? No. It quickly begins to repolarize.

## Repolarization of the Membrane

Each successive small area of neural membrane that has undergone the action potential now repolarizes. Now the cell undergoes yet another reversal of internal charge. This time, though, the charge reversal is from positive to negative. The charge reversal causes two things to happen:

1. Sodium channel gates close, making the cell impermeable to sodium.
2. Potassium gates open, allowing potassium to move out.

It's important to remember this: The depolarization and repolarization that follow a threshold-level stimulus occur as a result of the opening or closing of voltage-gated channels in the membrane. Voltage differences across the membrane induce a change in the conformation of sodium and potassium channels, permitting or inhibiting the flow of those ions.

## About The Refractory Period

There's one more thing we should mention: The repolarization events just described do not immediately restore the ions to their pre-threshold concentrations. If you look at the distribution of ions just after repolarization, there's a greater concentration of sodium on the inside and a greater concentration of potassium on the outside. So how does the axonal membrane reestablish its original resting state? Well, the sodium-potassium pump pumps sodium out of the cell and potassium back into the cell. This period of transition is called the refractory period; no stimulus can elicit a neural response during this time. As soon as the charge distribution is reestablished, the neuron is once again capable of responding to stimuli.

## Myelinated Neurons Lead to Saltatory Conduction

Some neurons have myelin surrounding their axons. *Schwann cells* encase long, discrete sections of the axon, creating *myelin sheaths*. It turns out, however, that small areas of the exposed axon (unmyelinated areas) remain. These are called the *nodes of Ranvier*. The highly insular properties of the Schwann cells block transmission of the nerve impulse where they are located. This makes the exposed nodes of Ranvier the only sites available for electrical propagation along the axon. Impulse transmission is accelerated as the impulse jumps from node to node. This is how myelination allows the axonal membrane to conduct impulses faster and more efficiently than can an unmyelinated axon.

Diseases involving demyelination of neurons produce devastating results.

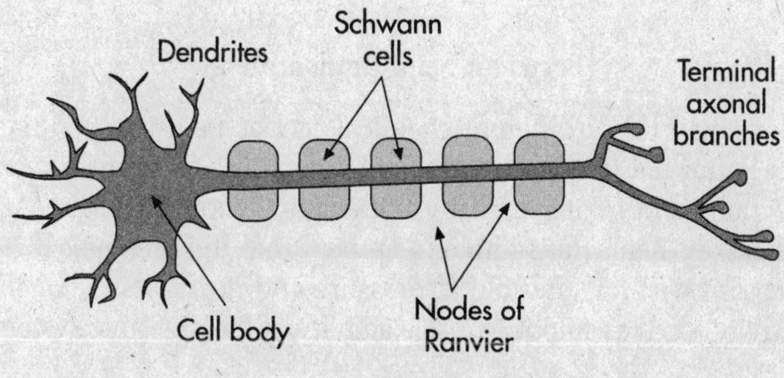


Your Average Myelinated Neuron

Okay, so our nerve impulse has made it across the entire neuron at this point. What happens when the impulse reaches the end of the neuron?

## It Gets Transmitted Across The Synapse

Once the nerve impulse arrives at the end of the neuron, which is called the synaptic knob, it triggers fusion of the synaptic vesicles with the terminal end of the axonal membrane, which is called the presynaptic membrane.

Fusion of the synaptic vesicles with the cell membrane causes the release of neurotransmitters from the synaptic vesicles into the synaptic cleft—the space between the presynaptic membrane and the postsynaptic membrane. The postsynaptic membrane is the membrane of a second neuron.

Neurotransmitters diffuse across the synaptic cleft and bind to receptor molecules on the postsynaptic membrane. These receptors are specific to the neurotransmitter released.

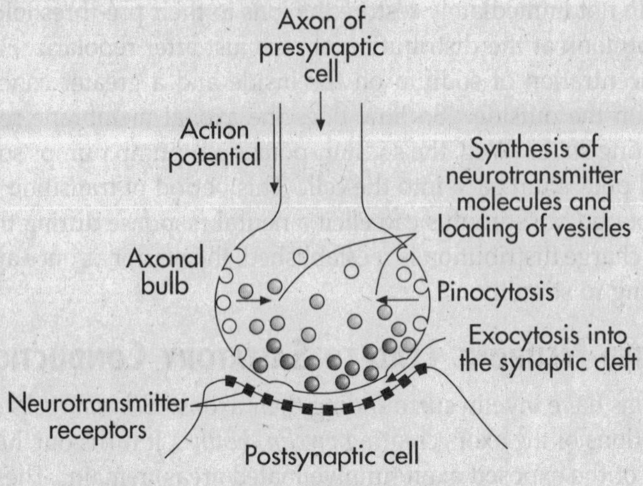


Recall that postsynaptic receptors are ligand-gated. That means that when the receptor binds to a neurotransmitter, a conformational change takes place which opens channels for ion flow. The ion flow produces the electrical impulse that acts as a signal to the neuron. The signal that is below threshold will produce only a small, localized depolarization of the neuron's axon. The signal that reaches threshold level will stimulate the action potential.

**Focus on Neurotransmitters**

More than thirty different chemicals act as neurotransmitters. An important one is acetylcholine, which triggers muscle contractions and is degraded by the enzyme cholinesterase. Another key neurotransmitter is epinephrine (adrenaline); it increases heart rate and blood pressure and decreases metabolic activity, such as smooth muscle activity of the digestive system.

**Other key neurotransmitters are serotonin and dopamine, both of which act on the central nervous system.**

## SENSORY ORGANS

Humans have five senses: tactile (touch), olfactory (smell), gustatory (taste), auditory (hearing), and vision. How are we able to experience these senses? By way of our sense organs. Sense organs are made up mostly of receptor cells called sensory receptors. Sensory receptors are important because they convey information from the environment (in the form of electrical impulses) to the central nervous system.

There are several types of sensory receptors. *Mechanoreceptors* respond to mechanical pressure or distortion and include stretch receptors, tactile receptors, proprioceptors (which provide cues to changes in pressure or tension in muscles), and auditory receptors. *Chemoreceptors* register taste and smell. Thermo-, electro-, and photoreceptors register heat, electrical energy, and light energy, respectively. *Sensory receptors,* located in the olfactory epithelium of the nasal cavity, detect odors. The hairlike projections of the taste receptors, located in the taste buds, detect molecules in the mouth. The four tastes are sour, sweet, salty, and bitter.

## The Vestibular and Auditory Systems of The Ear

"Of all the noises, I think music is the least disagreeable."
–Samuel Johnson

The ear actually has two functions: It maintains equilibrium and transmits sound. The three divisions of the ear are the *outer*, *middle*, and *inner ear*. The external ear is made up of the pinna, which funnels sound waves into the auditory canal. At the middle ear, sound waves vibrate the *tympanic membrane*, setting into motion the three auditory bones; the *malleus, incus*, and *stapes*. These bones are arranged like levers: The movement of the first bone is amplified by the second, and the second by the third.

Movement of the stapes starts vibrations in the fluid of the *cochlea*, a structure found in the inner ear. This action causes *hair cells* in the cochlea to bend. These hairs are the dendrites of the *cochlear nerve*, through which sound waves are transmitted to the auditory center of the brain.

The inner ear also contains the vestibular apparatus, which helps maintain equilibrium. The vestibular apparatus consists of a *membranous labyrinth* situated within the three *semicircular canals*. The semicircular canals are perpendicular to one another. When you move your head, you cause fluid to move around within the labyrinths. Depending on the direction of movement, different hair cells are stimulated by the fluid, sending sensory information (via the vestibular nerve) to the brain center. At the brain center directional movement and position are interpreted.

## The Eye

Our vision is the result of the transmission of light through the eye. The eye, of course, is composed of many structures. Light enters the eye through a transparent layer called the cornea. The iris, a smooth muscle, determines how much light will enter the eye. How does it do that? By regulating the size of the pupil. Light that enters the eye reaches the retina, which contains two types of photoreceptors: *rods* (specialized to register dim light) and *cones* (specialized to register bright light and color). Both rods and cones contain pigment (mostly rhodopsin) that allows them to absorb the energy from light rays.

How does the eye change focus? By relying on the action of an eye muscle called the ciliary muscle. This muscle governs the shape of the lens, a transparent structure that focuses light rays on the retina.

The actual sequence of light transmission through the eye looks like this:

> Light → cornea → aqueous humor → pupil → lens → vitreous humor → light receptors of the retina → optic nerve (as an electrical signal) → central nervous system (also as an electrical signal).

"You can't depend on your eyes when your imagination is out of focus"
– Mark Twain

**Focus on Nearsightedness and Farsightedness**

Myopia (nearsightedness) occurs when light is focused in front of the retina when a distant object is viewed. Hypermetropia (farsightedness) occurs when light is focused behind the retina when a nearby object is viewed.

# 14

# The Respiratory System

# 4

# The Respiratory System

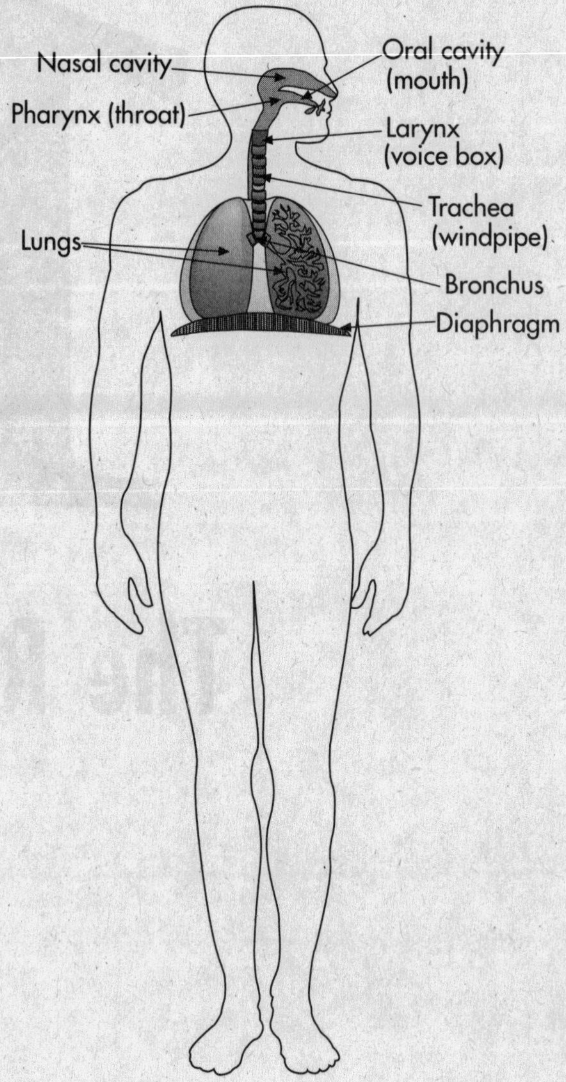


Take a deep breath. Every time you breathe your tissues are being oxygenated and getting rid of carbon dioxide. Gas exchange involves moving oxygen into the body, delivering it to the cells, and then removing carbon dioxide from cells and delivering it to the atmosphere.

## DIVINE INSPIRATION

Breathing is a normal involuntary behavior that is controlled by the medulla oblongata in the brain. The signal that initiates each cycle of breathing comes from the respiratory center within the medulla and is carried by the phrenic nerve to the diaphragm.

## THE INSPIRATION PROCESS

The diaphragm is a large, dome-shaped muscle positioned between the thorax and abdomen. Normally it is curved upwards toward the thorax. When the diaphragm contracts, it flattens out. This causes two things to happen:

- The amount of space between the lung and the diaphragm increases, and
- negative pressure is created in the extrapleural space.

Some people experience a disorder called sleep apnea. During sleep, they involuntarily stop breathing for a fraction of time. That brief interlude of oxygen deprivation is enough to trigger serious physiological consequences, like high blood pressure and strain on the heart.

To fill the space and reduce the negative pressure, the lungs begin to expand. Now, as the diaphragm contracts, the rib cage also expands due to the contraction of the intercostal muscles. This further increases the negative pressure within the thorax, contributing to even greater expansion of the lungs. The natural elasticity of the lung resists its own expansion. When the lungs expand, this creates a negative pressure inside the lungs themselves. The pressure differential between the inside and the outside of the lungs pulls air into the lungs through the respiratory tract. This air rushes to fill the expanding volume of the lungs. Once the air is in the lungs, of course, gas exchange occurs. (We'll get to that in a minute.) What happens to the inspired air after gas exchange occurs?

## IT GETS EXPIRED

Expiration occurs when the medulla sends a signal via the phrenic nerve to the diaphragm, causing the muscle to relax. Without the pull of the diaphragm, the lungs recoil due to the force of their elasticity. This recoil forces air from the lung tissue upward through the respiratory tract and out of the body. Let's talk now about what makes up the respiratory tract.

## STRUCTURAL FEATURES OF THE RESPIRATORY TRACT

The respiratory tract includes the *pharynx*, the *larynx*, the *trachea*, the *bronchi*, and the *alveoli*. Air first enters the respiratory tract through the nose. The hairs lining the nostrils and mucous membranes in the nasal cavity filter and trap large particles in the incoming air. Air travels from the nose through the nasopharynx and continues through the oropharynx. Air then travels through the larynx and into the *trachea* (windpipe). The trachea is a mucous membrane-lined tube with cartilaginous rings encircling it. These rings provide semirigid support to the tracheal wall and prevent the trachea from collapsing from the negative pressure that is generated during inspiration. At its terminus, the trachea branches into a left and a right *bronchus*. When the air reaches the bronchi, it can enter either the left or right branch. Like the trachea, the bronchi also have cartilaginous rings. After a distance of several centimeters the bronchi begin dividing into smaller and smaller branches; the smallest of these branches are called bronchi called bronchioles. At the termini of the bronchioles are tiny air sacs called alveoli.

Suppose small particles enter the lower respiratory tract. How does the body get rid of them? By trapping them in mucous. From there the particles are removed by the upward beating action of cilia. If even smaller particles escape these defenses and enter the alveoli, they are phagocytized by macrophages (immune cells specialized to engulf foreign particles).

The volume of air that enters and exits the lungs each time you breathe in and out is called the tidal volume.

Once air reaches the alveoli, gas exchange occurs.

## GAS EXCHANGE AT THE ALVEOLI

Each alveolus is surrounded by a network of pulmonary capillaries. The respiratory tract transports atmospheric oxygen to the alveoli, where it is picked up by the blood and circulated to the cells of the body. Carbon dioxide is picked up at the alveoli and transported out of the body.

The blood entering these capillaries from the right side of the heart contains more carbon dioxide than oxygen, since the blood has returned from systemic circulation (where it has picked up carbon dioxide and dropped off oxygen to the cells).

Carbon dioxide and oxygen travel by passive diffusion across the pulmonary capillary wall and alveolar wall. Remember that, in diffusion, molecules move from regions of high concentration to regions of low concentration, down a gradient. Oxygen passes from the alveolus, where its concentration is higher, to the capillary blood. Carbon dioxide diffuses down its concentration gradient across the capillary and alveolar membranes and into the alveolar air space.

We are now left with this question: How, then, is the concentration gradient restored? Here's how: Pulmonary capillary blood flow brings a constant blood supply that has high carbon dioxide and low oxygen content to the alveolus. Meanwhile, expiration flushes the high-carbon dioxide, low-oxygen content from the alveoli, thus renewing the concentration gradient from the atmospheric side.

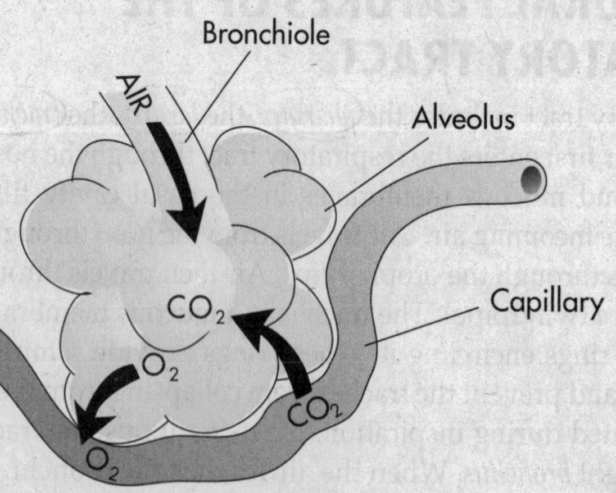

## SURFACE TENSION

The numerous alveoli clusters in the lung provide an enormous total surface area. This generates a large surface tension which must be overcome to keep the alveoli inflated. To lower the surface tension, specialized cells in the lung secrete surfactant. Surfactant, a mixture composed mostly of phospholipids, is added to the fluid that coats the inner side of the alveolar membrane to lower surface tension.

Certain alveoli cells produce and secrete surfactant. The surfactant's half-life is approximately half a day.

## BIOCHEMISTRY OF THE BLOOD GASES

Carbon dioxide can travel in many disguises in the blood. When $CO_2$ enters the circulation, it combines with water to form carbonic acid ($H_2CO_3$). Carbonic acid, in turn, can then dissociate into hydrogen ions ($H^+$) and bicarbonate ions ($HCO_3^-$). The release of lots of $H^+$ into circulation will lower the pH of the blood stream. What effect will this have on the blood? An increase in $CO_2$ levels in the blood will lead to an increase in the acidity of the blood. Carbon dioxide can also combine with hemoglobin to form carboxyhemoglobin.

These reactions are also reversible. At the alveolus, carbonic acid, bicarbonate, and carboxyhemoglobin all revert to give up the carbon dioxide, which then readily diffuses out of the alveolus.

## WHAT REGULATES THE CONTROL OF BLOOD GAS LEVELS?

The respiratory center in the medulla monitors blood carbon dioxide and oxygen levels.

**Respiratory rate INCREASES in response to:**

1. low blood oxygen levels
2. increased blood carbon dioxide levels
3. increased hydrogen ion concentration (low blood pH).

**Respiratory rate DECREASES in response to:**

1. high blood oxygen content
2. high blood pH
3. low blood carbon dioxide content.

# PART IV

# Organismal Biology

# 15

# Plants

In this chapter, we'll talk about some important features of plants that the GRE writers expect you to be familiar with. We'll discuss photosynthesis, which is the process by which plants manufacture their food. We'll review the structures and functions of the parts of a plant, proceeding from leaf to root and including herbaceous plant structures and woody plant structures. We'll talk about how a plant's life cycle includes alteration of generations. In our discussion of plant classification, we'll go over the differences between angiosperms and gymnosperms and between monocots and dicots. We'll finish the chapter with a review of plant behaviors and plant hormones.

## REMEMBER PHOTOSYNTHESIS?

In chapter 2, we learned that plant cells differ from animal cells primarily in that they contain chloroplasts and are enclosed by rigid cell walls that are made of cellulose.

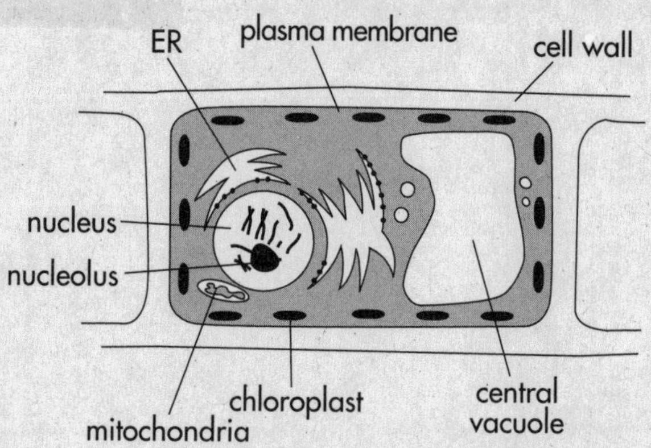


Chloroplasts enable the plant to conduct photosynthesis. Here's how photosynthesis works: Chloroplasts contain a green pigment called chlorophyll, which absorbs primarily blue, violet, and red light. Energy derived from the absorbed light rays is then used to synthesize sugar molecules for fuel. The general equation for photosynthesis is:

$$6CO_2 + 12H_2O \longrightarrow C_6H_{12}O_6 + 6O_2 + 6H_2O$$

**ATP and NADPH are both generated during the light reactions. Glucose is generated during the dark reactions**

The whole process of photosynthesis can be broken down into the light reactions and the dark reactions. The light reactions occur on the thylakoid membranes of the grana. There, chlorophyll and other molecules make up a system called a photosystem. There are actually two photosystems located on the thylakoid membrane: photosystems I and II. Together they carry out the light reactions. During the light reactions, chlorophyll absorbs light of specific wavelengths and this energy is used to split water molecules into their component hydrogen ions and molecular oxygen. The light reactions also generate ATP and NADPH.

Now what about the dark reactions? This series of reactions occurs in the stroma (the fluid-filled area surrounding the grana, as we discussed in chapter 2). During the dark reactions, the newly available hydrogen atoms combine with carbon dioxide to eventually form glucose. The series of dark reactions is also called *carbon fixation*.

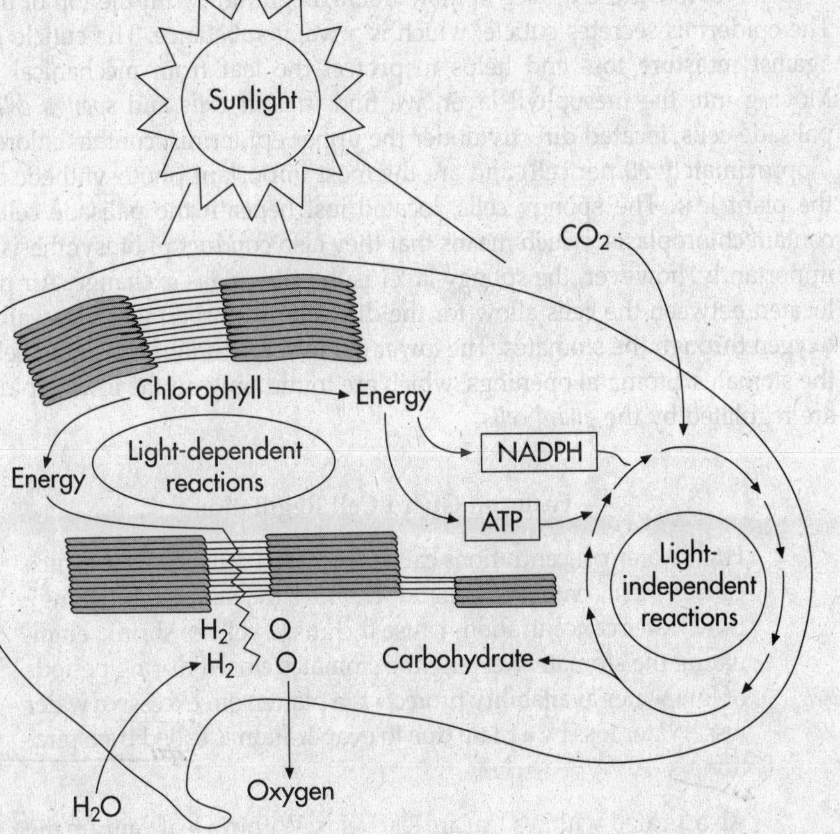


We've talked a bit about what photosynthesis is and how it works. Now let's talk about where in a plant it takes place. Most photosynthesis takes place in certain cell layers of a leaf. We'll show you what we mean.

## HERE'S A CROSS-SECTIONAL VIEW OF A LEAF

Consider a cross-sectional image of a leaf as it appears under a microscope, shown below. You'll notice that the leaf is composed of distinct layers of plant cells. The outer layer of cells at either face of the leaf is called the *epidermis*. Enclosed in the protective epidermis is the *mesophyll* layer. *Xylem* and *phloem* cells are also present, and each cell type is specialized.

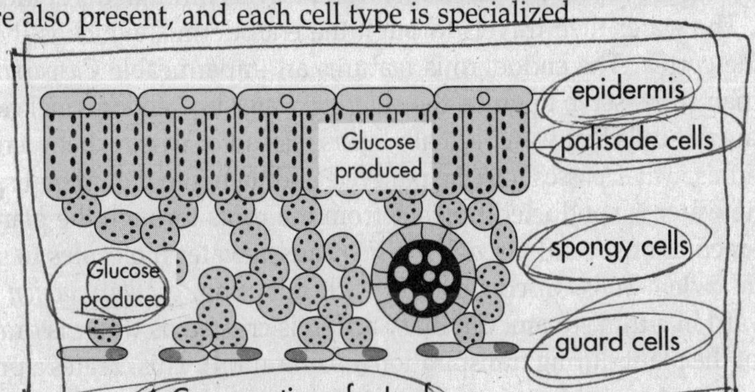


**From top to bottom, the tissue layers of a leaf are: upper epidermis; mesophyll layer containing palisade cells, spongy cells, and vascular tissue; lower epidermis, including guard cells.**

When the temperature climbs and humidity falls, plant cells' stomates nearly shut down in order to conserve water. As a result, very little carbon dioxide can enter the cell, causing photosynthesis to shut down.

Let's review these tissues in more detail, beginning with the top of the leaf. The epidermis secretes cuticle, which is a waxy substance. The cuticle guards against moisture loss and helps to protect the leaf from mechanical injury. Moving into the mesophyll layer, we find *palisade cells* and *spongy cells*. The palisade cells, located directly under the upper epidermis, contain chloroplasts (approximately 30 per cell) and are the most important photosynthetic cells of the plant leaf. The spongy cells, located just beneath the palisade cells, also contain chloroplasts, which means that they also conduct photosynthesis. More importantly, however, the spongy layer is the site of gas exchange. Air pockets located between the cells allow for the diffusion of carbon dioxide, water, and oxygen through the stomates. The lower epidermis contains the guard cells and the stomates. Stomatal openings, which are found only on the lower epidermis, are regulated by the *guard cells*.

**Focus on Guard Cell Regulation**

High water concentrations cause the guard cells to swell, which causes their centers to expand, creating the stomate (opening). Low water concentrations cause the guard cells to shrink, eliminating the stomate. Keeping the stomates closed during periods of low water availability protects the plant from excessive water loss. Water loss by a plant due to evaporation is called transpiration.

Also located within a leaf are leaf veins. Within a leaf vein are the conducting tissues phloem and xylem. The phloem transports the food that's produced by photosynthesis to all of the cells of the plant. The xylem transports water and minerals that entered the plant through the roots. Let's examine the way in which water enters the plant roots and makes its way up to the leaf.

## How Water Gets From the Soil to the Leaf Vein

A plant's roots anchor it in the ground and act to prevent soil erosion. Roots contain root hairs, which absorb water, minerals, and essential elements from the surrounding soil. From the root hairs, water travels through the epidermis to the cortex. The water then travels through the endodermis, which is the inner lining of the cortex. The endodermis features an impermeable *Casparian strip*. The Casparian strips serve to guide the entering water into endodermal cells, the very first layer of cells that water actually *enters* instead of passing between. From the endodermis, water passes into the pericycle and then into the xylem tissue.

Now the water is conducted upward from the roots through the plant stem by the interaction of several forces. *Adhesion* causes water molecules to stick to the walls of xylem cells. In conjunction with adhesion, *capillary action* draws water upward in a thin stream. Capillary action is created as water is drawn off of the top of the plant during transpiration (evaporation). This creates a pressure that draws water toward the top of the plant.

Now let's consider all of the other parts of the plant. The plant that we're looking at, by the way, is an herbaceous plant, which means that it does not contain woody structures.

## HERBACEOUS PLANT STRUCTURES

Take a look at the herbaceous plant structures in the typical dicot plant that's shown in the illustration below.

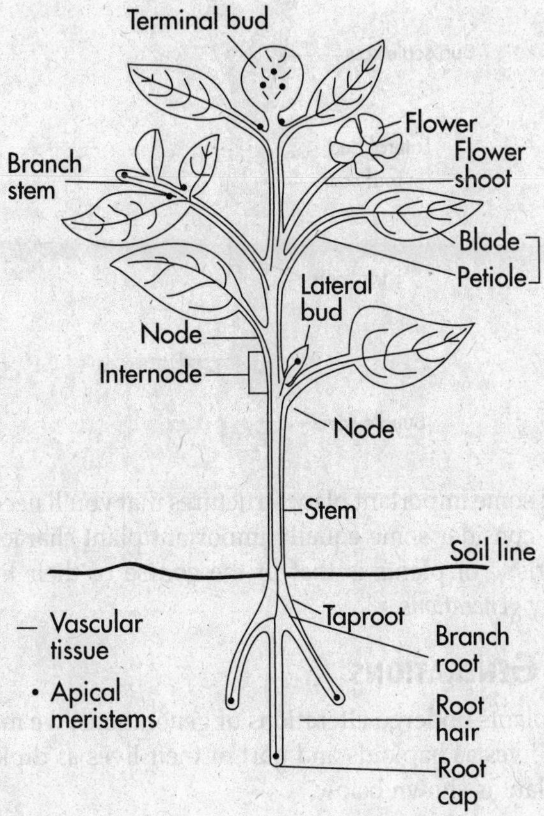


A herbaceous plant only undergoes primary growth; it only increases in length.

The plant has a taproot, which is also known as a primary root. (An alternate type of root is the fibrous root, which is seen in grasses, for example.) Our herbaceous plant also has a shoot, which is composed of the stem, leaves, flowers, and fruits. The shoot features a number of specialized structures. Its nodes serve as sites of leaf attachment. Its internodes are spaces between attached leaves. Its terminal bud is the site of plant growth. When the plant is not growing, the meristematic tissue (tissue capable of dividing to create growth) at the bud is covered by a bud scale. Lastly, its lenticels are the sites of gas exchange.

As we said, the structures just discussed belong to herbaceous plants. The following types of structures are found on woody plants.

## Woody Plant Structures

Take a look at the terminal twig featured in the illustration below.

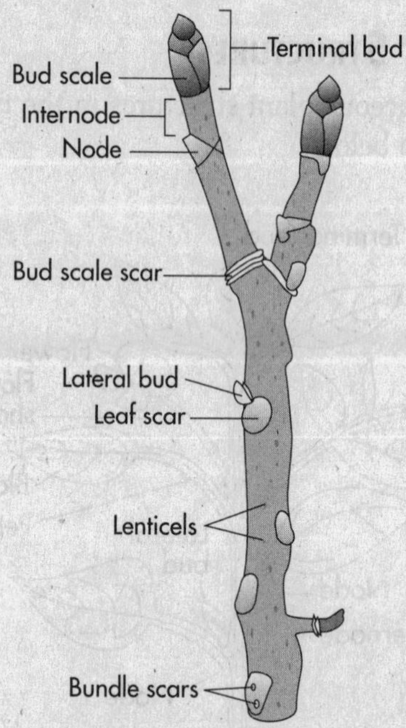


Woody plants undergo both primary growth and secondary growth. Secondary growth is an increase in width. (This is how trees get their rings over the years.)

We've reviewed some important plant structures that you'll need to know for the GRE; now let's consider some equally important plant characteristics. One definitive characteristic of plants is that in the course of their life cycle they undergo *alteration of generations*.

## Alteration of Generations

When we say that plants undergo alterations of generations, we mean that they spend part of their lives as haploids and part of their lives as diploids. The life cycle of a typical plant is shown below.

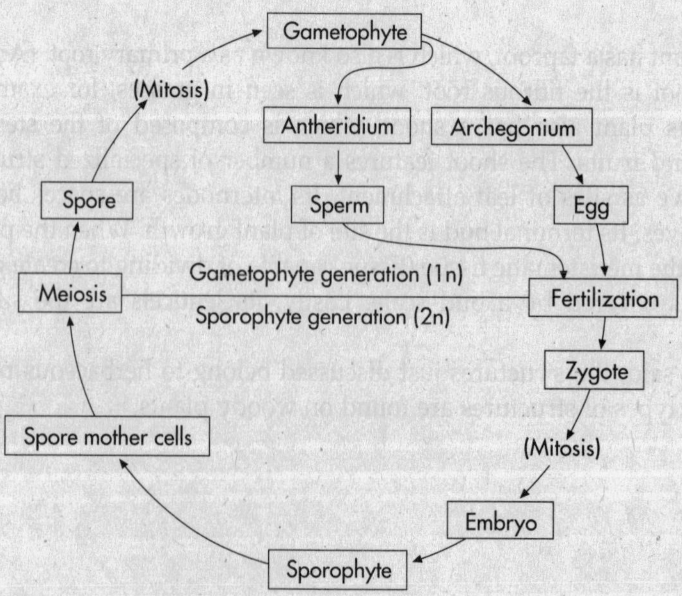

### Focus on Alteration of Generations in a Moss

Here's what the life cycle of a moss looks like:

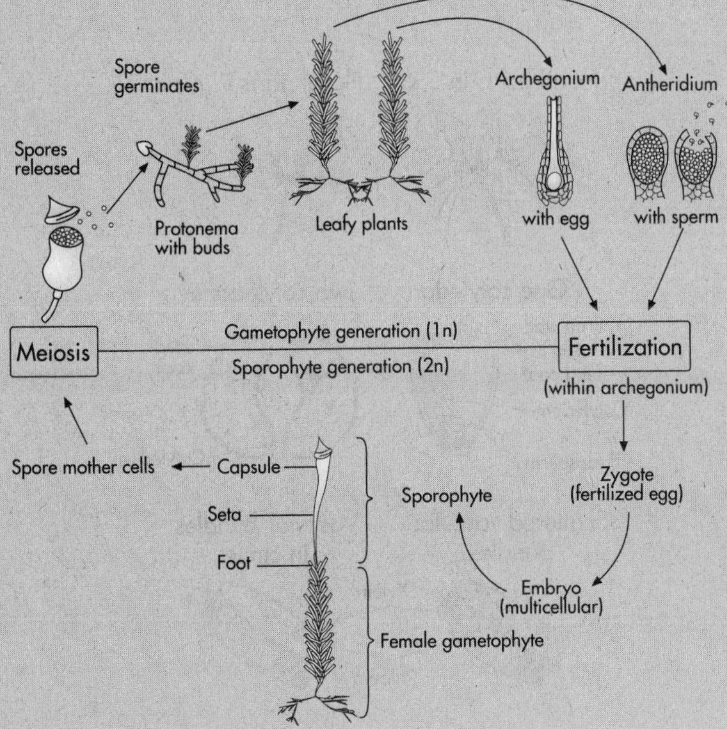


Browse these illustrations long enough to become familiar with important GRE terms like "antheridium" and "archegonium." If they don't ring a bell, haul out a related textbook and take a minute or two to brush up on these cycles in more detail.

## REMEMBERING ANGIOSPERMS

Vascular plants–those that contain conducting tissue–may be classified as either *gymnosperms* or *angiosperms*. Gymnosperms (such as conifers) do not have enclosed seeds, while angiosperms (flowering plants) do. Angiosperms possess a number of specialized features that facilitate fertilization, which may occur through self-pollination or cross-pollination. Structures of a typical complete flower are illustrated below.

All sorts of things act as pollinators of flowering plants, like bees and other insects, bats, birds, and the wind.

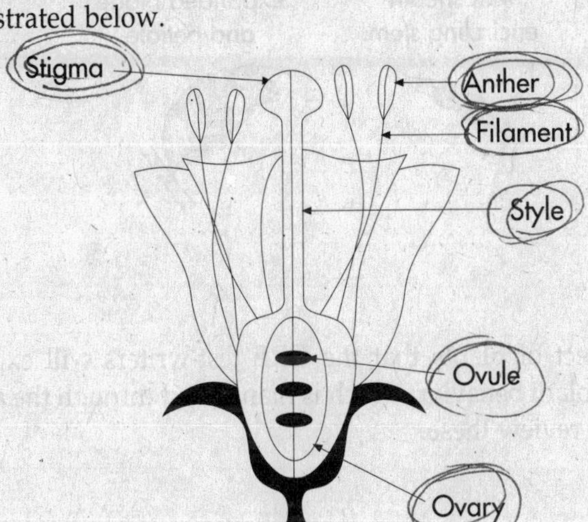

## What's the Difference Between a Monocot and a Dicot?

Angiosperms are classified as either monocots or dicots. Look at the chart below to refresh your memory on the differences between the two groups.

**What is a cotyledon? It's the seed leaf of a plant. Its job? To store food for germination.**

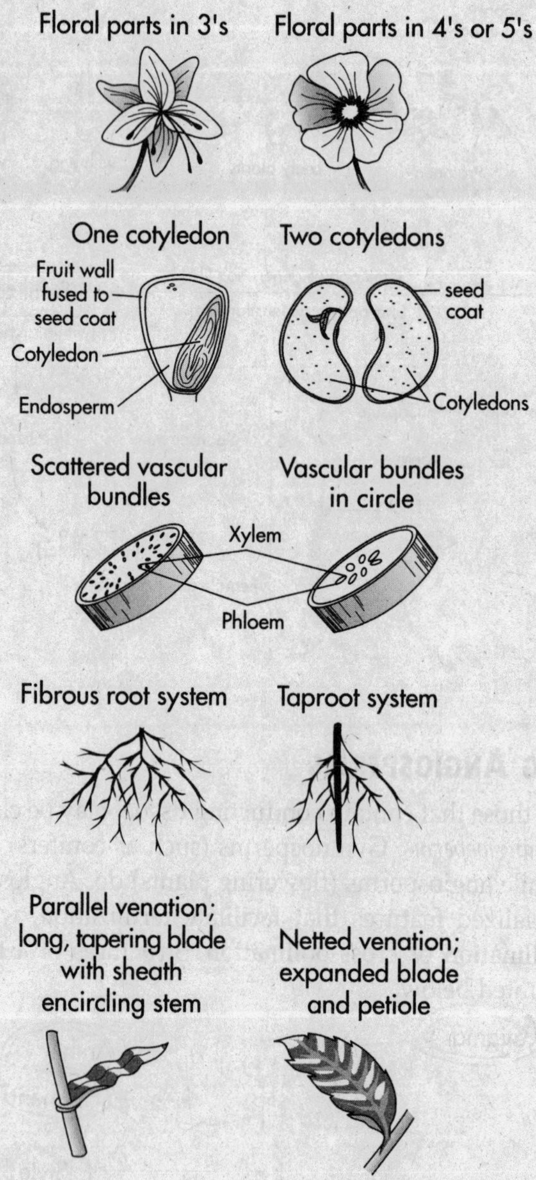


Another aspect of plants that the GRE test-writers will expect you to be familiar with is plant behavior, which is manifested through the actions of plant hormones. Let's review these.

## Plant Behaviors

Although plants are sessile (they can't move about), they are able to exhibit a variety of behaviors (called *tropisms*) in response to specific stimuli in their environment. In *thigmotropism*, a plant grows in along a solid object (i.e., a trellis). In *phototropism*, a plant grows in the direction of sunlight. In *gravitropism*, a plant's roots grow downward in the direction of gravity. In *negative gravitropism*, a plant's stem grows away from the direction of gravity. In *hydrotropism*, a plant's roots grow in the direction of water.

## Plant Hormones

Plant hormones influence plant behavior and plant growth, which are interconnected. Some important plant hormones are *auxins*, *gibberellins*, *cytokinins*, *ethylene*, and *abscisic acid*. Auxin induces plant growth through cell elongation. Uneven distributions of auxin in a plant produces unequal growth of plant sections; unequal production of this hormone underlies phototropism. Gibberellin also influences plant growth, most specifically stem elongation. Excess gibberellin produces tall, spindly plant stems. Cytokinin induces division and differentiation of plant cells. It is synthesized in the roots and conducted by the xylem to the rest of the plant. Ethylene acts to ripen fruit and initiates leaf abscission. Abscisic acid has a less well-known role and is produced by plants in response to stress (i.e., water stress).

**Based on his first-hand observations, the first person to posit that plants have hormones was none other than Charles Darwin.**

# 16

# Genetics and Evolution

In this chapter we'll talk about some of the basic concepts of heredity and review the relevant genetic terms. We'll look at mutations and how they alter the genome. We'll discuss sex-linked traits and their phenomic effects. Next we'll discuss how populations evolve, review the various forms of evolution, investigate population genetics and, finally, discuss how organisms are classified according to their evolutionary histories.

## About Alleles, Loci, and Homologous Chromosomes

The first things we need to tackle are a few relevant genetic terms. You learned about homologous chromosomes in chapter 5 when we told you that they are similar but not identical to each other. Now we have more information to add. Homologous chromosomes have their loci aligned at the same point on each strand. A locus is the physical site occupied by a gene on a chromosome. The aligned genes are called *alleles* and they code for the same trait.

Two alleles for a given trait may code for the same version of the trait, meaning that the organism is *homozygous* for the trait. Alternatively, two alleles for a trait may code for alternate expressions for a trait. When this happens, the organism is considered *heterozygous* with respect to the trait. Of course, if an organism is homozygous for a trait, there's no argument about which version of the trait will actually be expressed. It doesn't matter, because both alleles code for the same product.

"With a good heredity, nature deals you a fine hand at cards, and with a good environment, you can learn to play the hand well."
—Walter C. Alvarez, M.D.

But what happens when an organism is heterozygous for a trait? Which of its two alternate forms of expression will be expressed? The dominant allele will. A dominant gene overrides a recessive gene in expression of a trait. For instance, for the eye color trait, an allele that codes for brown eyes (B) will always be expressed over an allele that codes for blue eyes (b) because the allele for brown eyes is dominant and the one for blue eyes is recessive.

Here's something else to think about when it comes to dominant versus recessive alleles: In the presence of a dominant allele, a recessive allele for a trait does not show up in the organism's phenotype, but it will show up in its genotype.

## Genotype and Phenotype

The total alleles of an organism represent the organism's *genotype*. A set of alleles for a single trait represents the organism's genotype for the trait. The expression, or discernible appearance of a trait in an organism, is called the organism's *phenotype*. For example, an organism that has two alleles for brown eye color has the genotype (BB) and the phenotype "brown eyes." An organism having one allele for brown eyes and one allele for blue eyes has a genotype (Bb) and a phenotype "brown eyes."

Now let's say that we want to predict what genotype a child may have with regard to eye color based on his parents' genotypes for the trait. What we'll want to employ to arrive at this prediction is a…

## Punnett Square

The Punnett square helps to predict the statistical probability of genotypes and phenotypes of progeny resulting from a cross between two individuals. Even though it considers a mating between two individuals, it can be used to predict allele frequencies in an entire population of organisms. Consider two parents, each having the genotype (Bb) for eye color. If we want to predict the genotypes of their offspring, we would work out a Punnett square. The Punnett square would show that four possible offspring genotypes may result: (BB), (Bb), (Bb), and (bb). What phenotypes are we talking about here? Three brown-eyed children and one blue-eyed child. The offspring of the first generation are called the $F_1$ generation. If we then wanted to consider a generation of offspring arising from a member of the $F_1$ generation, we would be considering the $F_2$ generation.

Monohybrid crosses involve one pair of alleles that represent a single locus. A dihybrid cross involves alleles that represent two loci.

No review of the Punnett square, with its concept of parental contribution of alleles to offspring, would be complete without also reviewing Mendel's two laws.

## The Law of Segregation and The Law of Independent Assortment

For single-locus traits, alleles for a trait that are on separate homologs separate into different gametes during meiosis. In this way each new gamete contains a different allele for a trait. That's Mendel's first law, which is also known as the *law of segregation*. What's more, the alleles for two different traits carried on separate chromosomes will *assort* (separate into gametes) independently of each other during meiosis. In other words, the assortment of alleles of one trait does not influence the assortment of alleles of the other trait. That's Mendel's second law, which is also called the *law of independent assortment*.

It so happens that alleles for two traits don't always assort independently. Sometimes Mendel's law of independent assortment gets violated. When does that happen?

## When Genes Are Linked

Sometimes the genes that code for two or more traits are linked. Linked genes exist on the same chromosome, so that the traits they code for are inherited together. When linked genes are far apart on homologous chromosomes, crossing over occurs. We talked about crossing over when we reviewed meiosis in chapter 5. We said that during crossing over, equal regions of chromatid between homologous chromosomes are exchanged. We also said that crossing over happens during prophase I of meiosis, when tetrads form. Because crossing over involves breaking and rejoining reciprocal regions of DNA, each crossing over event leads to genetic recombination (a new combination of genes in the cells than was originally present) and increases genetic variability.

Sometimes, during chromosome exchange, things can get out of hand. Instead of the usual reciprocal exchange of sections of chromatid during crossing over, something goes amiss. As a result, the daughter cells take on chromosomal aberrations. Take a look at some of the ways in which chromosomes can develop these aberrations; they're all important terms to know for the GRE.

**Focus on Chromosomal Aberrations**

- A *translocation* occurs when part of a chromosome breaks off and attaches to another (nonhomologous) chromosome
- *Duplication* (extra copies of genes) arises on the too-long chromosome produced from translocation
- *Deletion* (missing genes) arises on the too-short chromosome produced from translocation
- *Robertsonian translocations* produce a chromosome made up of two long arms, each from a different chromosome
- *Reciprocal translocations* don't result in a loss of genetic material
- *Nondisjunction* occurs when chromosomes don't separate properly during anaphase
- An *inversion* occurs when a chromosome breaks in two places and reforms with the pieces rotated so that the order of genes in the area is reversed

It turns out that crossing over is not the only source of genetic variability. Another potent source of genetic variability is...

## MUTATIONS

Just as with crossing over, mutations increase genetic variability by producing new combinations of genes. In a mutation, one or more nucleotides on DNA are inserted, transferred, rearranged, or deleted. If the mutation is advantageous to an organism, it is only by chance; if it is disadvantageous, that, too, is by chance and not by design. Recall that mutations are heritable: they are transmitted from parent to offspring. Also recall that the more deleterious the mutation, the less likely it is to remain in the gene pool, since the affected organism doesn't usually survive long enough to reach reproductive age.

When a mutation involves a change to the chromosome structure, it tends to affect many genes, rather than only a few.

Here's how a mutation works. Because it changes the nucleotide sequence, it may alter a gene's production of product. As a result, a mutation can alter production of a protein or enzyme in any of three ways: It can halt production of the protein entirely, it can code for the synthesis of an alternate protein, or it can have no effect on production of the protein. Another thing to keep in mind about mutations is that most occur spontaneously. They can also be triggered by environmental factors, such as sunlight, or induced by chemical mutagens. For the GRE, you'll need to know a few specific types of mutations:

- In a *frameshift* mutation, a base pair is inserted or deleted in a gene, causing a shift in the reading frame of all subsequent codons.
- The *initial* (first) mutation is called a forward mutation.
- A *back* mutation reverses an initial mutation.

- A *missense* mutation initiates production of a different protein than the original protein produced.
- A *nonsense* mutation halts production of the original protein.

So far we've been talking about autosomal traits, which are traits carried on the autosomal chromosomes (in humans, those are chromosomes 1-22). Eye color and height are two good examples. Next, we'll go over *sex-linked traits*.

## Sex-linked Traits

Sex-linked traits are carried on the sex chromosomes, which are the X and Y chromosomes. Sex-linked traits, like hemophilia and color blindness, are typically carried by the X chromosome. We know that males have the sex chromosomes XY because they received one X chromosome from their mother and one Y chromosome from their father. We also know that females have the sex chromosomes XX because they receive one X chromosome from their mother and another X chromosome from their father. Since females have two X chromosomes but only need one active X chromosome, one X exists as euchromatin (loosely packed chromatin that is transcribed), while the other exists as heterochromatin (tightly packed chromatin that is not transcribed). The extra X chromosome that exists as heterochromatin is called a Barr body.

**In Klinefelter syndrome, a person has two X and one Y chromosome. In Turner syndrome, a person has an X and no Y chromosome.**

Now let's figure out what effects sex-linked traits have on males and females. Since a sex-linked gene is carried on the X chromosome, and males and females do not receive the same sex chromosomes, sex-linked traits have different consequences for each sex. What happens, for instance, to a female who receives an X chromosome from her mother that carries a sex-linked trait? If her second X chromosome, received from her father, doesn't carry the trait, then she won't express the trait. In other words, she won't show the trait in her phenotype, because her paternally derived second X chromosome overrides expression of the maternally derived sex-linked trait. She will, however, be a carrier of the sex-linked trait, and can potentially pass the trait on to her offspring. If, on the other hand, she also receives from her father an X chromosome that carries the same sex-linked trait, she will express the trait in her phenotype.

Now, what about the consequences of sex-linked traits for males? First of all, a male can only receive an X chromosome from his mother. That means that if the X chromosome he receives from her carries a sex-linked trait, he will express that trait. That's because the Y chromosome he receives from his father doesn't influence sex-linked traits one way or another.

So far we've been looking at heredity in individuals. Now let's broaden our outlook and consider heredity in a population.

## Population Genetics

To investigate *population genetics*, we need to review what a population is. A population is a subgroup of a species, and a species is a group of organisms that can mate and bear offspring. To help ensure that mating is appropriate to species, mechanisms exist that help to foster reproductive isolation. Reproductive isolation can be temporal, by which breeding is confined to a specific time frame or season; ecological, by which different niches are filled by two species in the same area; or behavioral, by which courtship rituals act to initiate matings. Other forms of reproductive isolation also exist.

Now that we have a better understanding of what a population is, we can consider a population's gene pool. A gene pool is the total assortment of genes found in a population of a species. Since members of a population have different genotypes, there's a fair amount of genetic variability in the population. Genetic variability is also increased by way of mutations, which introduce new alleles into the gene pool.

When the frequencies of alleles in a population's gene pool changes over successive generations, we call that change…

## Evolution

According to Lamarck, evolution worked this way: Traits were acquired during an organism's lifetime, directly in response to the environment, and then were passed on to offspring. Of course, that view of evolution has been rejected in favor of Darwin's view. Darwin proposed that only heritable traits can be passed down to offspring, and that new traits were the result of mutation, which is random. He also maintained that whether a new trait was advantageous depended on the environment of the organism, which is subject to random change.

"Theory without fact is fantasy, but facts without theory is chaos."
—C. O. Whitman

Another important thing to recall is that evolution takes place only in a population of organisms. It does not take place in an individual. In a process called natural selection, the environment acts upon a population's alleles, selecting for alleles that increase the fitness of an organism relative to its environment. According to Darwin, natural selection works according to the following set of conditions:

- Genetic variability exists in a population.
- There is an overproduction of offspring in a population.
- There is competition among the offspring for limited resources.
- Not all of the offspring will survive long enough to reproduce.

These conditions allow natural selection to select for those alleles that are most favorable to the population, at the expense of those alleles that are less favorable to the population. Darwin's theory of evolution was closely tied to his concept of the relative fitness of organisms.

### Darwinian Fitness

Fitness refers to how successful an organism is at propagating its genotype in successive generations. Competition for alleles in a gene pool means that not all alleles remain in a population. The alleles that do persist in the gene pool have been "selected" by the environment and will replace alternative forms of the gene. An organism that is able to survive to reproductive age is able to pass on to its progeny whatever trait or traits helped it to survive. Keep in mind, of course, that an organism's fitness depends on the interplay between its environment and its phenotype.

### Focus on Optimality Theory

According to the optimality theory, the best version of a trait is selected over all alternative versions. That means that if two or more alternate alleles for a trait are beneficial to an organism, only one will eventually be predominant—the one that out performs all other possible versions, even when other versions may also be advantageous. (Think of this as cost-cutting at its most ruthlessly efficient.)

So far we have been talking of evolution as a single process. Well, evolution is a complex process that can actually be divided into subcategories. The two predominant forms of evolution are *divergent evolution* and *convergent evolution.*

## Divergent Evolution

In divergent evolution, a new species evolves from a preexisting species. The evolution of the two populations takes place over a long period of time. *Speciation,* in which a new species arises, is a form of divergent evolution. Another term for speciation is *adaptive radiation.* In adaptive radiation, the genotypes of two populations eventually grow so far apart from one another that the two sets of organisms can no longer interbreed. Adaptive radiation reduces competition, expands potential niches, and increases biological diversity. Two forms of adaptive radiation are allopatric speciation and sympatric speciation. Allopatric speciation is usually prompted by geographical separation (i.e., a mountain range or a land bridge). Sympatric speciation unfolds in one locale shared by the parent and offshoot species. Two closely related populations of one species can diverge; this affords them the opportunity for establishing new niches in the same limited environment.

File all of these processes under divergent evolution: speciation, adaptive radiation, allopatric speciation, and sympatric speciation.

## Convergent Evolution

In convergent evolution, unrelated species without a common ancestor evolve similar structures. Their similar structures evolve from their being subjected to similar selection pressures from the environment. Convergent evolution gives rise to *analogous structures,* while divergent evolution gives rise to *homologous structures.*

### Focus on Homologous and Analogous Structures

Analogous structures arise in the course of convergent evolution. The analogous structures of two unrelated organisms are similar in function. Examples of analogous structures are the lungs of mammals and the trachea of insects.

Homologous structures arise in the course of divergent evolution. Homologous structures are similar to one another because the organisms share a common ancestor. Examples of homologous structures are the wings of a bird or a bat and the forearm of a human.

We've just looked at some broad categories of evolution. Now we are going to zero in on a few specific cases of evolution—cases in which we are able make some predictions concerning the gene frequency in a population. We can only predict what the gene frequencies might be under certain conditions. One set of conditions allows us to employ the *Hardy-Weinberg law*, and the other set of conditions lets us know we're dealing with *genetic drift*.

### The Hardy-Weinberg Law

According to the Hardy-Weinberg law, the frequency with which an allele occurs in a population does not change. The conditions that must prevail in order for the Hardy-Weinberg law to apply are:

- a large population
- no mutations
- no immigration or emigration
- random reproduction
- no natural selection

The equation used to apply the Hardy-Weinberg Law is $p^2 + 2pq + q^2 = 1$, or $p + q = 1$, where $p^2$ is the frequency of homozygous dominant condition, pq is the frequency of the heterozygous condition, and $q^2$ is the frequency of the homozygous recessive condition.

While Mendel's laws zero in on genotype frequencies generated by a single set of parents, the Hardy-Weinberg law views genotype frequencies generated by a whole population.

### Genetic Drift

While the Hardy-Weinberg law deals with large populations, genetic drift involves small populations. In genetic drift, chance matings can produce a change in the initial frequency of alleles. The important thing to remember here is that variation in gene frequency is due to chance. It's not caused by natural selection, which operates on the premise of survival of the fittest. In genetic drift, a random event such as a storm can act to increase or decrease the gene frequency of a trait in a completely random manner.

## Classification of Organisms

Evolution has given rise to a diverse number of closely related and unrelated organisms, which are classified by taxonomists based on their similarities and differences. In this way taxonomists attempt to piece together the evolutionary histories and relationships of organisms. Two important systems of classification are those of *protostomes* versus *deuterostomes*, and the *binomial system of classification*.

### Protostomes versus Deuterostomes

Here, organisms are classified based on patterns of their embryonic development. While both types of organisms develop a blastopore as early embryos, in protostomes, the blastopore forms the mouth of the organism while in deuterostomes, the blastopore develops into the anus and the mouth develops afterwards. While protostomes undergo spiral cleavage, deuterostomes undergo radial cleavage. Protostomes have determinate (more specialized) developing cells, while deuterostomes have indeterminate developing cells. What's more, since deuterostomes' cells are less specialized at cleavage, the cells are capable of giving rise to a complete organism if separated. Organisms belonging to each category are shown in the diagram below.

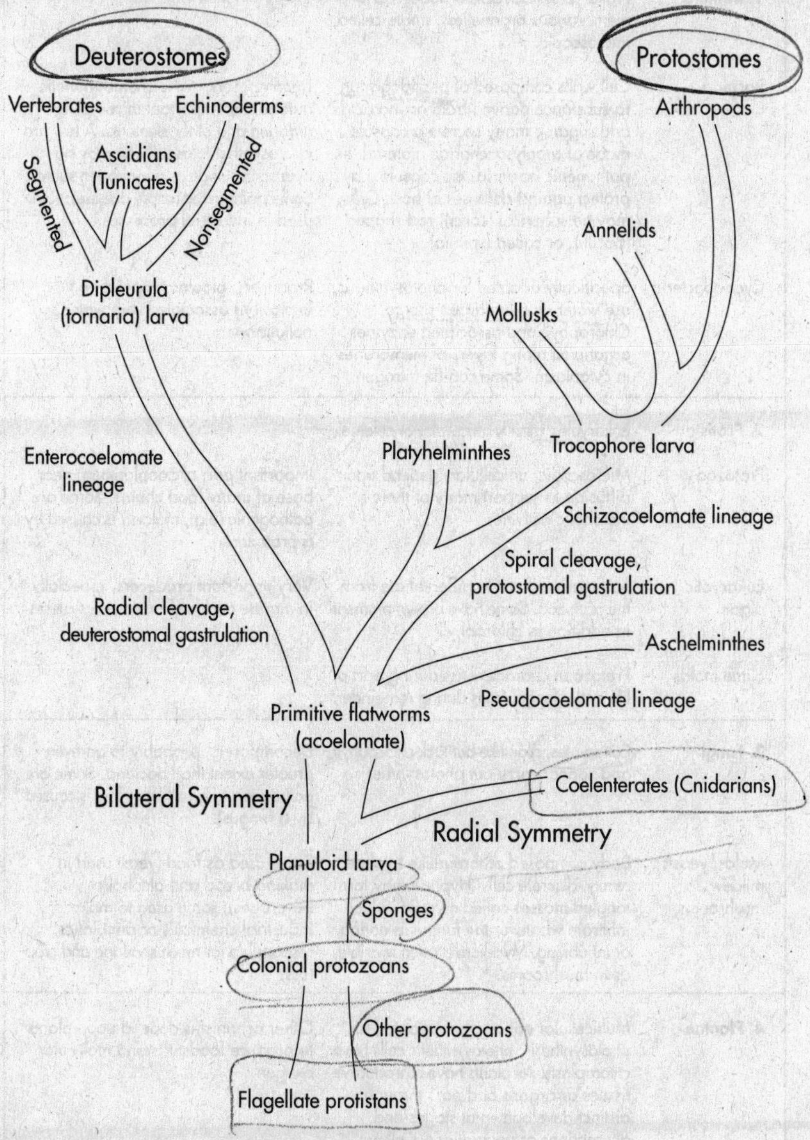


Notice that vertebrates and chordates are deuterostomes, and mollusks, annelids, and arthropods are protostomes.

## The Binomial System of Classification

Organisms can also be classified according to the binomial system developed by Carolus Linnaeus. An organism is classified based on a hierarchical framework that compares certain features of the organism to features of other organisms. The orders of classification from fewest to most characteristics in common are: kingdom, phylum, class, order, family, genus, and species. The broadest system of classification is the kingdom; all organisms belong to one of the five kingdoms.

Take a moment here to review the kingdoms shown in the table below.

One more time: The five kingdoms are Monera, Protista, Fungi, Plantae, and Animalia.

| 5 Kingdoms | Characteristics | Ecological Role |
|---|---|---|
| **1. Monera** | Prokaryotes (lack distinct nuclei and other membranous organelles); single-celled; microscopic. | |
| Bacteria | Cell walls composed of peptidoglycan (a substance derived from amino acids and sugars); many secrete a capsule made of a polysaccharide material. In pathogenic bacteria, the capsule may protect against defenses of host. Cells may be spherical (cocci), rod-shaped (bacilli), or coiled (spirilla). | Decomposers; some chemosynthetic autotrophs; important in recycling nitrogen and other elements. A few are photosynthetic, usually employing hydrogen sulfide as a hydrogen source. Some pathogenic (cause disease); some used in industrial processes. |
| Cyanobacteria | Specifically adapted for photosynthesis; use water as a hydrogen source. Chlorophyll and associated enzymes organized along layers of membranes in cytoplasm. Some can fix nitrogen. | Producers; blooms (population explosion) associated with water pollution. |
| **2. Protista** | Eukaryotes; mainly unicellular or colonial. | |
| Protozoa | Microscopic; unicellular; depend upon diffusion to support many of their metabolic activities. | Important part of zooplankton; near base of many food chains. Some are pathogenic (e.g., malaria is caused by a protozoan). |
| Eukaryotic algae | Some are difficult to differentiate from the protozoa. Some have brown pigment in addition to chlorophyll. | Very important producers, especially in marine and fresh-water ecosystems. |
| Slime molds | Protozoan characteristics during part of life cycle; fungal traits during remainder. | |
| **3. Fungi** | Eukaryotes; plantlike but lack chlorophyll and cannot carry out photosynthesis. | Decomposers, probably to an even greater extent than bacteria. Some are pathogenic (e.g., athlete's foot is caused by a fungus). |
| Molds, yeasts, mildew, mushrooms | Body composed of threadlike hyphae; rarely, discrete cells. Hyphae may form tangled masses called mycelia, which infiltrate whatever the fungus is eating or inhabiting. Mycelium is often invisible, as in mushrooms. | Some used as food (yeast used in making bread and alcoholic beverages); some used to make industrial chemicals or antibiotics; responsible for much spoilage and crop loss. |
| **4. Plantae** | Multicellular eukaryotes; adapted for photosynthesis; photosynthetic cells have chloroplasts. All plants have reproductive tissues or organs and pass through distinct developmental stages and alternations of generations. Cell walls of cellulose; cells often have large central vacuole. Indeterminate growth; often no fixed body size or exact shape. | Other organisms depend upon plants to produce foodstuffs and molecular oxygen. |
| **5. Animalia** | Multicellular eukaryotic heterotrophs, many of which exhibit advanced tissue differentiation and complex organ systems. Lack cell walls. Able as a rule to move about by muscle contraction; extremely and quickly responsive to stimuli, with specialized nervous tissue to coordinate responses; determinate growth. | Almost the sole consuming organisms in the biosphere, some being specialized herbivores, carnivores, and detrivores (eating dead organisms or organic material such as dead leaves). |

Moving downward on the classification hierarchy, we take a look at *phyla*. Distinguishing features of some complex animals categorized by phylum are outlined below.

| | Phylum | Body Symmetry | Gas Exchange | Waste Disposal | Nervous System | Circulation | Reproduction | Other Characteristics |
|---|---|---|---|---|---|---|---|---|
| Protostomes | **Mollusca** Clams Snails Squids | Bilateral | Gills and mantle | Metanephridia | Three pairs of ganglia; simple sense organs | Open system | Sexual; sexes separate; fertilization in water | Soft-bodied; usually have shell and ventral foot for locomotion |
| | **Annelida** (segmented worms) Earthworms Leeches Marine worms | Bilateral | Diffusion through moist skin; oxygen circulated by blood | Pair of metanephridia in each segment | Simple brain; ventral nerve chord; well-developed sense organs | Closed system | Sexual; hermaphroditic but cross-fertilize | Earthworms till soil |
| | **Arthropoda** (joint-footed animals) Crustaceans Insects Spiders | Bilateral | Trachae in insects, gills in crustaceans; book lungs or trachae in spider group | Malphigian tubules in insects; antennal (green) glands in crustaceans | Simple brain; ventral nerve chord; well-developed sense organs | Open system | Sexual; sexes separate | Hard exoskeleton; most diverse and numerous group of animals |
| Deuterostomes | **Echinodermata** (spiny-skinned animals) Sea stars Sea urchins Sand dollars | Embryo: bilateral; adult: modified radial | Skin gills | Diffusion | Nerve rings; no brain | Open system; reduced | Sexual; sexes almost always separate | Water vascular system; tube feet |
| | **Chordata** Tunicates Lancelets Vertebrates | Bilateral | Gills or lungs | Kidneys and other organs | Dorsal nerve chord with brain at anterior end | Closed system; ventral heart | Sexual; sexes separate | (1) Notochord; (2) dorsal, tubular chord; (3) pharyngeal gill slits |

"We hope that, when the insects take over the world, they will remember with gratitude how we took them along on all our picnics."
—Bill Vaughan

# 17

# Ecology and Animal Behavior

Ecology is a study of how organisms interact with one another and their environments. In this chapter, we review some key ecological concepts and define terms such as niche, competition, and fitness. We'll talk about the food chain and we'll consider each associated trophic level's significance. We'll revisit the various types of intimate relationships that organisms form in symbiosis. Next we'll tackle the stages of an ecological succession and then we'll give you a quick review of biomes. During our discussion of ecosystems, we'll consider the carbon and nitrogen cycle, and discuss both lake and ocean ecosystems. We'll wrap up with a talk on animal behavior, distinguishing between various forms of learned and instinctive behaviors.

## LET'S START BY DEFINING SOME TERMS

In order to consider how organisms interact with one another and their environment, we need to review the relevant vocabulary. The first of these terms is species. A species is a group of organisms that can mate successfully and produce offspring. Members of the same species share a number of genes in common. In considering a species more closely, we can also say that a species may contain a number of populations. A population is a group of organisms within a species that share the same habitat. An important point to keep in mind is that while different populations can exist within a species, all members of a species can successfully interbreed.

Now let's think about niches.

A niche defines an organism's lifestyle. The term refers to an organism's territory, food source, habitat, routines…in effect, everything the organism does or makes use of each day. Organisms of closely related species may occupy separate niches. When they do, they coexist in the same or overlapping regions. Generally it is said that organisms of two different species cannot occupy the same niche (although there is some debate about the point). Because different organisms occupy different niches, they face reduced competition with one another.

### O.K. NOW, WHAT EXACTLY IS COMPETITION?

It refers to the fact that organisms compete with one another for limited resources. The resources may include food, mates, habitat, territory, or other necessities. Competition may be either *intraspecific* or *interspecific*. Intraspecific competition is competition between two members of the same species. Interspecific competition is competition between two members of different species.

**Competition for limited resources can get fierce. Here's what one New Yorker has to say with respect to habitat: "When I was kidnapped, my parents snapped into action. They rented out my room." —Woody Allen**

Competition relates closely to the word fitness. Fitness has to do with how well an organism is able to compete for resources. As competitors, the more fit organism will be more successful than the less fit organism in obtaining the resource. That's because the more fit organism carries genes that confer an added advantage over the other organisms with whom it competes. Thus the more fit organism has a higher likelihood of surviving to reproductive age and bearing offspring. The offspring, of course, will also carry the successful genes.

Fitness, however, is a fluid concept. It is the environment that influences whether traits are advantageous or not, and the environment is subject to change. When the environment changes, a trait that was once advantageous to an organism might suddenly become irrelevant or even detrimental to the organism's chances of survival and reproduction.

Much of the competitive process concerns the quest for food. Let's now look at the ways in which organisms obtain their food.

## THE FOOD CHAIN

Any discussion of the food chain must start out by distinguishing between producers and consumers.

Producers synthesize their own food, using energy derived from sunlight. Another term for producers is autotrophs. Most (but not all) autotrophs are plants and blue-green algae. Another type of autotroph is the chemosynthetic organism. Like other autotrophs, chemosynthetic organisms produce their own food. But they don't rely on the sun as their energy source. Instead, they produce their own food from inorganic compounds. The rest of the food chain is composed of the consumers.

**"I've known what it is to be hungry, but I always went right to a restaurant."**
**—Ring Lardner**

Consumers must obtain their nutrition from an outside source; they cannot manufacture their own food the way producers can. Another term for consumers is heterotrophs.

Consumers include many types of bacteria, fungi, and animals. Since the range of food sources available to consumers is so diverse, not all consumers have the same diet. For this reason, consumers are grouped into separate categories according to their primary diet. These categories include herbivore, carnivore, omnivore, saprophyte, and decomposer. Herbivores eat plants. Carnivores eat meat. Omnivores eat both plants and meat. Saprophytes, which lack digestive structures, absorb their food from dead organisms. Decomposers degrade organisms, releasing minerals, carbon dioxide, and water for recycling.

In the food chain, producers and consumers are arranged according to a hierarchy based upon who eats whom.

## About the Hierarchy: Trophic Levels

Producers represent the first trophic level and are located at the bottom of the food chain. Directly above the producers, in sequential order, are the primary consumers, secondary consumers, and tertiary consumers. Each order of consumer constitutes a separate trophic level. Primary consumers constitute the second trophic level and feed upon the producers. Secondary consumers constitute the third trophic level and feed upon the primary consumers. Tertiary consumers constitute the fourth trophic level and feed upon the secondary consumers.

**In the opinion of one dubious primary consumer, "A cucumber should be well-sliced, dressed with pepper and vinegar, and then thrown out." —Samuel Johnson**

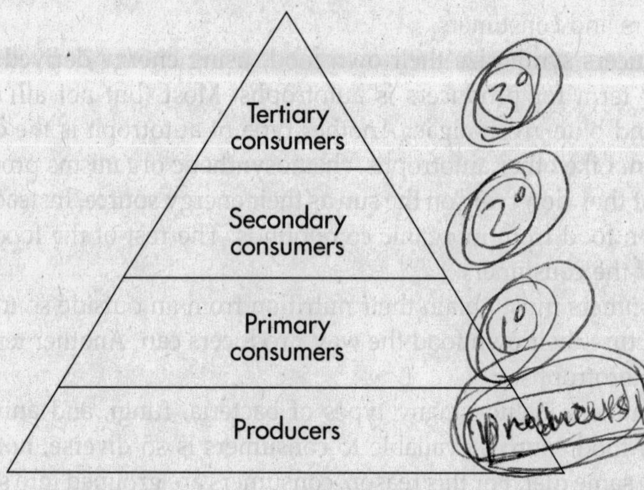


## The Pyramid of Numbers

The pyramid of numbers characterizes the relative numbers of organisms that exist at each trophic (feeding) level. The largest numbers of organisms belong to the producers. As trophic level increases, the number of individuals decreases.

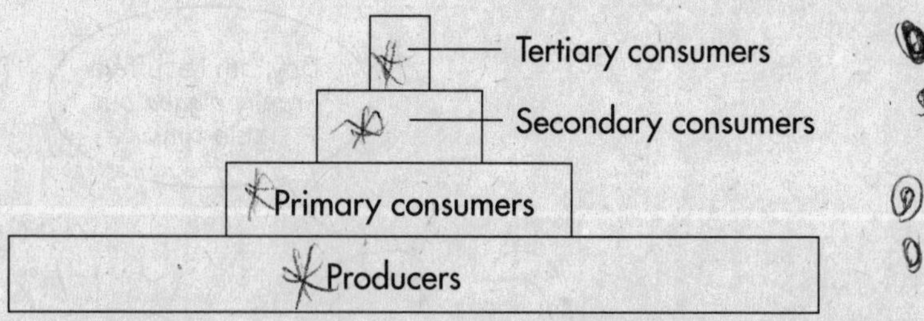


Just as the number of organisms declines at each higher trophic level, so does the amount of energy that is available to organisms. The energy originally made available by the producers undergoes successive reductions at each trophic level. It is depleted at each trophic level for two reasons: It is either used by the consumer to produce protoplasm, or is lost as heat during metabolic activities.

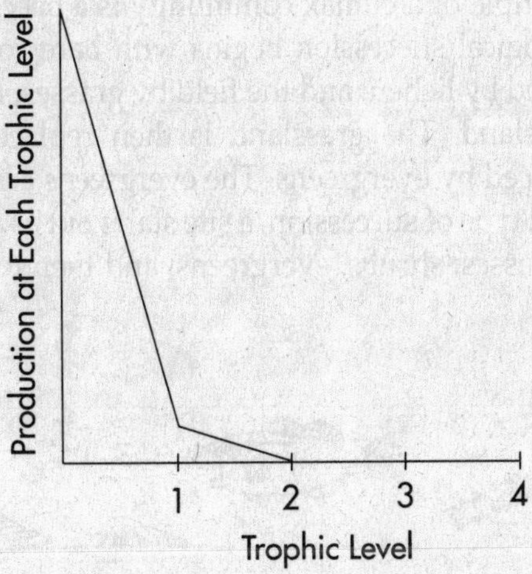


We've reviewed a variety of terms. We've talked about the ways in which organisms compete and the ways in which they (unwittingly) cooperate to form a food chain and a series of trophic levels. Let's talk now about how they do and do not interact with one another.

## SYMBIOSIS

Symbiosis is characterized by a long-standing and intimate interspecies relationship between two organisms. Its forms are *parasitism*, *commensalism*, and *mutualism*. In parasitism, one organism benefits and the other organism is harmed. Examples of parasitic relationships include those between canines and ticks, and tapeworms and humans. In commensalism, one organism benefits, and the other neither benefits nor is harmed by the association. Examples include epiphytes and trees, bird nests and trees, and pilotfish and sharks. In mutualism, both organisms derive benefit from the relationship. Examples include the root nodules of legumes and nitrogen-fixing bacteria, and angiosperms and pollinating insects.

**Viruses are considered obligate parasites because they require a host organism in order to reproduce.**

We've reviewed the interactions between individual organisms, both animals and plants. Now we'll turn to a topic that primarily concerns plants. It pertains not so much to the individual organism or species but to the way in which whole communities of plants take their turn at inhabiting a particular site.

## ECOLOGICAL SUCCESSIONS

During an ecological succession, transient plant communities alter a site in such a way that the site becomes less hospitable to them and more hospitable to a succeeding plant community. The shifts in plant communities occur, on average, every few decades. As the plant community in the site changes, the animal communities inhabiting the site change as well.

The initial plant community to inhabit a site is called the *pioneer community*. Lichen, a symbiotic arrangement of bacteria and algae, is a good example of a pioneer species. Lichen typically colonizes bare rock. At the other end of the continuum is the *climax community*. The climax community, which represents the final stage of an ecological succession, is a generally stable and diverse plant community. An example of a climax community is a beech-maple forest.

One typical ecological succession begins with bare rock or bare field. The rock may be colonized by lichen, and the field by grasses. Eventually, either site will become a grassland. The grassland is then replaced by shrubs, which themselves are replaced by evergreens. The evergreens are replaced by deciduous trees. In a second type of succession, a site starts out as a pond-water site and proceeds through grasses, shrubs, evergreens, and then to deciduous trees.

One typical succession: grasses—shrubs—conifers—deciduous trees.

We've talked about how relatively small regions undergo succession to ultimately create climax communities. Let's look now at how relatively large areas of the Earth are grouped according to their climax communities.

## BIOMES

*Biomes* are large geographical areas characterized by climate, weather, plant life (flora), and animal life (fauna). Biomes include the tundra, taiga, temperate deciduous forest, grasslands, deserts, and tropical rain forests. It may have been a while since you've thought about this subject. If you feel the need, study the chart provided below.

## Major Biomes

**Tundra**
*Regions*–northernmost regions
*Plant life*–few, if any, trees; primarily grasses and wildflowers
*Characteristics*–contains permafrost (a layer of permanently frozen soil); has a short growing season
*Animal life*–includes lemmings, arctic foxes, snowy owls, caribou, and reindeer

**Taiga**
*Region*–northern forests
*Plant life*–wind-blown conifers (evergreens), stunted in growth, possess modified spikes for leaves
*Characteristics*–very cold, long winters
*Animal life*–includes caribou, wolves, moose, bear, rabbits, and lynx

**Temperate Deciduous Forest**
*Regions*–northeast and middle eastern U.S., western Europe
*Plant life*–deciduous trees which drop their leaves in winter
*Characteristics*–moderate precipitation; warm summers, cold winters
*Animal life*–includes deer, wolves, bear, small mammals, birds

**Grasslands**
*Regions*–American midwest, Eurasia, Africa, South America
*Plant life*–grasses
*Characteristics*–hot summers, cold winters; unpredictable rainfall
*Animal life*–includes prairie dogs, bison, foxes, ferrets, grouse, snakes, and lizards

**Deserts**
*Regions*–western North America, Arctic
*Plant life*–sparse, includes cacti, drought-resistant plants
*Characteristics*–arid, low rainfall; extreme diurnal temperature shifts
*Animal life*–includes jackrabbits (in North America), owls, kangaroo rats, lizards, snakes, tortoises
Tropical Rain Forests
*Regions*–South America, Colombia.
*Plant life*–high biomass; diverse types
*Characteristics*–high rainfall and temperatures; impoverished soil
*Animal life*–includes sloths, snakes, monkeys, birds, leopards, and insects

The permafrost soil of the tundra is surprisingly delicate and easily disturbed; it can still bear the imprint of tire tracks long after the vehicle has left the area.

(*) (Tundra)
(*) (Tiaga)
(*) (Temp-Decid. Forest)
(*) (Grasslands)
(*) - (Deserts)

We've talked about biomes. They are relatively stable and contain a variety of interactions among their living and non-living elements. Materials and resources important to the maintenance of life are used, reused, and recycled within and among their communities. To study that phenomenon is to study the ecosystem.

## ECOSYSTEMS

Ecosystems are self-contained regions that include *biotic* (living) and *abiotic* (non-living) factors. Energy from an ecosystem is lost as heat and must be replaced by energy provided by the sun. Ecosystems depend on a continuous recycling of materials to perpetuate. Two important recycled materials are carbon and nitrogen; the ways in which they are recycled through the ecosystem are shown below:

Carbon, of course, is the key element in all organic molecules which make up organisms. Most of the carbon available to us exists in the atmosphere.

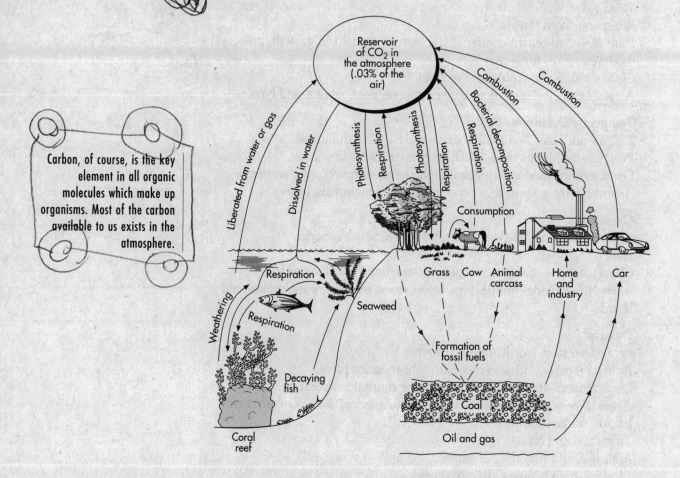

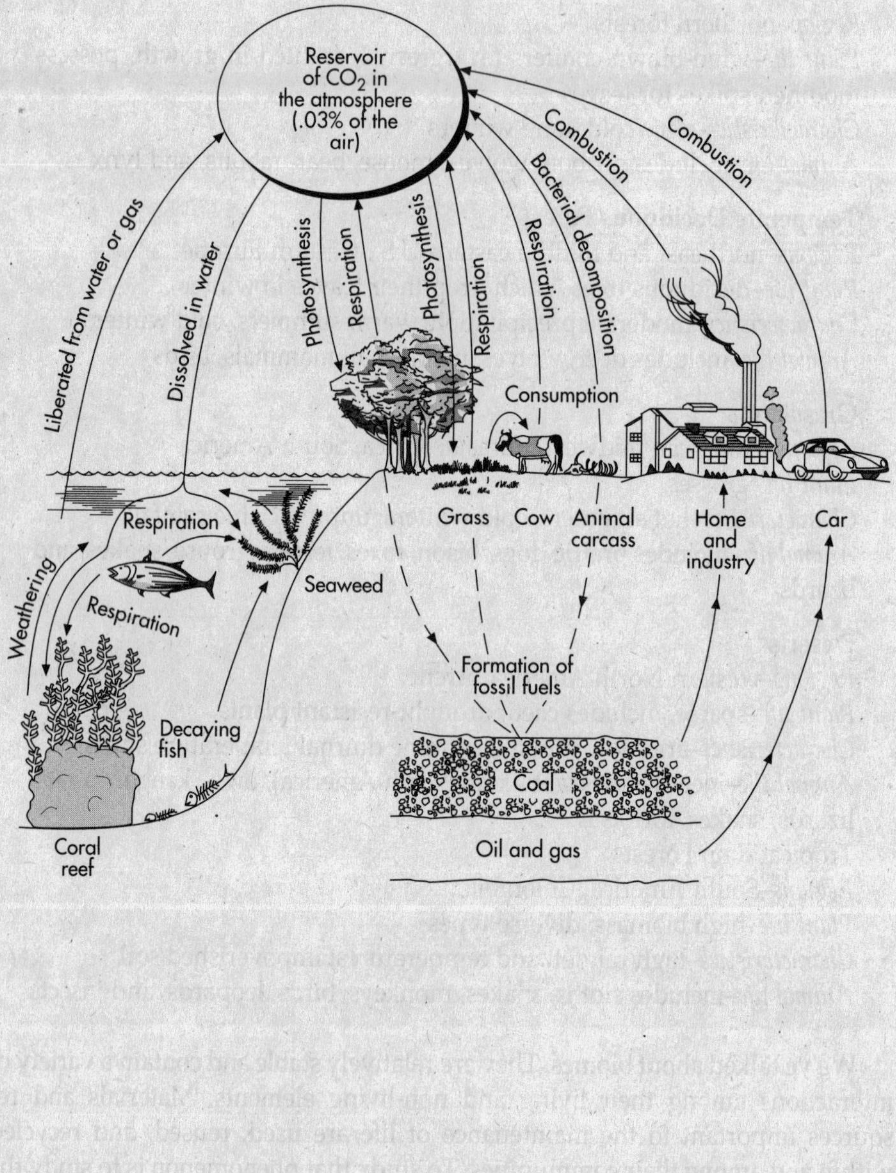

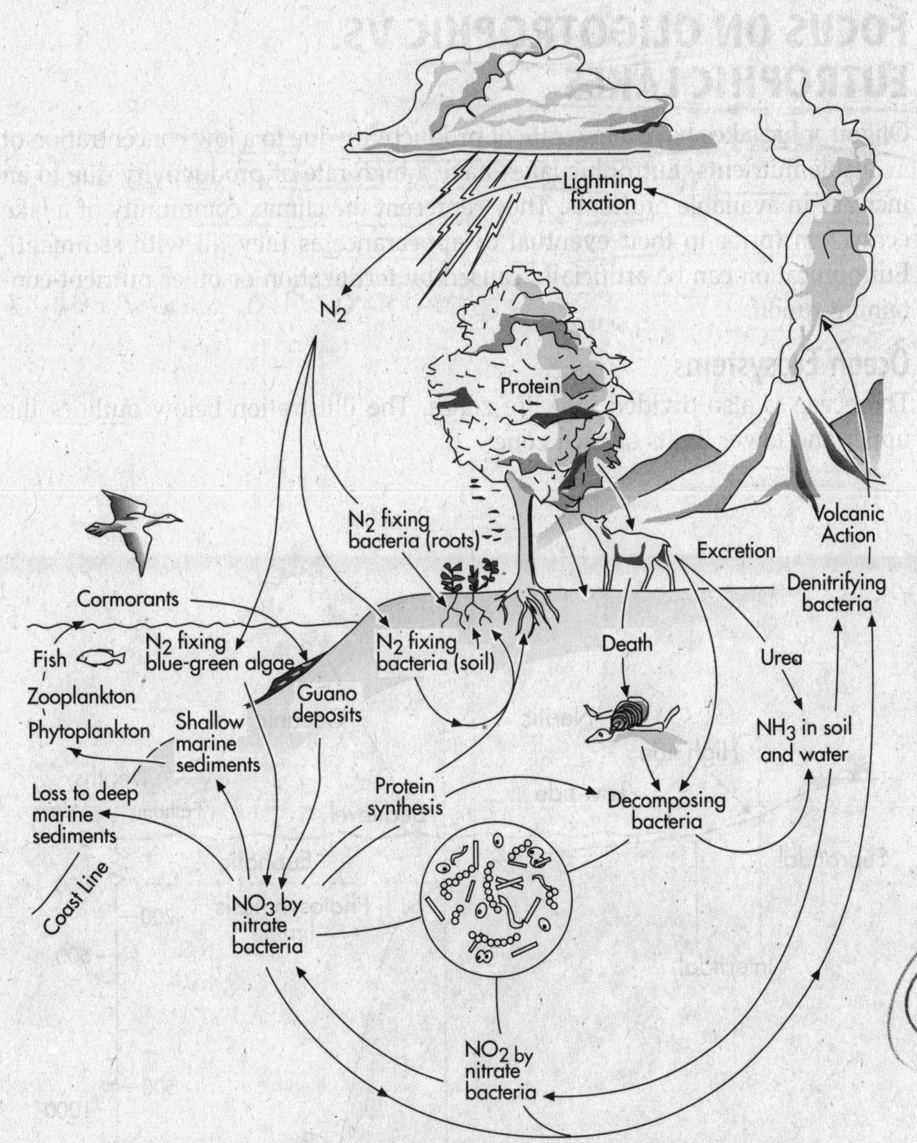

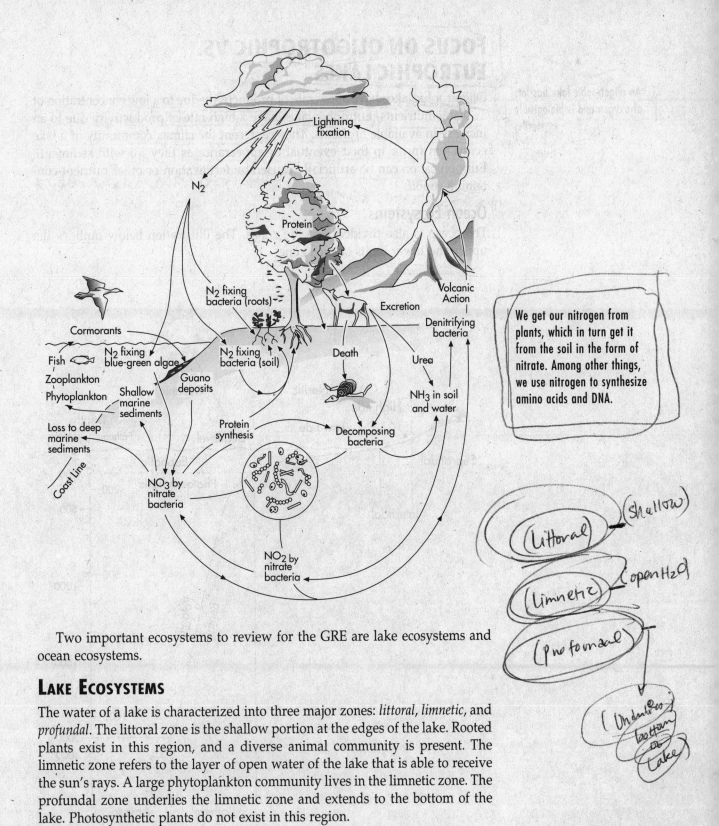

We get our nitrogen from plants, which in turn get it from the soil in the form of nitrate. Among other things, we use nitrogen to synthesize amino acids and DNA.

Two important ecosystems to review for the GRE are lake ecosystems and ocean ecosystems.

## LAKE ECOSYSTEMS

The water of a lake is characterized into three major zones: *littoral*, *limnetic*, and *profundal*. The littoral zone is the shallow portion at the edges of the lake. Rooted plants exist in this region, and a diverse animal community is present. The limnetic zone refers to the layer of open water of the lake that is able to receive the sun's rays. A large phytoplankton community lives in the limnetic zone. The profundal zone underlies the limnetic zone and extends to the bottom of the lake. Photosynthetic plants do not exist in this region.

An oligotrophic lake has lots of oxygen and is biologically sterile.

## FOCUS ON OLIGOTROPHIC VS. EUTROPHIC LAKES

Oligotrophic lakes have a low rate of productivity due to a low concentration of available nutrients. Eutrophic lakes have a high rate of productivity due to an increase in available nutrients. They represent the climax community of a lake ecosystem (prior to their eventual disappearance as they fill with sediment). Eutrophication can be artificially caused by fertilization or other nutrient-containing runoff.

### Ocean Ecosystems

The ocean is also divided into life zones. The illustration below outlines the upper and lower limits of each zone.

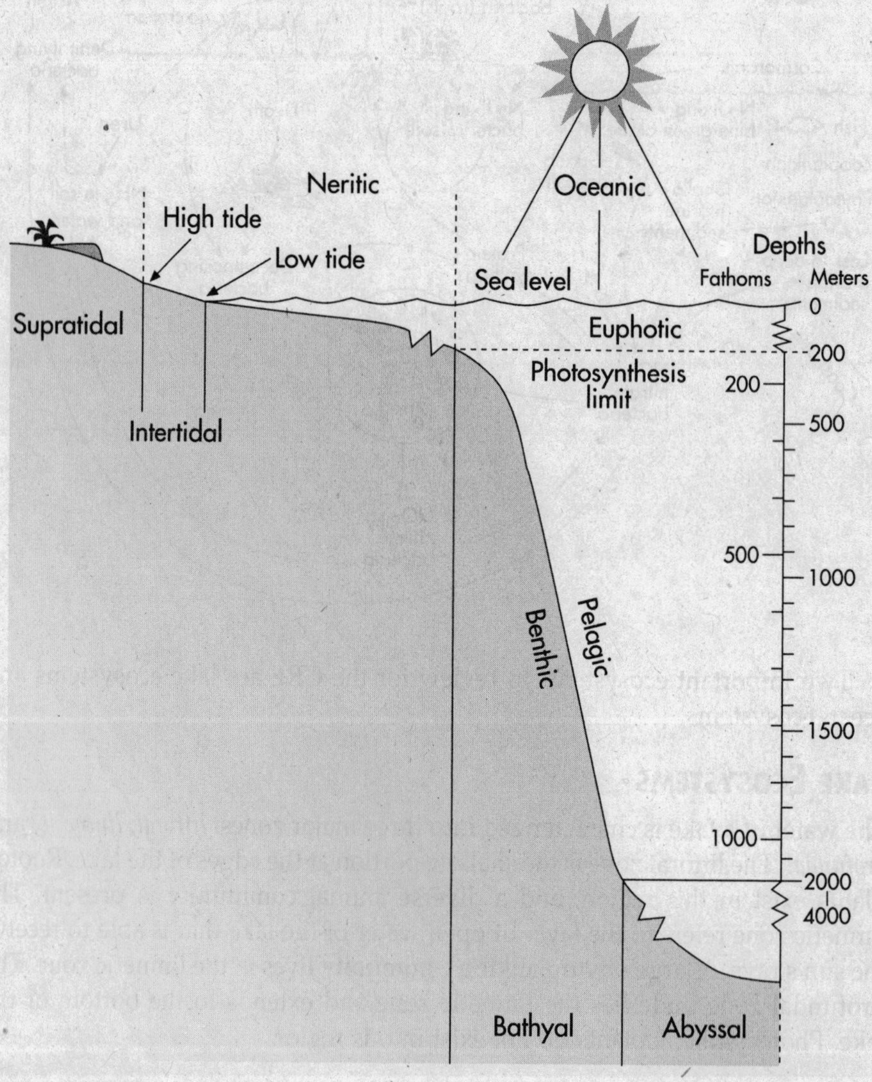


Many ecosystems, of course, involve animals. For the GRE, you'll want to review what you've learned about animal behavior. So let's do it.

## BEHAVING LIKE AN ANIMAL: LEARNING AND INSTINCT

Animal behavior is fairly complex; however, we broadly may divide animal behavior into those behaviors that are learned, and those that are instinctive, or innate.

*Innate behaviors* are behaviors that an animal is born with. This means that specific cues in the environment can trigger an animal's innate response the very first time that the animal is exposed to the stimulus. Innate responses tend to be well-choreographed, neurologically resistant to alteration, and predictable. *Learned behaviors,* on the other hand, are more flexible. Here, an animal's first reaction to a stimulus will not necessarily be the same as its second, third, or fourth reaction to the same stimulus.

Four important types of learned behaviors are *trial and error, conditioning, imprinting,* and *insight.*

- trial/error
- conditioning
- imprinting
- insight

Trial and error learning allows an animal to behave a certain way with a reasonable expectation of the outcome based on previous experience.

In conditioning (associative learning), an animal learns to associate a stimulus with a particular outcome. An example is Pavlov's dogs, who were taught to associate the ringing of a bell with delivery of food. As a result, they salivated at the sound of the bell. Imprinting occurs during a critical period in a young animal's life. At this time it learns to associate a particular environmental cue with an important aspect of its life. For instance, a chick fixes on a moving object in its path and equates that object with its mother. A bird hears a particular sequence of notes and is able to reproduce that sequence as its species-specific song. A salmon is able to imprint, using its olfactory senses, the stream in which it was hatched, so that it can return to spawn. Each of these associations must occur during the critical period, or they will not form. Imprinted learnings last throughout the organism's lifetime.

Insight learning is associated with "higher" animals. An animal can respond to a new stimulus despite the fact that the animal hasn't previously encountered it. This can be paraphrased as "figuring out what to do when confronted with a new problem."

"The measure of success is not whether you have a tough problem to deal with, but whether it's the same problem you had last year."
—John Foster Dulles

## FOCUS ON BATESIAN MIMICRY

Batesian mimicry is an adaptive feature of certain prey animals. The adaptation exploits a predator's learned association of a noxious food source with the food's distinctive coloration, shape, or behavior. Once the predator makes the mistake of trying to eat the noxious prey, the consequences will cause the predator to avoid in the future any prey organism that resembles the noxious prey. Benign prey species then exploit the predator's learned aversion by mimicking the color, form, or behavior of the noxious prey species.

# PART V

# GRE Biology Lab

Step into our Biology Lab and try your hand at these questions:

## Specimen 1

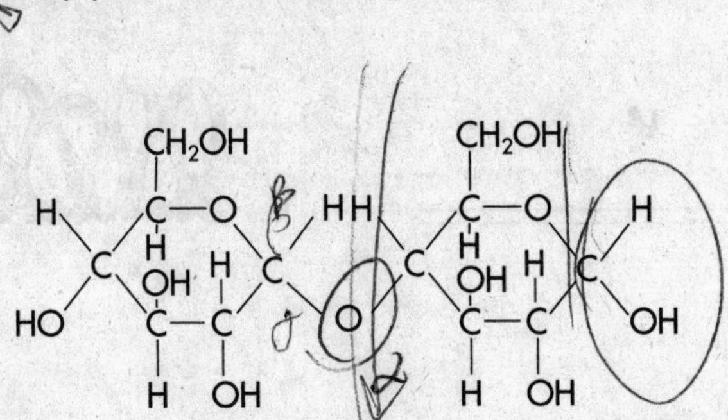

1. What monosaccharide subunits produce this molecule? Glucose
2. What enzyme hydrolyzes this disaccharide? Maltose

## Specimen 2

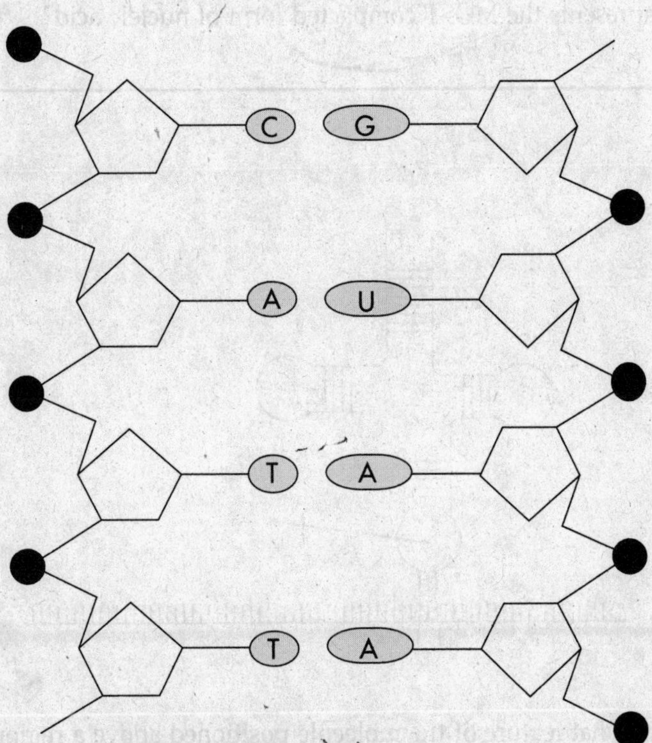


1. What structure is this? DNA -RNA hy
2. What nuclear process has just been completed? transc

## Specimen 3

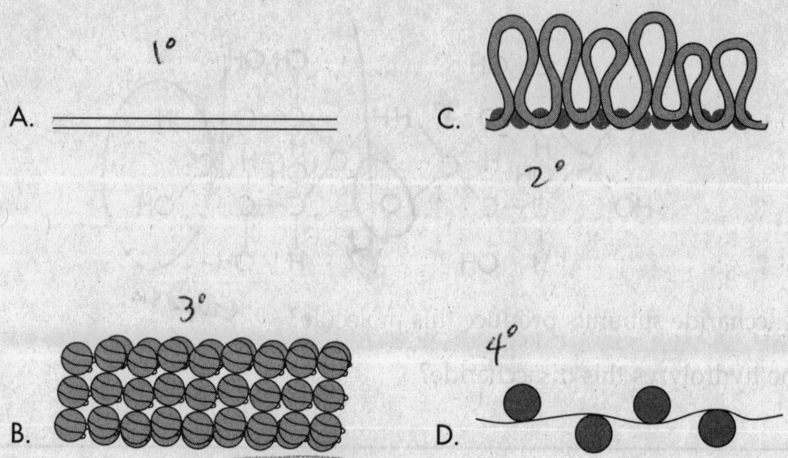


1. Which structure represents the LEAST compacted form of nucleic acid?
2. Which structure represents the MOST compacted form of nucleic acid?

## Specimen 4

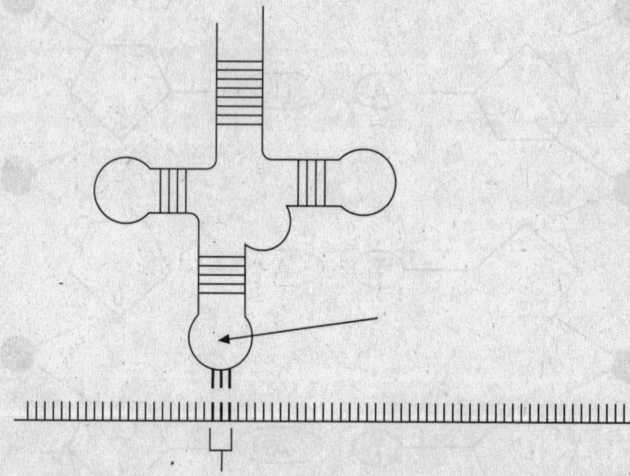

1. The arrow points to what feature of the molecule positioned above a region of mRNA?
2. In what part of the cell are these two structures located?

## Specimen 5

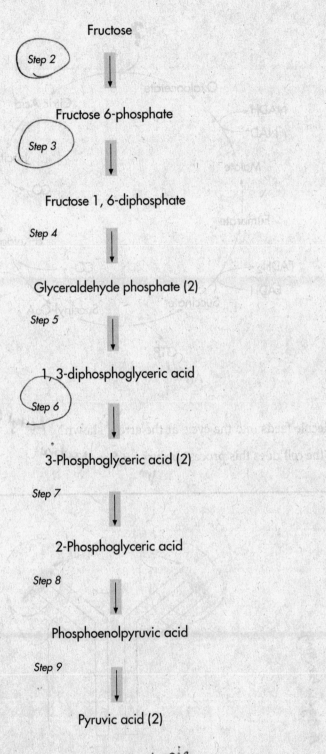

Fructose

Step 2 ↓

Fructose 6-phosphate

Step 3 ↓

Fructose 1, 6-diphosphate

Step 4 ↓

Glyceraldehyde phosphate (2)

Step 5 ↓

1, 3-diphosphoglyceric acid

Step 6 ↓

3-Phosphoglyceric acid (2)

Step 7 ↓

2-Phosphoglyceric acid

Step 8 ↓

Phosphoenolpyruvic acid

Step 9 ↓

Pyruvic acid (2)

1. What process of cellular respiration is this? Glycolysis
2. At which step(s) is (are) input of ATP required?

## Specimen 6

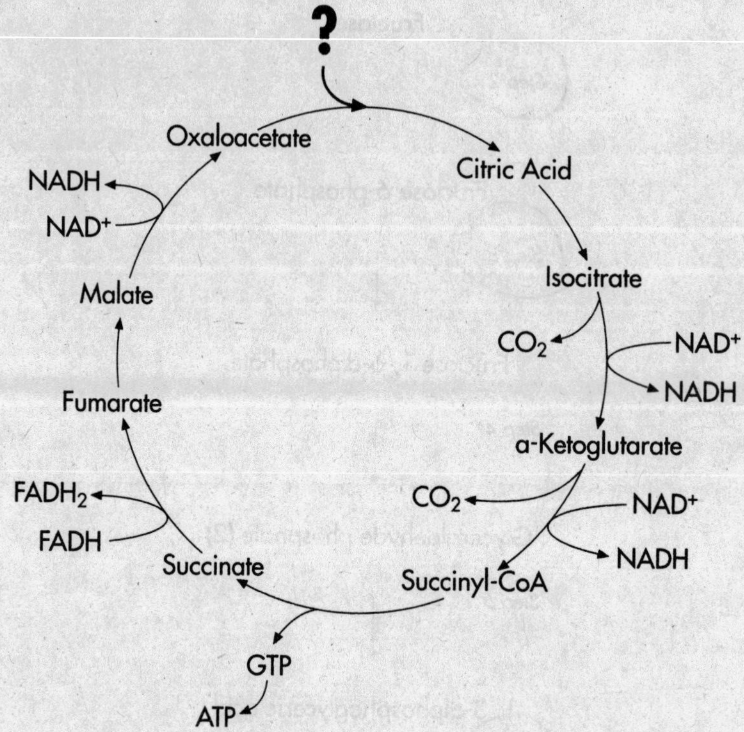


1. What molecule feeds into the cycle at the arrow shown? Acetyl CoA
2. Where in the cell does this process occur? Inn Mito Matrix

---

## Specimen 7

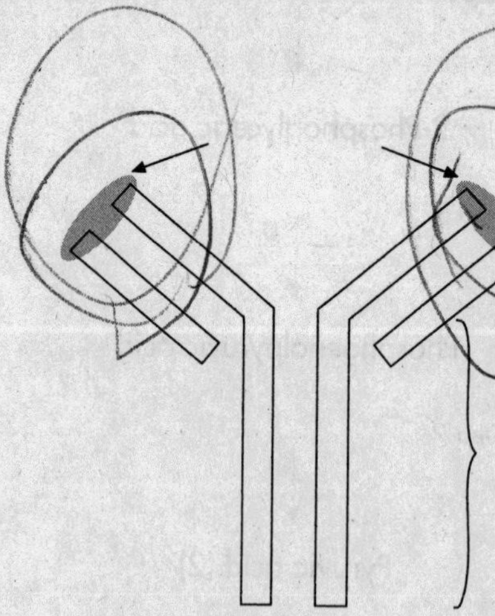

Antigen binding

Effector sides

1. The arrows point to what feature of the immunoglobulin shown? Variable Region
2. The bracket encompasses the portion of immunoglobulin responsible for what function?

Constant Region

---

## Specimen 8

I.

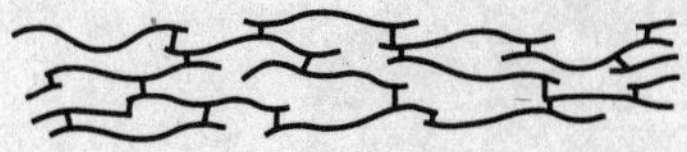

II.

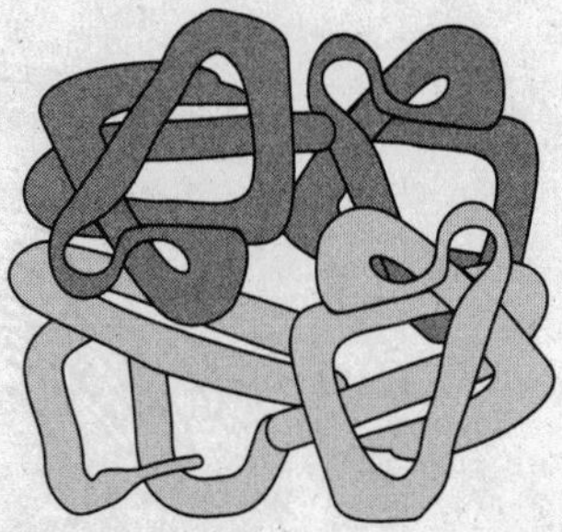

1. Which of the two proteins shown is more likely to have a regulatory function? II (glob.)
2. Which protein is most likely found in connective tissue? (I) (elastin)

---

## Specimen 9

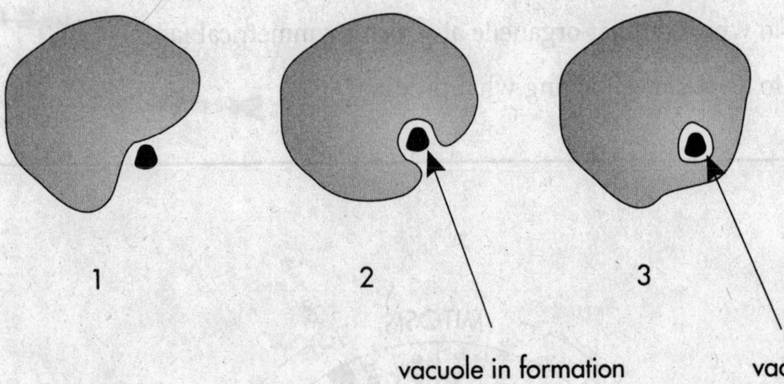


1. What cellular process is this? Endocytosis
2. This form of cell uptake is associated with the presence of what protein on the intracellular phospholipid face? Clathrin Receptor pits

---

## Specimen 10

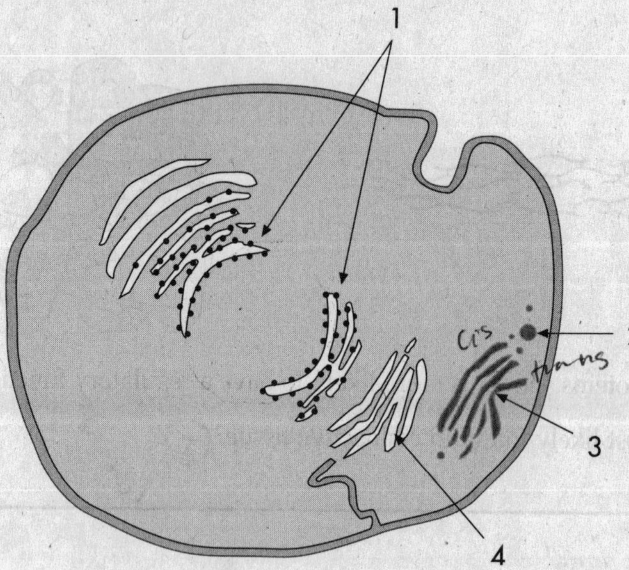


1. Arrow 3 points to which cellular organelle at which asymmetrical face? ~~Rough ER~~ sec. vesicle
2. Arrow 2 points to a vesicle containing what product? ~~sec. vesicle~~. Golgi

---

## Specimen 11

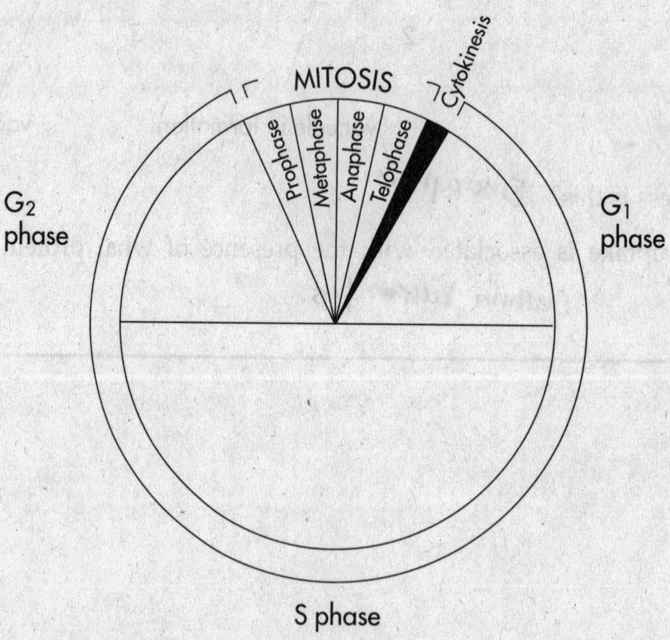


1. Replication occurs during which of the indicated cell phases? S
2. Protein synthesis is conducted during which of the indicated cell phases? G2

---

## Specimen 12

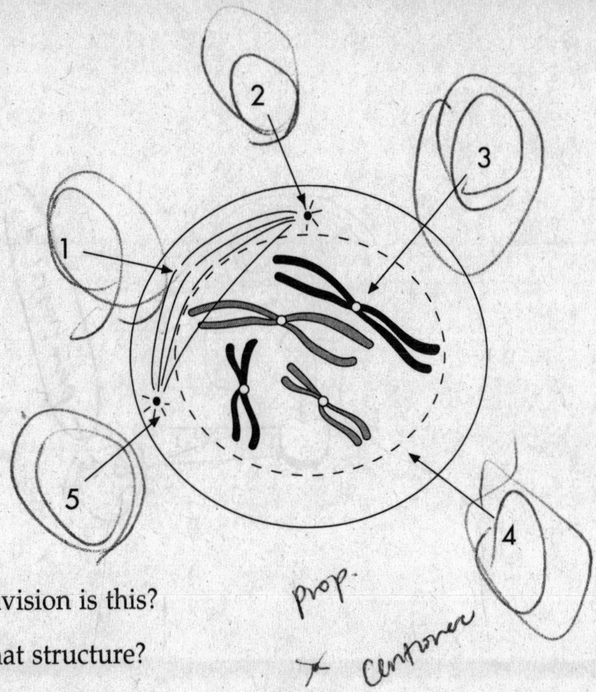


1. Which stage of cell division is this? prop.
2. Arrow 3 points to what structure? centromere

---

## Specimen 13

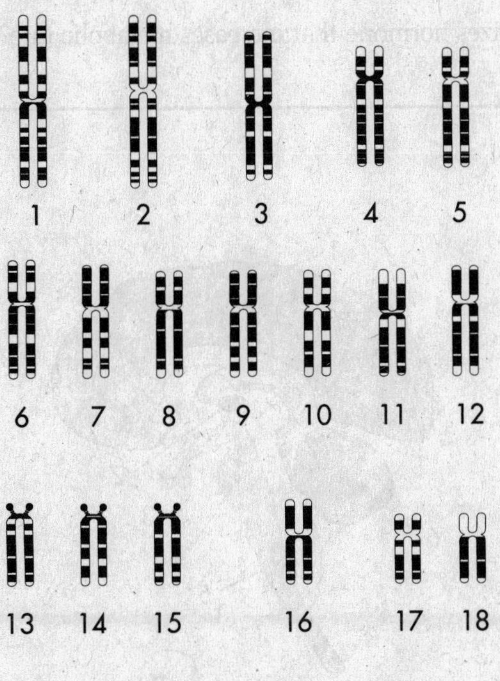

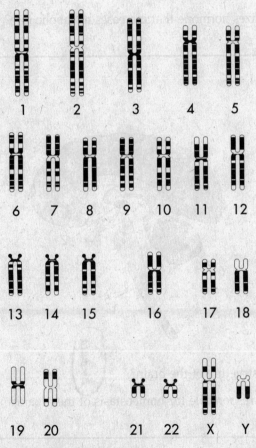

1. What is the name given to this chromosomal lineup? karyotype
2. What (if any) is the significance of the banding patterns?

---

## Specimen 14

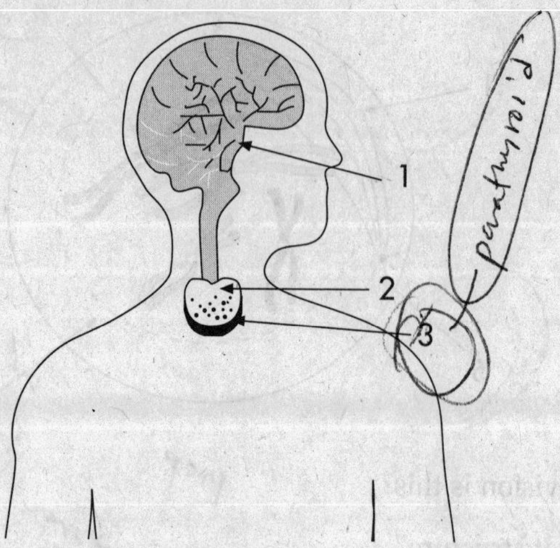


1. Arrow 3 points to what endocrine gland?
2. Which structure synthesizes hormone that increases metabolic rate?

---

## Specimen 15

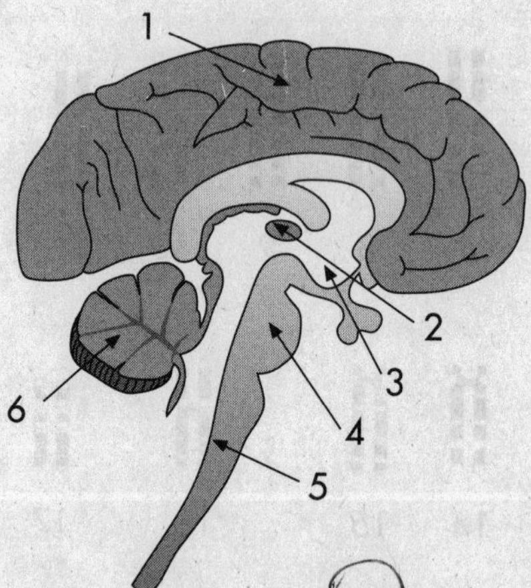


1. Arrow 5 points to what structure of the brain?
2. Which brain structure is responsible for homeostasis of the organism?

---

## Specimen 16

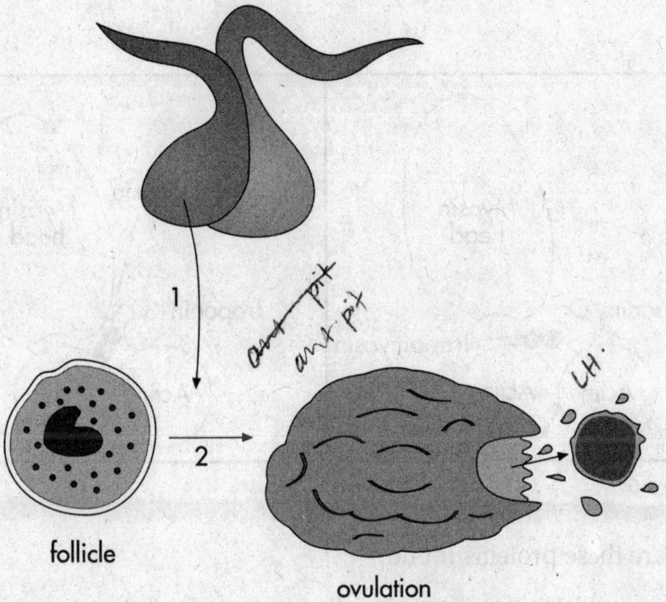


1. What two hormones are indicated by arrow 1? LH
2. What endocrine organ produces the hormones indicated by arrow 1?

---

## Specimen 17

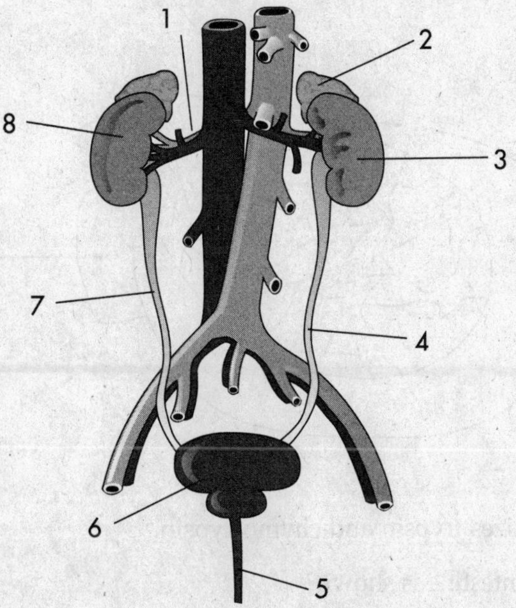


1. Arrow 5 points to what urinary structure? urethra
2. Arrow 4 points to what urinary structure? ureter

---

## Specimen 18

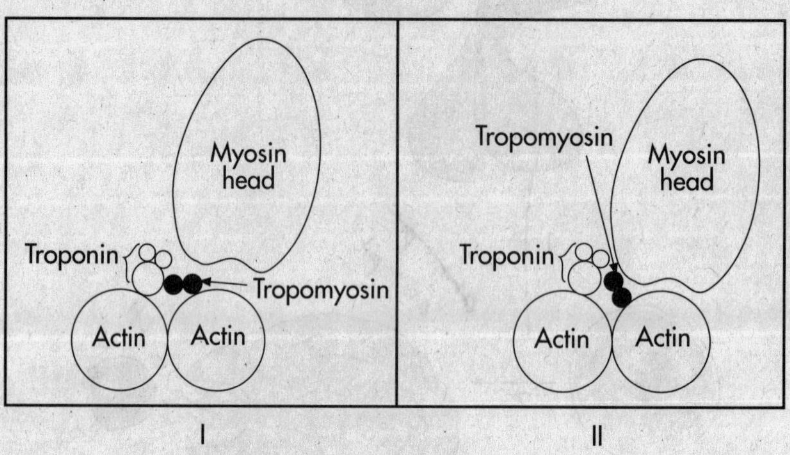


1. In what cell type are these proteins found?
2. The protein arrangement shown in stage II follows an intracellular rise in what ion?

---

## Specimen 19

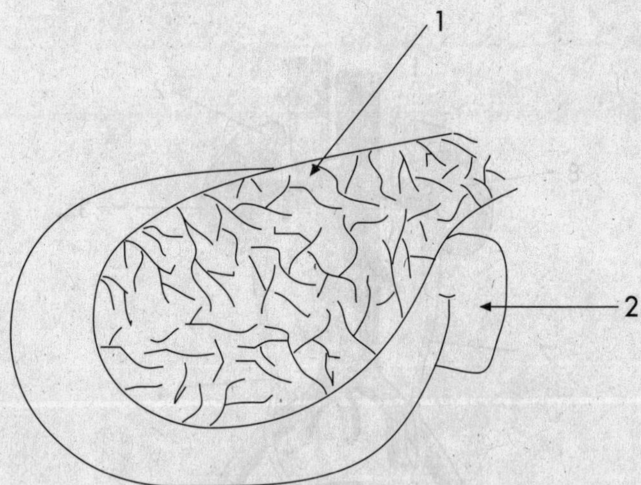


1. Which structure synthesizes trypsin and chymotrypsin?
2. Which section of small intestine is shown?

---

## Specimen 20

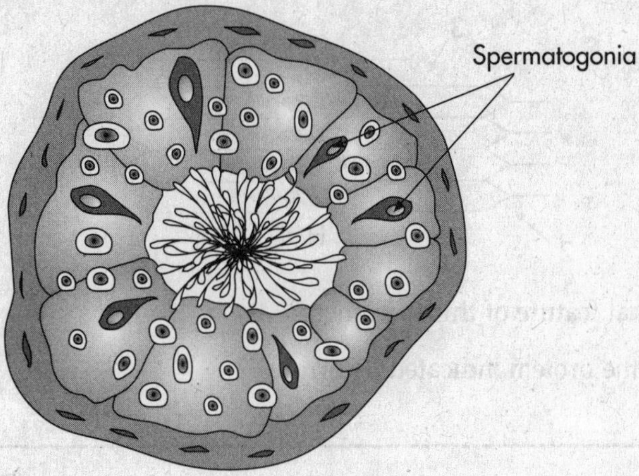


1. This cross-sectional view presents what tubular structure?
2. This tubular structure is located in what organ of the body?

---

## Specimen 21

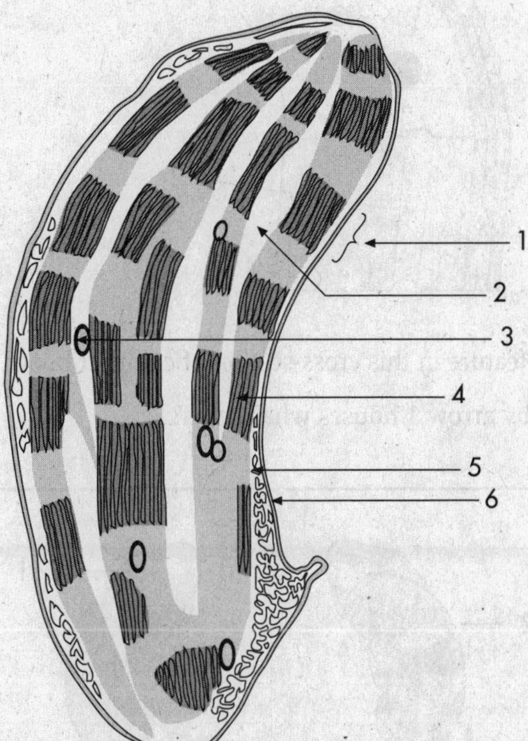


1. Arrow 1 points to what structure of this plastid?
2. Carbon dioxide is converted into glucose in which of the structures shown?

---

## Specimen 22

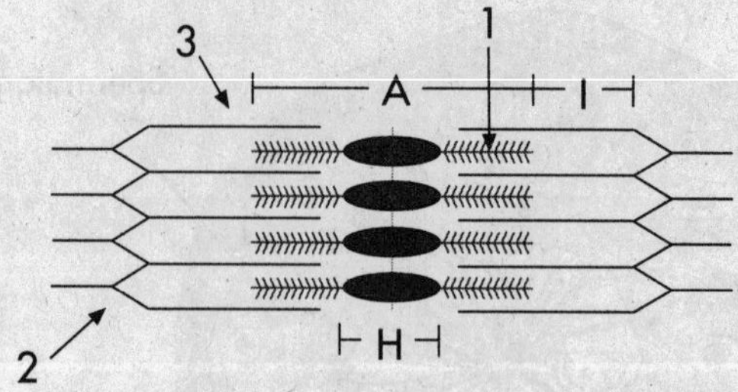


1. Arrow 2 points to what feature of this sarcomere?
2. What is the name of the protein indicated by arrow 3?

---

## Specimen 23

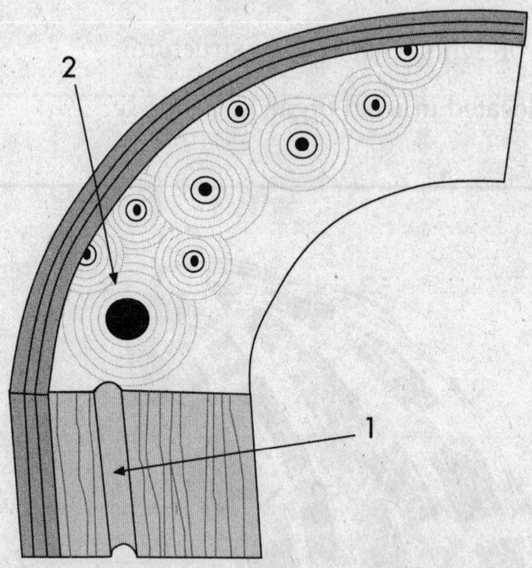


1. Arrow 1 points to what feature in this cross-section of compact bone?
2. The structure indicated by arrow 1 houses what items?

---

## Specimen 24

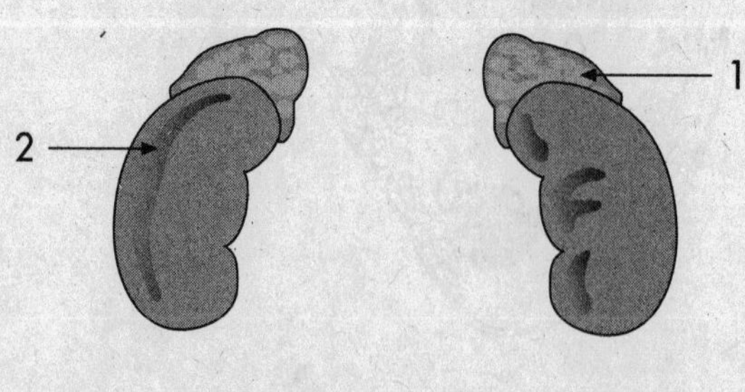


1. Arrow 1 points to what organ?
2. The medulla of the organ indicated by arrow 1 secretes what catecholamines?

---

## Specimen 25

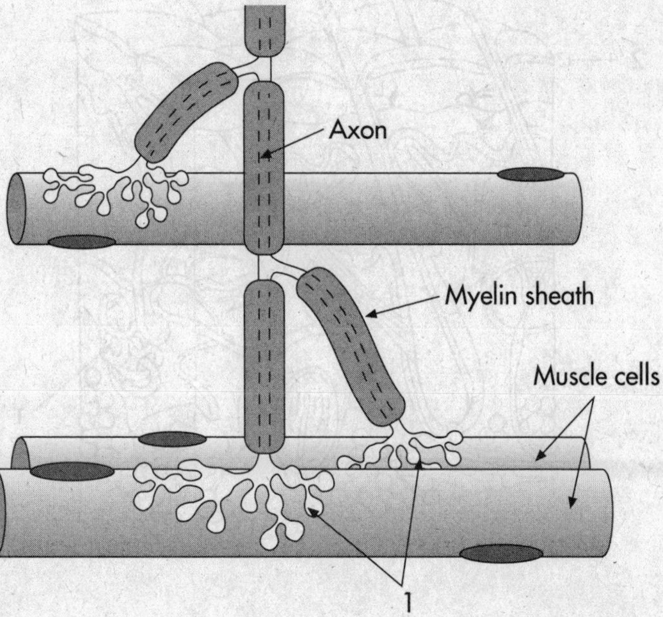


1. What is the name of the sites where the motor neuron synapses on myofibrils?
2. What neurotransmitter is released at the site indicated by arrow 1?

## Specimen 26

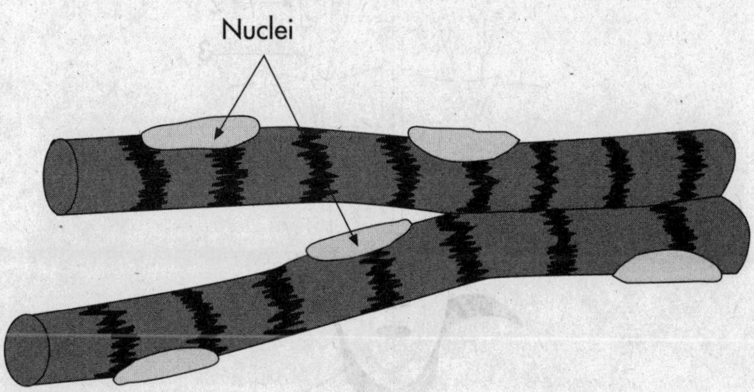


1. What type of muscle is shown?
2. Where in the body might this type of muscle fiber be found?

## Specimen 27

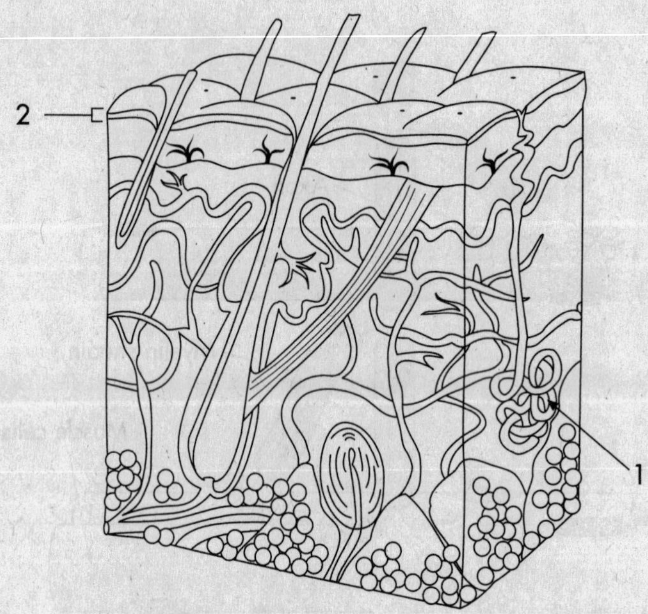


1. Arrow 1 points to what structure of the skin?
2. What protein predominates in the epithelial cells of the epidermis shown at arrow 2?

---

## Specimen 28

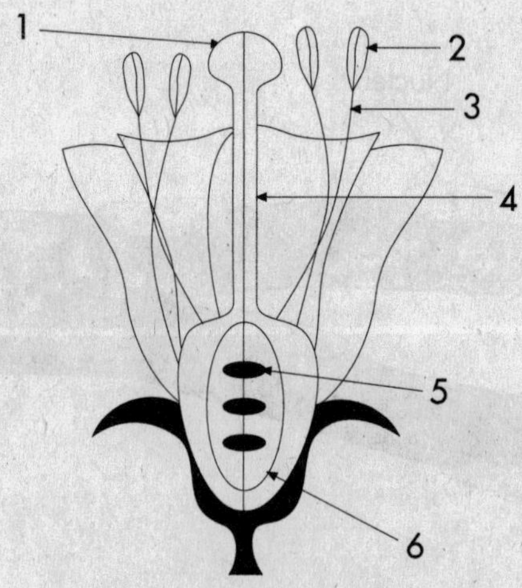


1. The stamen consists of which of the numbered structures?
2. Arrow 6 points to what structure on this angiosperm?

---

## Specimen 29

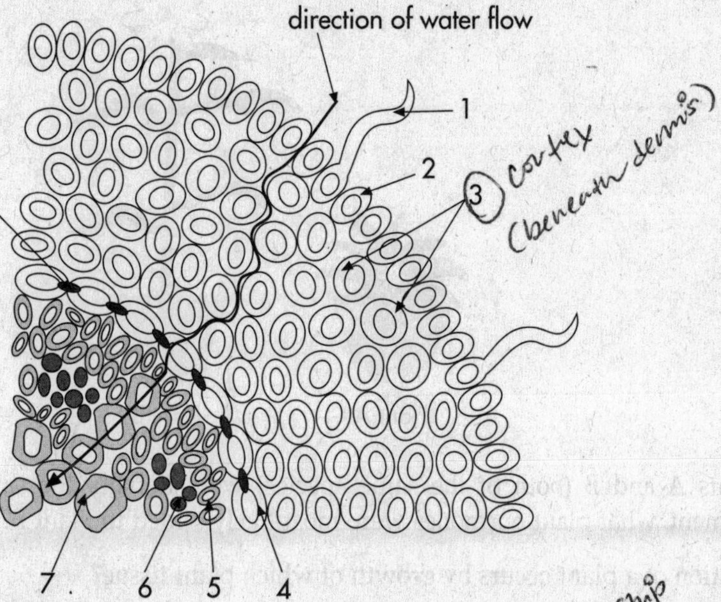


1. Arrow 8 points to what structure in this cross-section of a plant root? Casp Strip
2. Which numbered structure indicates the cortex?

---

## Specimen 30

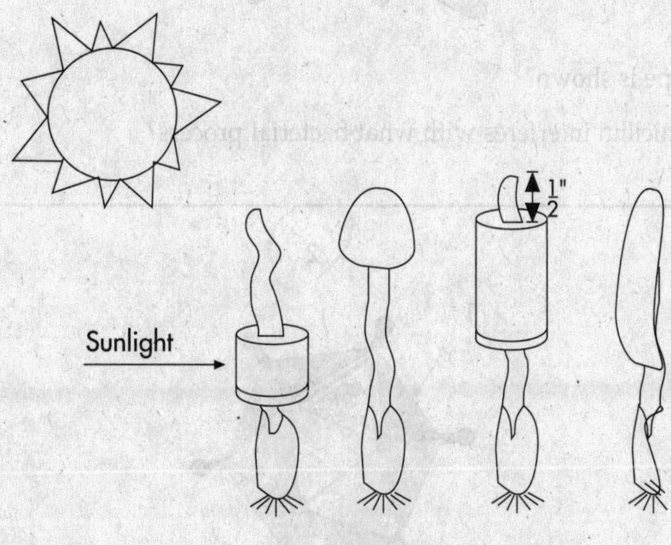


1. Which plant(s) will cease to exhibit phototropism under the experimental conditions shown?
2. What plant hormones are primarily responsible for the phototropism? auxin

---

## Specimen 31

1. If Plants A and B (both of the same species) were initially the same size at the onset of the experiment, what plant hormones were most likely added to Plant B?
2. Elongation of a plant occurs by growth of which plant tissue?

---

## Specimen 32

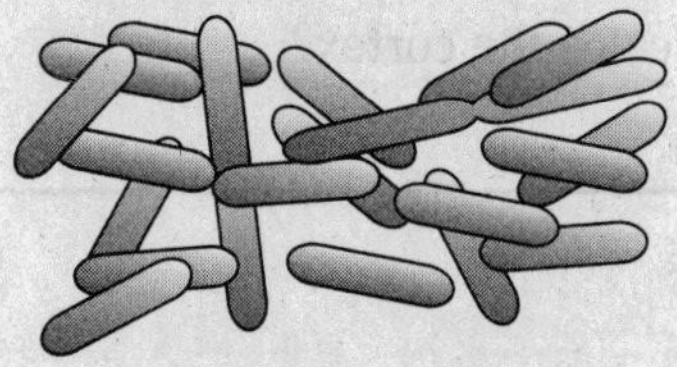

1. What bacterial type is shown?
2. The antibiotic penicillin interferes with what bacterial process?

---

## Specimen 33

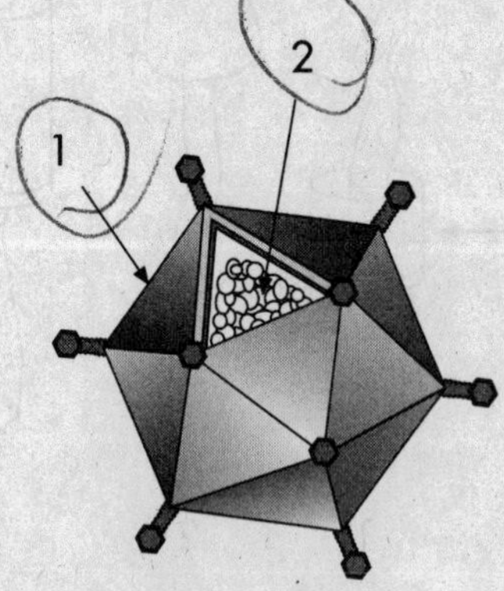


1. Arrow 1 points to what viral structure?
2. If arrow 2 points to an RNA viral core, what enzyme is required for successful viral reproduction?

---

## Specimen 34

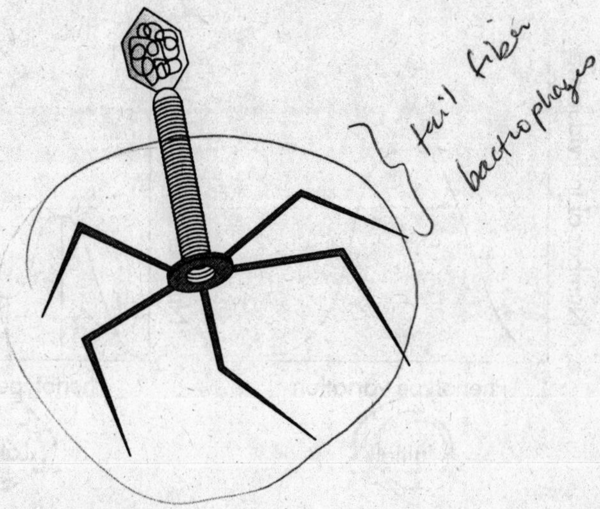

1. What is the name of the structure shown?
2. What is its target host?

---

## Specimen 35

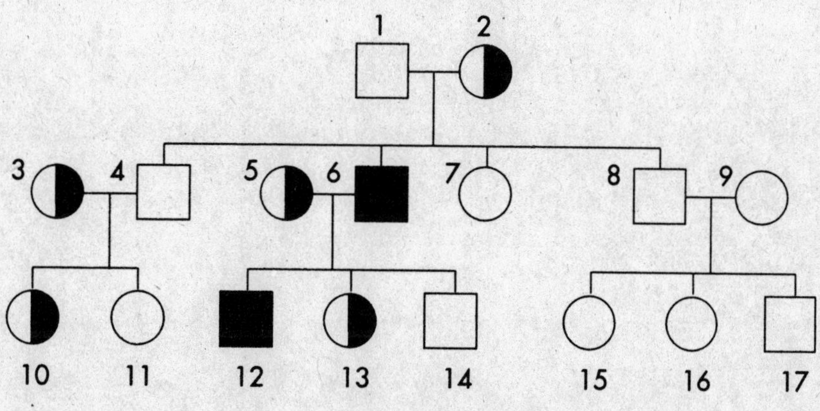


1. What form of inheritance is indicated for the trait covered in the pedigree?
2. What trait might conceivably be the focus of this pedigree?

---

## Specimen 36

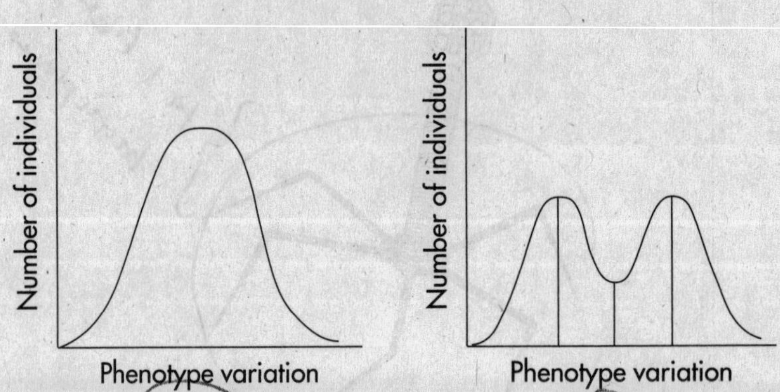


Initial    Later

1. Which form of selection acted upon the population shown in order to produce the phenotypic variation curve exhibited in the later stage?
2. Has the population undergone directional selection?

# BIOLOGY LAB ANSWER KEY

**Specimen 1**

1. Glucose
2. Maltase

**Specimen 2**

1. A DNA/RNA hybrid (note the T on one strand and the U on the other)
2. Transcription

**Specimen 3**

1. Structure A (a double-stranded DNA molecule)
2. Structure C (solonoid looped and bound to protein to form chromatin)

**Specimen 4**

1. Anticodon (of tRNA molecule)
2. Cytoplasm (on rough ER or free ribosome)

**Specimen 5**

1. Glycolysis (it's anaerobic)
2. Steps 2, 3, and 6

**Specimen 6**

1. Acetyl CoA
2. Mitochondria

**Specimen 7**

1. Antigen-binding sites
2. Effector sites (important in determining an antibody's function once it's bound to antigen)

**Specimen 8**

1. Protein II (globular proteins generally have regulatory functions; this is hemoglobin, which binds oxygen)
2. Protein I (fibrous proteins generally have structural functions; this is elastin, which confers strength and flexibility)

**Specimen 9**

1. Endocytosis
2. Clathrin

**Specimen 10**

1. Golgi apparatus (*trans* face)
2. Secretory enzyme

**Specimen 11**

1. S phase
2. $G_2$ phase

**Specimen 12**

1. Prophase
2. Centromere

**Specimen 13**

1. A karyotype
2. Banding provides distinctive identification for each chromosome

**Specimen 14**

1. Parathyroid glands
2. Structure 2 (thyroid gland)

**Specimen 15**

1. Medulla
2. Structure 3 (hypothalamus)

**Specimen 16**

1. LH and FSH (luteinizing hormone and follicle-stimulating hormone)
2. Anterior lobe of the pituitary

**Specimen 17**

1. Urethra
2. Ureter

**Specimen 18**

1. Muscle cells
2. Calcium

**Specimen 19**

1. Structure 1 (pancreas)
2. Duodenum

**Specimen 20**

1. Seminiferous tubule
2. Testes

**Specimen 21**

1. Grana
2. Structure 2 (stroma)

**Specimen 22**

1. Z line
2. Actin (thin filament)

**Specimen 23**

1. Haversian canal
2. Blood vessels and nerves

**Specimen 24**

1. Adrenal glands
2. Epinephrine and norepinephrine

**Specimen 25**

1. Neuromuscular junction
2. Acetylcholine

**Specimen 26**

1. Striated muscle
2. Skeletal muscle, heart muscle

**Specimen 27**

1. Sweat gland
2. Keratin (confers elasticity, water resistance, protection)

**Specimen 28**

1. Structures 2 and 3 (anther and filament; male parts of flower)
2. Receptacle

**Specimen 29**

1. Casparian strip
2. Tissue 3 (just beneath the epidermis)

**Specimen 30**

1. Plants 2 and 4
2. Auxins

**Specimen 31**

1. Gibberellins
2. Apical meristem

**Specimen 32**

1. Bacilli
2. Production of the bacterial cell wall (it's an irreversible inhibitor of transpeptidase)

**Specimen 33**

1. Protein capsid (outer protein coat)
2. Reverse transcriptase

**Specimen 34**

1. Bacteriophage (it's a specialized virus possessing a tail fiber)
2. Bacteria

**Specimen 35**

1. Sex-linked (note that male 6 has the condition from receiving a single X from his mother, and male 14 is spared the condition even though his father suffers from it)
2. Color-blindness; hemophilia

**Specimen 36**

1. Disruptive selection
2. Yes

# PART VI

# Word Watch

**These terms frequently appear on the GRE Biology Subject Test.**

Actinomycin D
: inhibits RNA polymerase.

Action potential
: voltage reversal that rapidly moves along axonal membrane surfaces.

Allen's rule
: pattern of geographical variation within a species that results in attenuated extremities in hot environments.

Allelopathy
: secretion by plants (desert plants in particular) of a toxic substance into the soil that repels other plants from growing near them.

Allozymes
: alternate forms of an enzyme due to alleles that code for slightly different versions of the enzyme.

Axoneme
: structural core of cilium made of microtubule doublets.

Basal body
: cytoplasmic organelle of microtubules found at base of eukaryotic flagella and cilia.

Bergmann's rule
: pattern of geographical variation within a species resulting in large body size in cold environments.

Biotic potential
: measures how many young are produced in a litter, how often, and female's reproductive age span (organisms with high biotic potential generate a lot of offspring; those with low biotic potential generate few).

Carrying capacity
: maximum number of individuals of a species that an environment can support.

Chiasmata
: microscopically visible sites where chromatid exchanges occur during meiosis.

Chromosomes
: nuclear structures that contain hereditary material.

Chromatin
: nucleic acids and proteins that together make up chromosomes.

Cistron
: DNA segment that encodes a polypeptide chain.

Clade
: monophyletic group of species that are descendants of a single ancestor.

Cline
: variation in phenotypes of the members of a species that is geographically based; there is a steady and gradual difference in phenotype that corresponds to shifts across geographical regions.

Codon
: grouping of three individual nucleic acids in DNA or mRNA that specify a certain amino acid.

Colchicine
: poison that binds to tubulin and prevents microtubule assembly.

Deme
: local population of organisms.

Depolarization
: reduction in negative electrical potential of axon membrane.

Directional selection
: population phenotype changes over time to another phenotype that had previously been only marginally represented in the gene pool; directional selection occurs in response to change in the environment.

Disruptive selection
: more than one phenotype predominates in a population.

DNA polymerase
: DNA replication enzyme.

**Dyad**
pair of chromosomes that is separated from the tetrad formed during prophase I of meiosis.

**Ecotone**
overlapping plant communities in nearby regions.

**Ecotypes**
geographic races of a species that change phenotypes in order to accommodate different environmental pressures.

**Euchromatin**
extended, active portion of chromatin.

**Exon**
regions of transcribed gene that are present in mature mRNA.

**Gause's competitive exclusion theory**
competition for limited resources in which the more fit organism will obtain the desired resource and the less fit organism will become locally extinct; alternatively, less fit organisms will establish an alternative niche.

**Heterochromatin**
condensed, inactive portion of chromatin.

**Histones**
proteins associated with DNA in eukaryotic chromosomes.

**Home range**
area an animal utilizes during its routine activities; may overlap with home ranges of other animals; is not defended.

**Intron**
segments of gene that are transcribed, but subsequently excised from mRNA.

**Juvenile hormone**
insect hormone responsible for developmental staging.

**Lampbrush chromosome**
found especially in amphibian oocytes; chromosome in diplotene stage of first meiotic division characterized by paired lateral loops.

**Monophyletic species**
derive from one common ancestor.

**Mutation**
heritable change in sequence of genomic DNA.

**Nondisjunction**
meiotic error in which one gamete receives two homologous chromosomes and the other gamete receives none.

**Oncogenes**
normal vertebrate genes involved in regulation of growth that may lead to neoplastic transformation if overexpressed or mutated.

**Operon**
group of adjacent coregulated genes.

**Optimality theory**
only most beneficial of all possible beneficial phenotypes prevail in gene pool.

**Peptidoglycan**
material of bacterial cell walls.

**Phylogeny**
relates to the evolutionary history of a species.

**Phylogenetic species**
derive from more than one ancestor.

**Pleiotrophic genes**
exert an effect on more than one trait.

**Promoter**
DNA site for RNA polymerase to initiate transcription.

**Pseudogenes**
DNA sequences that appear to be once functional genes which acquired mutations during evolution rendering them nonfunctional.

**Regulatory genes**
genes that encode proteins that regulate other genes.

**Resting Potential**
–70mV (i.e., electrical potential of nerve cell membrane in resting state).

**RNA polymerase**
RNA transcription enzyme utilizing DNA template.

**Stabilizing selection**
intermediate variants of a distribution of phenotypes favored over extreme variants; occurs in stable populations.

Synapsis
: pairing of homologous chromosomes during meiosis.

Territory
: area that an animal defends against intruders.

Thermocline
: temperature gradient of more than one degree Celsius per meter (i.e., as occurs in lakes in the summer).

Translocation
: exchange of chromosomal material between nonhomologous chromosomes.

# PART VII

# The Princeton Review Diagnostic Test

# GRE BIOLOGY SUBJECT TEST

You are about to take The Princeton Review's simulated GRE Biology Subject Test. You'll find an answer sheet at the very back of this book. When you're ready to score yourself, refer to the scoring instructions and answer key on pages 230 and 231. Full explanations regarding the correct answers to all questions start on page 233.

Biology Test
Time–170 minutes
200 Questions

Directions: Each of the questions or incomplete statements below is followed by five suggested answers or completions. Select the one that is best in each case and then completely fill in the corresponding space on the answer sheet.

1. Which of the following is NOT a correct statement concerning elastin?
   (A) It is a component of large blood vessels.
   (B) Its secondary structure consists primarily of alpha helices.
   (C) It is secreted into the extracellular matrix of tissues.
   (D) It is a globular protein found in connective tissue.
   (E) It forms covalent cross-links with other elastin molecules to generate a fibrous network.

2. Which of the following is true of an enzyme that has undergone denaturation?
   (A) its primary structure has not been disrupted
   (B) it is still able to catalyze the reaction for which it is specific
   (C) it is capable of lowering the activation energy of a reaction
   (D) its active site can still bind to a ligand
   (E) if the denaturation is reversible, it is incapable of spontaneously reforming its three-dimensional shape

3.

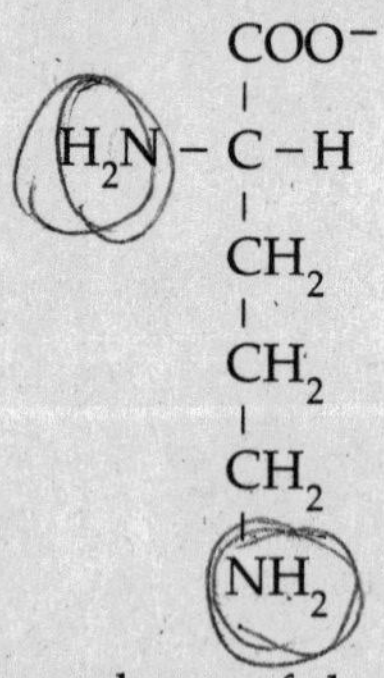


The structure above of the amino acid lysine is shown
   (A) at physiological pH
   (B) at neutral pH
   (C) at alkaline pH
   (D) at acidic pH
   (E) as a zwitterion

4. The Barr body found within female mammalian cells' nuclei is an example of
   (A) euchromatin
   (B) heterochromatin
   (C) a cistron
   (D) pseudogenes
   (E) polytene chromosomes

5. A subunit of DNA and protein consisting of 134-base-pair long stretches of DNA surrounding a protein octomer is called (a)
   (A) histone
   (B) chromatin
   (C) nucleosome
   (D) solenoid
   (E) nucleoid

6. A fluorescent molecule of 1,000 daltons injected into one cell is observed to enter an adjacent cell by passing through a
   (A) spot desmosome
   (B) belt desmosome
   (C) gap junction
   (D) tight junction
   (E) septate junction

7. A competitive inhibitor of an enzyme exerts its effect by
   (A) irreversibly forming covalent links with the enzyme, effectively preventing the enzyme's dissociation from it
   (B) irreversibly modifying some of the amino acid residues that help to comprise the enzyme's active site
   (C) competing with the substrate molecule for the same enzyme but a different binding site than the substrate binding site
   (D) reversibly decreasing the number of enzyme molecules that are available to bind substrates
   (E) reversibly decreasing the enzyme's turnover number

GO ON TO THE NEXT PAGE.

8. Immunoglobulins having epsilon heavy chains and located on the plasma membranes of mast cells and basophilic leukocytes belong to the class of antibodies called

(A) IgG
(B) IgM
(C) IgD
(D) IgA
(E) IgE

9. All of the following are true concerning mitochondria and chloroplasts EXCEPT:

(A) They possess a circular chromosome.
(B) They reproduce by binary fission.
(C) They divide at the same time that the cells in which they are situated divide.
(D) They both employ chemiosmotic energy transduction to fuel the biochemical reactions that take place within their structures.
(E) They are double-membraned organelles.

10. The basal body, a specialized structure found at the base of the axonemes of eukaryotic cilia and flagella, acts to

(A) organize microtubules into a 9 + 2 arrangement and gives rise to the doublet microtubules
(B) organize microfilaments into a 9 + 2 arrangement and gives rise to the doublet microfilaments
(C) assemble α-tubulin and β-tubulin molecules into heterodimers and arrange them into protofilaments
(D) assemble actin molecules into actin filaments and arrange them into a double-stranded helix
(E) initiate elongation of ciliary and flagellar subunits by causing the addition of new protein at the base of the axoneme

11. Which of the following traits do prokaryotes and eukaryotes have in common?

(A) A single chromosome carries the entire genome.
(B) Chromosomes are circular.
(C) Replication is bidirectional.
(D) Molecular weight of respective DNA is comparable.
(E) Number of origins of replication along the chromosome is comparable.

12.

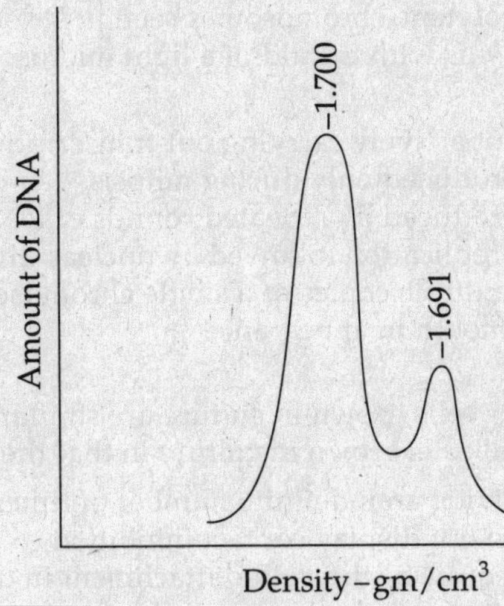


Centrifugation of mouse DNA in a CsCl gradient produces the two peaks in the profile shown above. Which of the following is a correct interpretation of the smaller peak?

(A) It is composed of unique sequences of DNA.
(B) It contains the same overall base sequence composition as the main band.
(C) It contains a higher overall G-C content and thus has a higher average density than the main band DNA.
(D) It represents euchromatin.
(E) It represents satellite DNA.

13. Synthesis of an RNA/DNA hybrid from a single-stranded RNA template requires

(A) a DNA or RNA primer and reverse transcriptase
(B) a DNA or RNA primer and DNA polymerase
(C) RNase only
(D) reverse transcriptase only
(E) DNA polymerase only

14. The amino acid ornithine is regenerated during each turn of the urea cycle in a similar manner to which of the following participants in the citric acid cycle?

(A) Succinate
(B) Fumarate
(C) Oxaloacetate
(D) Citrate
(E) Acetyl CoA

GO ON TO THE NEXT PAGE.

15. The polytene chromosomes seen in *Drosophila silvarentis* with the aid of a light microscope are

(A) not actively carrying out transcription
(B) produced only during mitosis
(C) produced by repeated rounds of DNA replication followed by nuclear division
(D) multiple copies of a single chromosome
(E) smooth in appearance

16. Cancer cells grown in culture are similar to normal cells grown in culture in that they

(A) divide an indefinite number of times
(B) do not display contact inhibition
(C) require a surface for attachment in order to grow
(D) proliferate to the same cell density
(E) require similar levels of growth factors for proliferation

17. Which of the following is NOT a characteristic of introns?

(A) They occur only in eukaryotes.
(B) They represent noncoding regions.
(C) They are found interspersed with exons on a region of DNA that codes for a polypeptide chain.
(D) They are excised from the primary transcript before it gains a 5' cap and a 3' poly(A)tail.
(E) They are transcribed along with exons to create the primary transcript.

18. Cellular uptake of cholesterol occurs through internalization of low density lipoprotein-cholesterol complexes. Cholesterol uptake involves all of the following EXCEPT

(A) cell-surface receptors
(B) clathrin-coated pits
(C) endosome formation
(D) receptor-mediated endocytosis
(E) adhesion plaques

19. A recent theory concerning an unusual rise in asthma attacks following a thunderstorm proposes that while pollen grains at 5 microns are too large to enter the airways, their exposure to water precipitates the release of starch granules as a result of osmotic shock. The starch granules are small enough to enter the lower airways and trigger an asthmatic attack. If this theory is true, which of the following is a correct statement?

(A) The interior of the pollen grains was hypotonic compared to the surrounding environment.
(B) The interior of the pollen grains had a higher osmotic pressure than did the surrounding environment.
(C) The pollen grains underwent plasmolysis prior to releasing their contents.
(D) The pollen grains underwent shrinking before they ruptured and released their contents.
(E) No net movement of water took place between the interior of the pollen grains and their surroundings.

20. (1) $E + S \underset{k_2}{\overset{k_1}{\rightleftharpoons}} ES \xrightarrow{k_3} E + P$

(2) $V = V_{max}\,[S]/[S] + k_m$

Which of the following statements is NOT true concerning the Michaelis-Menten equations of enzyme kinetics shown above?

(A) $k_m$ is equal to the substrate concentration at which the reaction rate is one-half of its maximal value.
(B) When $[S] = k_m$, $V = V_{max}/2$.
(C) When $k_3$ is smaller than $k_2$, $k_m$ is equal to the dissociation constant of the enzyme-substrate complex.
(D) When $k_3$ is smaller than $k_2$, a high $k_m$ indicates a strong binding affinity of enzyme and substrate.
(E) $k_3$ represents the number of substrate molecules that become product per unit time when the enzyme is saturated.

GO ON TO THE NEXT PAGE.

21. All of the following are excerpts from James D. Watson and F.H.C. Crick's "Molecular Structure of Nucleic Acids" published in *Nature* on April 25, 1953 EXCEPT:

(A) "This structure has two helical chains coiled round the same axis."
(B) "The novel feature of the structure is the manner in which the two chains are held together by the purine and pyrimidine bases."
(C) "Both members of a base pair must be either purines or pyrimidines for bonding to occur."
(D) "It follows that in a long molecule many different permutations are possible, and it therefore seems likely that the precise sequence of the bases is the code which carries the genetic information."
(E) "It has not escaped our notice that the specific pairing we have postulated immediately suggests a possible copying mechanism for the genetic material."

22. Proteins were shown to move about in a plane of the plasma membrane when mouse cell-surface proteins and human cell-surface proteins were observed to integrate along a fused mouse-human cell plasma membrane. Which of the following cell culture techniques was most likely employed in order to yield these results?

(A) Producing a heterokaryon
(B) Producing a hybrid cell
(C) Isolating an immortal variant cell from culture and using it to create a cell line
(D) Inserting a tumor-inducing virus into a normal cell to initiate transformation
(E) Cloning a cell population from a single ancestor cell

23. A frameshift mutation is created when

(A) an initial mutation is reversed by a second mutation
(B) telomeric sequences are removed from DNA
(C) a codon's nucleotide sequence changes so that it calls for production of a different amino acid than the original one
(D) a codon's nucleotide sequence is changed so that instead of coding for a given amino acid it acts to terminate translation
(E) a base pair is either inserted or deleted in a gene

24. All of the following are required procedures in order to clone specific mRNA molecules EXCEPT

(A) extracting mRNA from cells
(B) cleaving the full genome of a cell into fragments
(C) creating a cDNA molecule
(D) converting single-stranded cDNA into double-stranded cDNA
(E) inserting double-stranded cDNA into plasmids

25. Which of the following statements regarding antibody molecules in higher vertebrates is correct?

(A) Each antibody molecule is composed of identical H chains and identical L chains.
(B) The antigen-binding site on an antibody molecule is located on its H chain only.
(C) One L chain of an antibody molecule is a $\kappa$ chain and the other is a $\lambda$ chain.
(D) Antibodies are found only on B-cell plasma membranes as cell-surface receptors.
(E) The tail (Fc) region of an antibody is formed by both L and H chains.

GO ON TO THE NEXT PAGE.

26.

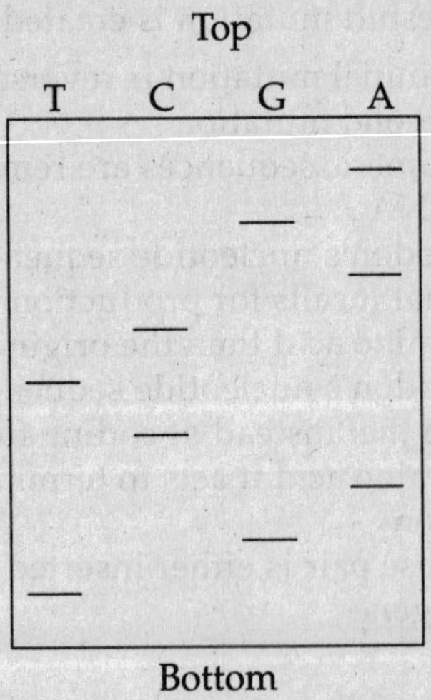


A cloned DNA fragment has been sequenced in gel as shown above. The correct nucleotide sequence corresponding to the pattern shown is

(A) 3′TTCCGGAAA5′
(B) 5′AGACTCAGT3′
(C) 3′AGACTCAGT5′
(D) 5′TGACTCAGA3′
(E) 3′TGACTCAGA3′

27. In order to study the decarboxylation process that yields succinate from oxaloacetate in the citric acid cycle, the carboxyl carbon furthest from the keto group of oxaloacetate has been labeled $^{14}C$. A subsequent analysis of α-ketoglutarate shows the full measure of applied radioactivity. Following decarboxylation of the α-ketoglutarate, the resulting succinate molecule would reveal

(A) the full measure of the original radioactivity
(B) one-half the measure of the original radioactivity
(C) one-quarter the measure of the original radioactivity
(D) one-eighth the measure of the original radioactivity
(E) none of the original radioactivity

28. Which of the following is a second messenger that stimulates release of calcium ions into the cytoplasm?

(A) Prostaglandins
(B) Inositol triphosphate
(C) Cyclic AMP
(D) Calmodulin
(E) Antidiuretic hormone

29. Which of the following statements concerning a sarcomere of a striated muscle (such as skeletal muscle) is correct?

(A) During contraction H zones become elongated.
(B) In the relaxed position tropomyosin impedes myosin's access to the binding site of actin.
(C) Each myosin helical tail contains an actin-binding site and an ATP-hydrolyzing site.
(D) The proteins troponin and tropomyosin constitute the thick and thin filaments, respectively.
(E) The proteins actin and myosin constitute the thick and thin filaments of a sarcomere, respectively.

30. Cell motility, as viewed in a cultured fibroblast, encompasses all of the following EXCEPT

(A) adhesion plaques
(B) vinculin
(C) clathrin
(D) lamellipodia
(E) ruffled edges

31. Which of the following statements concerning the Golgi apparatus of a eukaryote is correct?

(A) It is oriented in the cytoplasm so that its *cis* face is closest to the endoplasmic reticulum.
(B) It is typically associated with small secretory vesicles located near its *cis* face.
(C) Its composite flattened cisternae are continuous with one another.
(D) Glycosylation of certain secretory proteins occurs prior to the protein's entry into its lumen.
(E) Transit of a secretory protein occurs in a direction from its *trans* face to its *cis* face.

32. The target of digestion of a nucleosome dimer to nucleosome monomers by DNase is

(A) the H1 histone
(B) histones H2A, H2B, H3, and H4
(C) the nucleosome core
(D) linker DNA
(E) the DNA that surrounds the nucleosome core protein

GO ON TO THE NEXT PAGE.

33. Which of the following does NOT occur as a result of the binding of 2,3-bisphosphoglycerate to beta chains of hemoglobin in red blood cells?

(A) It has the same effect on hemoglobin-oxygen affinity as does lowered pH.
(B) Its levels increase in response to high altitudes.
(C) Its levels increase in response to low blood oxygen levels.
(D) It increases hemoglobin's affinity for oxygen, increasing oxygen uptake at the lungs.
(E) It reduces hemoglobin's affinity for oxygen, so more oxygen is available to the tissues.

34. Mobile regions of DNA capable of inserting themselves into an existing genome are

(A) prions
(B) cistrons
(C) introns
(D) transposons
(E) transducers

35. A female fruit fly bearing linked genes that produce the phenotype gray body and normal wings mates with a male fruit fly of phenotype black body and vestigial wings. The presence of gray-bodied, vestigial-winged flies among the progeny is best explained by

(A) crossing over
(B) independent assortment
(C) segregation of alleles
(D) penetrance
(E) dominance

36. Which of the following agents will induce polyploidy in a dividing eukaryote?

(A) Actinomycin D
(B) Puromycin
(C) Tetracycline
(D) Penicillin
(E) Colchicine

37. The efficiency with which an immune response is mounted against an antigen to which an organism had been previously immunized can be traced most directly to which of the following pairs of immune response type and lymphocyte activation?

| Immune Response | Activated Lymphocyte |
|---|---|
| (A) Primary | T or B virgin cells |
| (B) Primary | T or B effector cells |
| (C) Secondary | T or B virgin cells |
| (D) Secondary | T or B effector cells |
| (E) Secondary | T or B memory cells |

38.

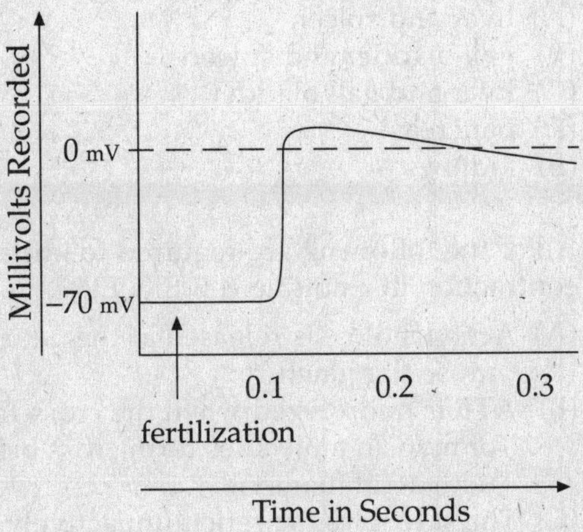


The figure above depicts the changes in the membrane potential of a sea urchin egg initiated by fertilization by a sperm cell. Which of the following statements is LEAST supported by the data?

(A) Fertilization produces a hyperpolarization of the egg membrane potential.
(B) Fertilization induces a transient reversal of the interior charge of the egg membrane from negative to positive.
(C) Fertilization causes a depolarization of the egg cell membrane.
(D) The resting membrane potential of a sea urchin egg is –70 millivolts.
(E) A sea urchin egg membrane at rest is polarized with respect to its interior and exterior surfaces.

GO ON TO THE NEXT PAGE.

39. Cell-mediated immune reactions such as cell-killing and suppression of B and T lymphocytes are carried out predominantly by

(A) B cells only
(B) both B cells and T cells
(C) both T cells and plasma cells
(D) a uniform population of T cells only
(E) different subpopulations of T cells only

40. In sickle cell anemia, an altered form of hemoglobin causes sickling of red blood cells. The sickled red blood cells are subject to degradation by the

(A) liver and spleen
(B) gall bladder and spleen
(C) liver and gall bladder
(D) pancreas
(E) kidneys

41. All of the following are required to initiate contraction in a muscle cell EXCEPT:

(A) Acetylcholine is released at the neuromuscular juncture.
(B) ATP is hydrolyzed when the cross-links of myosin molecules form cross bridges with actin filaments.
(C) The sarcoplasmic reticulum actively takes up intracellular calcium in response to an action potential.
(D) The sarcolemma transmits an action potential to the T tubules located in the interior of the cell.
(E) The sarcolemma undergoes depolarization in response to neurotransmitter released from a motor neuron.

42. Which of the following is an accurate statement about protists and plants?

(A) They are comprised only of autotrophs.
(B) They possess contractile vacuoles.
(C) They possess true nuclei and membrane-bound organelles.
(D) They form multicellular embryos.
(E) They are primarily multicellular.

43. In angiosperms, the embryo is nourished by which of the following structures?

(A) Endosperm
(B) Seed coat
(C) Antheridium
(D) Archegonium
(E) Embryo sac

44. In an oak leaf, plastid density is highest in the

(A) stomates
(B) palisade cells
(C) guard cells
(D) spongy cells
(E) epidermal cells

45. A fungus has which of the following features in common with arthropods?

(A) Hyphae
(B) Setae
(C) Mycelium
(D) Peptidyloglycan
(E) Chitin

46. The siphon of a bivalve serves primarily to

(A) propel the bivalve through water
(B) filter sediment from ingested water
(C) seize and grasp prey
(D) release sperm cells
(E) secrete calcium carbonate

47. A homeostatic response of an animal exposed to an external temperature lower than its established point for body heat may be

(A) dilating small blood vessels in the skin
(B) reducing food intake
(C) reducing involuntary muscle contraction
(D) increasing the overall rate of metabolism
(E) decreasing the production of thyroid hormone and epinephrine

48. Prior to their excretion, the nitrogenous wastes that accumulate in avians and reptiles as by-products of protein and nucleic acid metabolism are converted from

(A) ammonia to uric acid
(B) uric acid to ammonia
(C) urine to urea
(D) urea to urine
(E) urea to ammonia

49. The malpighian tubules of the grasshopper provide the same function as which of the following in an earthworm?

(A) Gizzard
(B) Crop
(C) Nephridia
(D) Esophagus
(E) Ganglia

GO ON TO THE NEXT PAGE.

50. Adequate serum levels of calcium are maintained in humans by the secretion of

(A) thyroxine
(B) glucagon
(C) growth hormone
(D) parathyroid hormone
(E) calcitonin

51. The chiasma of a tetrad is formed in meiosis during

(A) prophase I
(B) metaphase I
(C) anaphase I
(D) prophase II
(E) metaphase II

52. The section of chromosome that serves as the site of attachment by the mitotic spindle during cell division is the

(A) chromatophore
(B) chromomere
(C) kinetochore
(D) centriole
(E) chiasma

53. Bone cells which are actively involved in bone remodeling include which of the following?

I. Chondrocytes
II. Osteoblasts
III. Osteoclasts

(A) I only
(B) III only
(C) I and III only
(D) II and III only
(E) I, II, and III

54. A rise in intracellular free calcium in the sea urchin oocyte causes the release of proteolytic enzymes which act to prevent polyspermy. The events just described entail the

(A) zona reaction
(B) acrosomal reaction
(C) cortical reaction
(D) fertilization reaction
(E) fertilization cone

55. Which of the following statements about embryonic cleavage is NOT true?

(A) The presence of yolk inhibits cleavage.
(B) Telolecithal eggs undergo meroblastic cleavage.
(C) Cleavage pattern is determined by cytoplasmic factors and yolk proteins.
(D) The rapid mitotic divisions of cleavage directly give rise to blastomeres.
(E) The vegetal pole undergoes cleavage more readily than does the animal pole.

56. Cleavage symmetry arising from early cell divisions that occur at an oblique angle to the polar axis is known as

(A) meroblastic cleavage
(B) radial cleavage
(C) spiral cleavage
(D) superficial cleavage
(E) incomplete cleavage

57. Nerve outgrowth from a developing neuron begins at the growth cone, located at the tip of the axon. Microspikes of the growth cone extend and retract in order to move the growth cone forward. Exposure of the neuron to cytochasalin B at this stage of development causes

(A) microtubules in the axon to undergo reversible dissociation
(B) microtubules in the axon to undergo irreversible dissociation
(C) microfilaments in the microspike to undergo reversible depolymerization
(D) microfilaments in the microspike to undergo irreversible depolymerization
(E) no change in the developing neuron

58. A behavioral response called a fixed action pattern shown by animals

(A) occurs the second time an animal is exposed to the correct stimulus at the appropriate time in its life
(B) occurs in the absence of sensory feedback
(C) is a motor response which once released may be terminated spontaneously
(D) is triggered by a number of sensory signals in the animal's environment
(E) is a learned response

GO ON TO THE NEXT PAGE.

59. All of the following might be found in connective tissue EXCEPT

(A) fibroblasts
(B) mast cells
(C) collagens
(D) glycosaminoglycans
(E) thrombin

60. Which is a characteristic unique to angiosperms?

(A) Wind-borne pollen
(B) A dominant sporophyte life cycle
(C) Alteration of generations
(D) Double fertilization
(E) Heterosporous capability

61. Annelids and arthropods are similar to each other in that members of both phyla

(A) have segmented bodies
(B) have a closed circulatory system
(C) conduct gas exchange by diffusion through a moist membrane
(D) have well-developed sense organs
(E) reproduce asexually

62. The cell type comprising the pith tissue centered within a dicot stem is the

(A) parenchyma
(B) sclerenchyma
(C) vascular cambium
(D) vascular bundle
(E) epidermis

63. Root pressure created by a plant's roots causes water to enter the roots by

(A) translocation
(B) adhesion
(C) osmosis
(D) capillary action
(E) guttation

64. Which of the following depicts the correct sequence of membranes of the chloroplast, beginning with the innermost membrane and ending with the outermost membrane?

(A) Stroma, inner membrane, outer membrane
(B) Stroma, outer membrane, inner membrane
(C) Outer membrane, inner membrane, thylakoid membrane
(D) Inner membrane, outer membrane, thylakoid membrane
(E) Thylakoid membrane, inner membrane, outer membrane

65. A plant that grows along a trellis exhibits

(A) thigmotropism
(B) phototropism
(C) gravidotropism
(D) negative gravidotropism
(E) hydrotropism

66. An organism with a lobed thallus, rhizoids, and gemmae is a

(A) moss
(B) liverwort
(C) fern
(D) mushroom
(E) filamentous mold

67. Fungi participate in each of the following EXCEPT

(A) association with algae to form lichen
(B) association with the roots of plants to form mycorrhizae
(C) association with humans to produce ringworm
(D) fermentation to produce alcohol
(E) photosynthesis to produce glucose

68. Which of the following represents an accurate statement concerning arthropods?

(A) Classes are limited to arachnida and crustacea.
(B) They lack paired, jointed appendages.
(C) They are members of a biologically unsuccessful phylum incapable of exploiting diverse habitats and nutrition sources.
(D) They possess an exoskeleton composed primarily of peptidoglycan.
(E) They possess an open circulatory system with a dorsal heart.

69. To prevent desiccation and injury, the embryos of terrestrial vertebrates are encased within a fluid secreted by the

(A) amnion
(B) chorion
(C) allantois
(D) yolk sac
(E) placenta

GO ON TO THE NEXT PAGE.

70. An embryologist studying the development of a vertebrate organism from the zygote stage to fetus would be justified in drawing which of the following conclusions?

(A) Ontogeny recapitulates phylogeny.
(B) Early embryos display identical features of their class, order, and species.
(C) An early human embryo has features in common with early fish and avian embryos.
(D) A human embryo displays features of adult fish and birds in the course of its development.
(E) Development of an embryo proceeds in a direction from more specialized to more generalized features.

71. Which of the following is true of organisms belonging to the kingdom Protista?

(A) They are eukaryotic.
(B) They include the cyanobacteria.
(C) They are heterotrophic.
(D) They possess cell walls composed of peptidoglycan.
(E) They contain vascular tissue.

72. The first groups of animals to develop lung tissue adequate to support their respiratory requirements without the use of supplementary gas exchange organs were the

(A) amphibians
(B) reptiles
(C) mammals
(D) aves
(E) trematoda

73. Chemosynthetic bacteria can produce their own food despite their lack of photon-absorbing pigments because the chemosynthetic bacteria derive energy by

(A) oxidizing inorganic substances such as ammonia, sulfur, or hydrogen
(B) reducing inorganic substances such as ammonia, sulfur, or hydrogen
(C) oxidizing organic compounds
(D) transducing light energy into chemical energy
(E) supplying plants with nitrogen

74. Sugar is primarily transported through the phloem of plant tissue as

(A) a disaccharide
(B) a monosaccharide
(C) a polysaccharide
(D) glycogen
(E) fructose

75. The first point of entry of water at the roots of a monocot plant is through the cytoplasm of cells of the

(A) root cap
(B) Casparian strip
(C) pericycle
(D) endoderm
(E) cuticle

76. All of the following are true of monocots EXCEPT:

(A) They generally do not undergo secondary growth.
(B) Their vascular bundles are arranged in a circle.
(C) Their vascular tissue extends through the length of the stem.
(D) Their cortex and pith are not clearly defined.
(E) A bundle sheath encloses their vascular bundles.

77. As an adaptation to living in a fluid environment, the swim bladders of fish are

(A) compressible
(B) incompressible
(C) equivalent to the urinary bladder in humans
(D) maintained at an unvarying volume and pressure as a fish changes water depth
(E) filled with water

78. The structures that act as sites of gas exchange in a woody stem are the

(A) petioles
(B) internodes
(C) nodes
(D) terminal buds
(E) lenticels

GO ON TO THE NEXT PAGE.

79. All of the following environmental conditions increase the rate of transpiration from plants EXCEPT

(A) high temperature
(B) high relative humidity
(C) low relative humidity
(D) wind
(E) sunlight

80. Two xylem plant cell types that provide support and conduct water and minerals are the

(A) collenchyma and sclerenchyma
(B) parenchyma and collenchyma
(C) sieve tube members and companion cells
(D) vessel elements and companion cells
(E) tracheids and vessel elements

81. The sight organs of crustaceans and insects contain ommatidia, which make up the individual visual units of the

(A) eyespot
(B) simple eye
(C) compound eye
(D) binocular eye
(E) pit organ

82. The soils of which of the following biomes has the highest rate of leaching and cycling of nutrients?

(A) Savanna
(B) Desert
(C) Taiga
(D) Tundra
(E) Tropical rain forest

83. Charles Darwin's proposed conditions for natural selection encompass all of the following with regard to a given population EXCEPT

(A) genetic variability
(B) overproduction of offspring
(C) competition for limited resources
(D) differential survival and reproductive success
(E) inheritance of both "fit" and "unfit" genes

84. Which of the following must be true in order for evolution to have occurred?

(A) The frequencies of some alleles in an organism's genotype has changed during its lifetime.
(B) The frequencies of each allele in an organism's genotype has remained constant within the organism's lifetime.
(C) The frequencies of each allele in a population's gene pool has remained constant over successive generations.
(D) The frequencies of some alleles in a population's gene pool has changed during the organisms' lifetimes.
(E) The frequencies of some alleles in a population's gene pool has changed over successive generations.

85. A trait that is governed by polygenes displays a bell-shaped distribution of phenotypes within a population. If the trait is then subject to stabilizing selection, which of the following will result?

(A) Phenotypic variability of the population will be increased.
(B) Extremes of a bell-shaped distribution in the population will be favored.
(C) Its effects will tend to be more pronounced by genetic variability resulting from mutation and recombination.
(D) It is more likely to occur in an unstable environment.
(E) It is associated with a population that is well adapted to its environment.

GO ON TO THE NEXT PAGE.

86. A quote from a natural resources text states: "Whenever the original ecosystem becomes restructured by man, it tends to become simplified, with a resultant disruption of the stabilizing influences of density-dependent regulatory factors." This implies that in a disturbed ecosystem

(A) there exist large populations of a low number of species
(B) population levels of a species are kept at equilibrium through natural regulatory mechanisms
(C) a given prey organism is subject to higher predation rates by more diverse predators
(D) a given prey organism is less likely to undergo a population surge
(E) population fluctuations of species tend to be less extreme

87. One hypothesis posed by evolutionary biologists to account for an organism's altruistic behavior in social groups is that of kin selection. According to the kin selection theory, the risk incurred by a bird that sounds an alarm call due to a nearby predator may be offset by the fact that

(A) the alarm call induces the predator to abandon its hunt
(B) the alarm call allows the bird to gain protection at the center of a flock
(C) the alarm call benefits the species as a whole
(D) the bird will gain the same early warning advantage from another member of the flock at a future time
(E) the alarm call will benefit those members with whom the bird shares a percentage of its genes

88. Mimicry is a strategy that has evolved through natural selection to increase the fitness of organisms to their environment. Which of the following represents a form of Batesian mimicry?

(A) A type of millipede that is toxic to a toad is permanently avoided by the toad following the toad's initial attempt to consume it.
(B) A moth exhibits false eyes at its tail end in order to disorient predators.
(C) A moth exhibits nearly identical coloration to that of a stinging bee.
(D) A ground-nesting gull chick displays a coloration pattern that is nearly indistinguishable from its surroundings.
(E) A gull chick is able to elicit food from the mouth of a nonparent adult gull by pecking at the correct spot on the adult gull's bill.

89. In order for the Hardy-Weinberg law to operate with respect to a population of organisms, each of the following conditions must be met EXCEPT:

(A) Mutations do not occur.
(B) Matings are random.
(C) Natural selection does not take place.
(D) Population size is large.
(E) Genes are exchanged with other populations.

90. The members of a bird species capable of nesting in treetops or on the ledges of nearby cliffs make their homes only in the treetops due to the established presence of a more aggressive bird species on the cliff ledges. With respect to habitat, the treetop-nesting birds are utilizing

(A) their fundamental niche only
(B) their realistic niche only
(C) their ecological niche only
(D) neither their fundamental niche nor their realistic niche
(E) both their ecological and their realistic niches

GO ON TO THE NEXT PAGE.

91. Which of the following forms of nitrogen is taken up from the soil by plant roots?

(A) $N_2$
(B) NO
(C) $NO_2$
(D) $NO_3^-$
(E) $NO_4^+$

92. 1. Mosses and ferns
2. Oak seedlings
3. Pine seedlings
4. Lichen

Bare rock becomes colonized by windblown spores. As the rock undergoes an ecological succession, the correct sequence of plant colonies inhabiting the site is

(A) 1, 2, 3, 4
(B) 1, 3, 4, 2
(C) 3, 2, 1, 4
(D) 4, 1, 3, 2
(E) 4, 3, 2, 1

93. The allelopathy exhibited by desert plants is most likely responsible for their characteristic distribution pattern, which is

(A) clumped
(B) uniform
(C) random
(D) undetermined
(E) graded

94. Due to genetic load, some offspring of heterozygous parents for a given trait inherit

(A) only the poorly adaptive homozygous version of the trait
(B) only the better adapted homozygous version of the trait
(C) the heterozygous version of the trait
(D) alleles conferring hybrid vigor
(E) alleles subject to mutation

95.

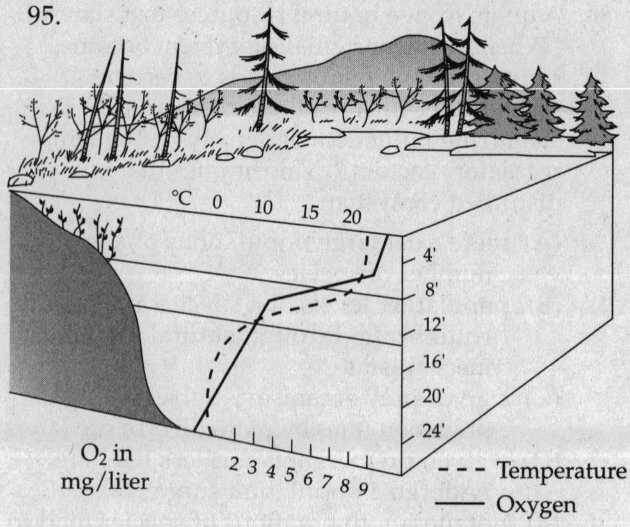


The graph above depicts both the distribution of dissolved oxygen (mg/liter) and the temperature in °C in the midsummer in a lake located in temperate latitudes. Which of the following statements is supported by the data?

(A) The surface water layer is cooler than the lower water layers.
(B) The upper stratum of the lake contains the lowest concentration of dissolved oxygen.
(C) The lower level of the lake is characterized by a thermocline.
(D) The upper, middle, and lower strata of the lake are of stratified density.
(E) Bacterial decomposers at the bottom of the lake contribute to the oxygen surplus there.

96. Gel electrophoresis was performed on the enzyme peroxidase, obtained from the tissue extracts of a single organism. The resulting bands indicate the presence of two slightly different forms of peroxidase. The LEAST likely explanation for the results is that the

(A) organism has two different allozymes for peroxidase
(B) organism is heterozygous for peroxidase
(C) organism received alternate versions of the enzyme from each parent
(D) locus for the peroxidase is polymorphic
(E) gene for the peroxidase is pleiotrophic

GO ON TO THE NEXT PAGE.

97. Which of the following best accounts for why, in certain geographical regions, having homozygous alleles for "normal" hemoglobin production is less advantageous than having heterozygous alleles for the sickle cell trait?

(A) Those regions in which the heterozygous condition is advantageous are associated with a high incidence of sickle cell disease.
(B) Those regions in which the heterozygous condition is advantageous are associated with frequent outbreaks of malaria.
(C) Those regions in which the heterozygous condition is advantageous are associated with lower binding affinities of hemoglobin moieties to oxygen.
(D) Those regions in which the homozygous condition is advantageous are associated with high incidence of sickle cell disease.
(E) Those areas in which the homozygous condition is advantageous are associated with frequent outbreaks of malaria.

98. All of the following may contribute to pesticide resistance in an insect species subjected to repeated exposures of insecticide EXCEPT

(A) mutation
(B) high reproductive potential
(C) reduced intraspecific competition
(D) lowered predation pressure due to effects of the pesticide
(E) acquired resistance by an exposed insect which is then inherited by future generations

99. Which of the following is NOT a characteristic of an oligotrophic lake?

(A) Low nutrient levels
(B) High altitudes
(C) Shallow water
(D) Sand or gravel bottom
(E) Few rooted plants

100. A marine ecosystem region characterized by penetrance of solar radiation and upwelling of nutrients is the

(A) bathyl zone
(B) neritic zone
(C) pelagic zone
(D) benthyl zone
(E) abyssal zone

101. Based on the characteristic population curves that result from plotting population growth of a species, the most effective means of controlling the mosquito population is to

(A) maintain the population at a point corresponding to the midpoint of its logistic curve
(B) opt for zero population control once the *K* value of the curve has been reached
(C) reduce the carrying capacity of the environment to lower the *K* value
(D) increase the mortality rate
(E) it is not possible to control the mosquito population

102. A sex-linked trait (such as hemophilia) may be transmitted from mother to daughter and appear in the daughter's phenotype if

(A) one of the mother's X chromosomes carries the trait and the father's X chromosome does not
(B) one of the mother's X chromosomes carries the trait and the father's Y chromosome carries the trait
(C) both of the mother's X chromosomes carry the trait and the father's X chromosome does not
(D) both of the mother's X chromosomes carry the trait and the father's Y chromosome carries the trait
(E) one of the mother's X chromosomes carries the trait and the father's X chromosome carries the trait

103. The presence of homologous structures in two different organisms, such as the humerus in the front limb of a human and a bird, indicates that

(A) the human and bird are polyphyletic species
(B) a human's and bird's evolution is convergent
(C) the human and bird belong to a clade
(D) the human and bird developed by analogy
(E) the human and bird did not evolve from a common ancestor

GO ON TO THE NEXT PAGE.

104. A high biotic potential typically occurs in

(A) only asexually reproducing organisms
(B) only sexually reproducing organisms
(C) large herbivores
(D) rodents
(E) carnivores

105. An organism belonging to the nekton is which one of the following?

(A) Whale
(B) Barnacle
(C) Cyanobacterium
(D) Protist
(E) Lobster

106. The change in a population's gene pool brought about by genetic drift will always

(A) occur in the same evolutionary direction as those changes effected by natural selection
(B) occur in the opposite evolutionary direction as those changes effected by natural selection
(C) occur in an evolutionary direction that is randomly determined
(D) replace an allele that has adaptive value with an allele that is poorly adaptive
(E) improve the overall fitness of the population

107. Which of the following is NOT a source of atmospheric carbon?

(A) Respiration
(B) Photosynthesis
(C) Bacterial decomposition
(D) Combustion of fossil fuels
(E) Vaporization from the oceans

108.

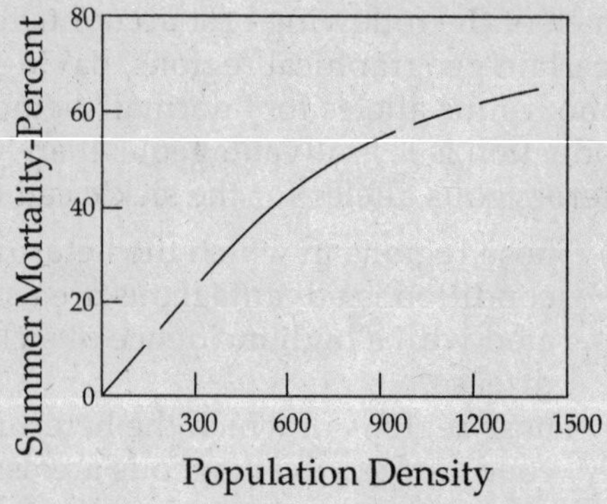


Late summer density-dependent mortality rates of a bobwhite quail population are indicated above. Compared to those members of the population when it reached a density of 300, bobwhites at a density of 1200 most likely experienced

(A) less intraspecific competition for food, water, and mates
(B) more predation pressure
(C) less intraspecific fighting
(D) increased fecundity
(E) less use of marginal habitat

109. Productivity of estuaries is high for all of the following reasons EXCEPT:

(A) Tidewaters flush out wastes and circulate nutrients.
(B) Incoming nutrients are brought in from land by tributary rivers and creeks.
(C) Plant communities have a high tolerance for changes in salinity and temperature.
(D) High plant biomass acts to trap nutrients.
(E) Decaying plants provide food for detritus feeders.

GO ON TO THE NEXT PAGE.

110. The brown fat cells of hibernating bears allows the bears to remain warm during a state of low metabolic activity because

(A) the electron transport chain and oxidative phosphorylation are uncoupled in their mitochondria, allowing for the production of heat
(B) glycolysis and aerobic respiration are more efficient in their mitochondria, so that more heat is produced as a by-product
(C) the brown fat cells form a thick layer of insulation just under the bear's fur
(D) unlike in other animal fats, the triglycerides found in brown fat cells are metabolized as fuel molecules
(E) their fat stores are slowly oxidized in order to produce a steady flow of heat

111. Brood parasites such as the cuckoo successfully trick other species of birds into rearing their young by exploiting the host birds' instinctive response to the loud begging cues of a fledgling in their nest. The genes that allow the host bird species to be duped into rearing the cuckoo fledglings to the detriment of their own offspring most likely remain in the gene pool of the population because

(A) on average, the host birds' response allows them to rear their own young efficiently by feeding only those who indicate they are hungry
(B) the maximum fitness of the duped bird is not compromised when the bird rears an interloper of another species
(C) on average, little energy is spent on rearing a fledgling bird, whether it is an interloper or one's own
(D) the maximum fitness of the cuckoo would then be reduced
(E) the cuckoo and the host bird share a percentage of genes in common

112.

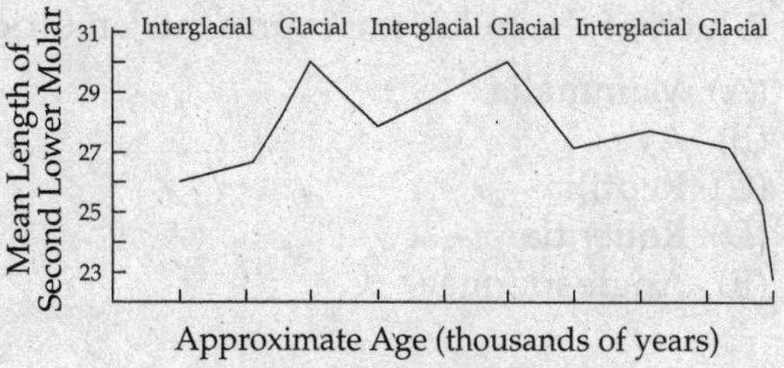


In geographic variation both phenotypes and genotypes in populations change across spatial parameters. The figure above can be used to identify a trend in the relative sizes of brown cave bears (as measured by molar size) in comparison to glacial cycles. The trend is consistent with which of the following?

(A) Kurten's rule
(B) Allen's rule
(C) Bergmann's rule
(D) Hardy-Weinberg equilibrium
(E) Davidson-Danielli theory

113. From an evolutionary perspective, the optimality theory as applied to a given trait is best represented by the idea that

(A) if the benefits gained from the trait exceed the cost of the trait to the animal performing them, that trait will persist in the genome
(B) if the trait reaps the best return for the cost relative to alternative forms of the trait, that trait will win out over the alternative forms
(C) beneficial traits are always worth the cost to the organism in energy and physiology, so those traits will persist in the genome
(D) the relative fitness of an organism must be improved due to a specific trait in order for the trait to remain in a population's gene pool
(E) any trait that does not actually reduce an organism's fitness is retained in the population's gene pool for its potential adaptive value

GO ON TO THE NEXT PAGE.

114. Which of the following represents an order?

(A) Mammalia
(B) Aves
(C) Reptilia
(D) Rodentia
(E) Angiospermae

115. Gene flow brought about by migration of organisms between neighboring demes has each of the following effects EXCEPT

(A) increasing the genetic variability within the receiving deme
(B) increasing the genetic variability between the migrating and the receiving demes
(C) opposing the effects of natural selection
(D) opposing the effects of genetic drift
(E) increasing the number of possible phenotypes within the receiving deme

116. Adaptations of plants to minimize water loss in environments with high temperatures include which of the following?

(A) Numerous stomata
(B) Thin cuticles
(C) Spines instead of leaves
(D) Large surface-to-volume ratios
(E) Stomata restricted to exposed portions of leaves

GO ON TO THE NEXT PAGE.

117. I

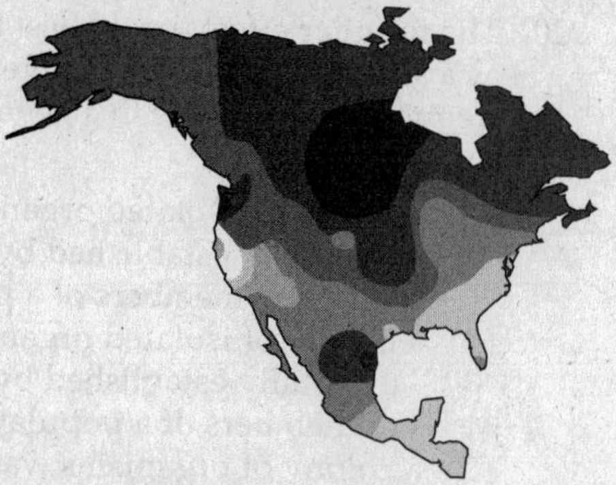

II

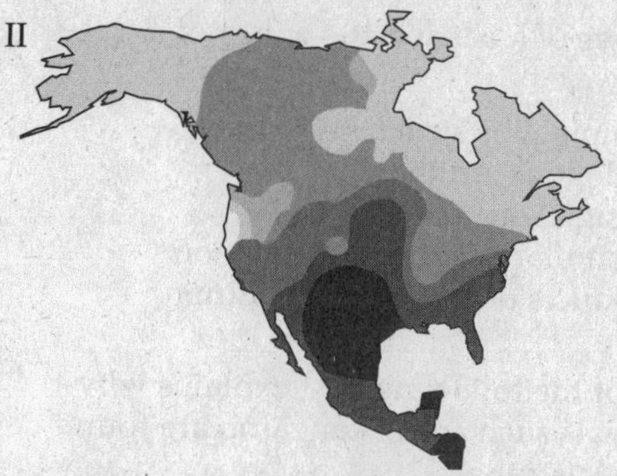

III

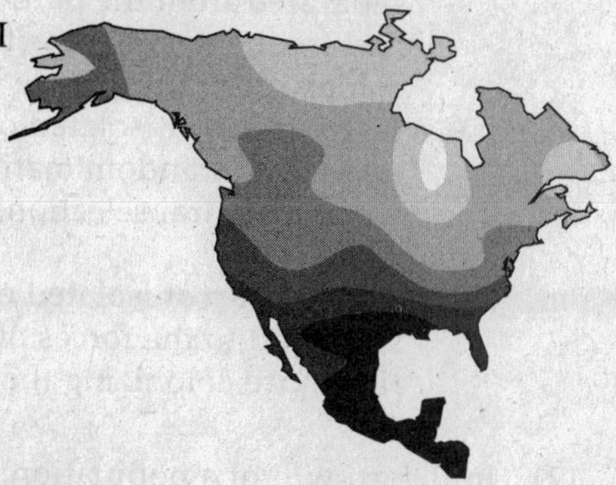

IV

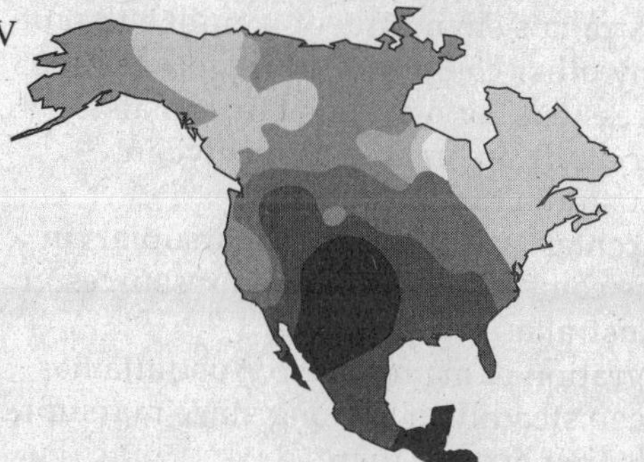

The regions shown in the maps of North America above represent geographical variation in the body size of a species of bird found throughout North America. Darkest regions correspond to largest body size. Which of the maps indicate(s) that variation in body size is clinal?

(A) I only
(B) II only
(C) III only
(D) IV only
(E) I and III only

GO ON TO THE NEXT PAGE.

118. The wings of a bat and the wings of a butterfly are

(A) homologous structures
(B) analogous structures
(C) vestigial structures
(D) dissimilar in form and function
(E) products of divergent evolution

119. Which of the following best explains why marsupials such as the kangaroo are found only in Australia?

(A) Australia's environment is unlike that of any other country, leading to selective pressures for marsupial mammals.
(B) Placentals are unable to survive in Australia's environment.
(C) Placentals are not as fit as marsupials in the competition for limited resources in Australia.
(D) Migration of mammals to Australia has been steadily increasing since marsupials first arrived there.
(E) Australia's isolated position has prevented marsupials from emigrating elsewhere.

120. The founder effect would best be determined as a source of influence in determining the frequency of an allele in a gene pool by looking for evidence that

(A) a colony of isolated organisms was originally established by a single or very few members of a population
(B) a colony of isolated organisms was originally established by a large number of members of a population
(C) a colony of organisms was geographically separated from the parent colony but had frequent contact with the parent colony, permitting gene flow
(D) a large group of isolated organisms underwent random matings, and there was no natural selection, and no mutations
(E) a large group of isolated organisms were subjected to the forces of natural selection since colonizing the area

121. In the growth of a population, the point at which natality and mortality rates are equal to one another is referred to as

(A) a population crash
(B) a population explosion
(C) zero population growth
(D) exponential growth
(E) intrinsic rate of increase

GO ON TO THE NEXT PAGE.

Directions: Each group of questions below consists of five lettered headings followed by a list of numbered phrases, sentences, or figures. For each numbered phrase, sentence, or figure, select the one heading that is most closely related to it and fill in completely the corresponding space on the answer sheet. One heading may be used once, more than once, or not at all in each group.

Questions 122-123

(A) B lymphocytes
(B) T lymphocytes
(C) Mast cells
(D) Megakaryocytes
(E) Plasma cells

122. Recognize histocompatibility antigens

123. Secrete immunoglobulins into the blood stream

Questions 124-125

(A) Ionic bonds
(B) Covalent bonds
(C) Hydrogen bonds
(D) Van der Waal's forces
(E) Brownian motion

124. These forces allow histone proteins to form complexes with the sugar-phosphate backbone of DNA.

125. These forces permit complementary base pairs of deoxyribonucleic acid strands to couple.

Questions 126-128

(A) Posterior pituitary
(B) Uterus
(C) Graafian follicle
(D) Corpus luteum
(E) Anterior pituitary

126. Target of follicle-stimulating hormone

127. Produces and secretes estradiol prior to ovulation

128. Post-ovulatory structure capable of secreting progesterone

Questions 129-130

(A) Pollen tube
(B) Endosperm
(C) Stigma
(D) Anther
(E) Stamen

129. Along with the style and the ovary, comprise the carpel

130. Site of pollen formation

Questions 131-133

(A) Symport
(B) Antiport
(C) Active transport
(D) Facilitated diffusion
(E) Osmosis

131. Movement of glucose into mucosal cells of the small intestine

(A)

132. Movement of glucose from mucosal cells of the small intestine into the bloodstream

(D)

133. Movement of calcium ions into the sarcoplasmic reticulum

(C) (C)

GO ON TO THE NEXT PAGE.

Questions 134-136 refer to the three-tiered arrangement of sensory cells in the vertebrate retina shown below; letters (A) through (E) indicate the sensory cell types or associated features.

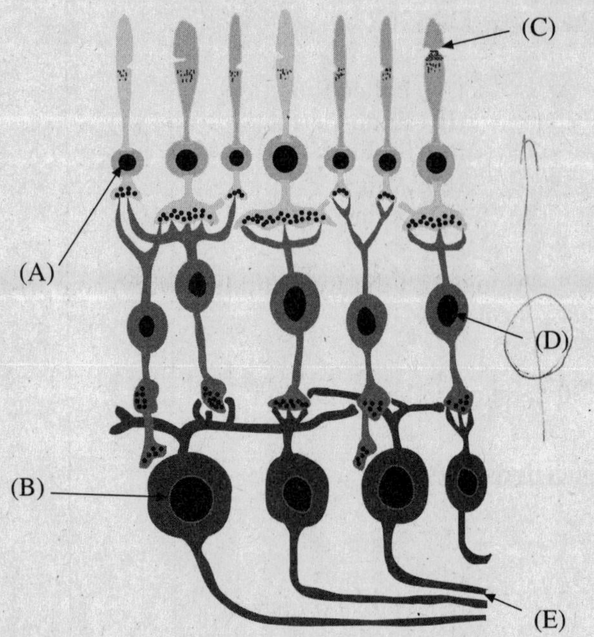


134. Contains a high density of photoexcitable molecules

135. First structure through which light rays pass

136. Consists of bipolar cells

Questions 137-139

(A) $W = 1 - S$
(B) $p^2 + 2pq + q^2 = 1$
(C) $p + q = 1$
(D) probability $(p)$ × probability $(q)$
(E) probability $(p) \times (q)$

137. Relative frequencies of each of two possible alleles in a population

138. Percentages of individuals in a population having different genotypes

139. The selective coefficient and the adaptive value of a given phenotype

Questions 140-143

(A) Polymorphism
(B) Convergent evolution
(C) Allopatric speciation
(D) Sympatric speciation
(E) Intraspecies competition

140. Species A and B do not share common ancestry yet display similar behavioral traits.

141. Species C and D do not share common ancestry and are subject to similar selection pressures.

142. Species E evolves from a parent species as a result of geographical isolation.

143. Alternative forms of a trait persist in successive generations.

Questions 144-146

(A) Countercurrent mechanism
(B) Chemiosmotic gradient
(C) Electrochemical gradient
(D) Intracellular second messenger
(E) Hydrolysis of an adenine nucleotide

144. Mechanism for maintaining a high salt concentration in the interstitial fluid of the renal medulla

145. Mechanism for causing depolarization of the T tubules of the sarcolemma

146. Mechanism for causing calcium influx into neurons

GO ON TO THE NEXT PAGE.

Questions 147-149: The graphs below show the rate of catalysis of enzymatic reactions under varying intracellular conditions over time.

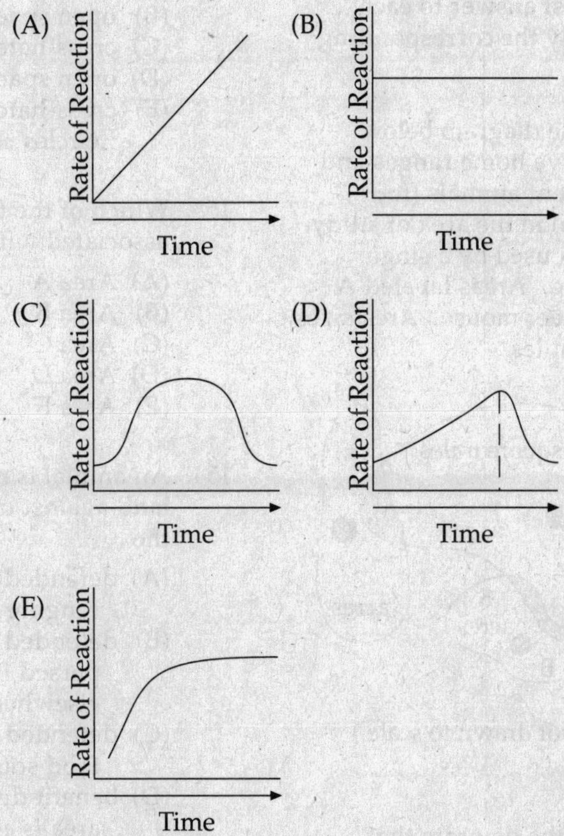


147. Which results show saturation kinetics over time?

148. Which results may be caused by increasingly higher temperature over time?

149. Which results may be caused by increasingly higher pH over time?

GO ON TO THE NEXT PAGE.

Directions: Each group of questions below concerns a laboratory or an experimental situation. In each case, first study the description of the situation. Then choose the one best answer to each question and fill in completely the corresponding space on the answer sheet.

Questions 150-154 refer to the diagram below which represents the respective home ranges and territories used by five different animals (four herbivores and one carnivore) in the area of study. Each letter represents an area used by a single individual, with some overlap. Areas labeled A and B are each used by one deer mouse. Area sizes are given in acres or square miles.

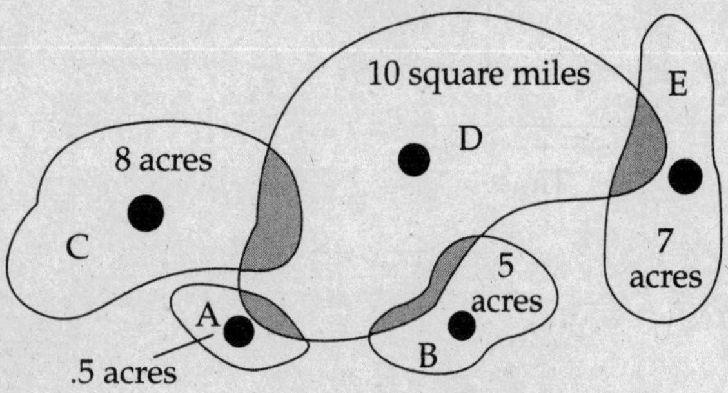


(Note: figure not drawn to scale.)

150. It can be inferred from the diagram that animals inhabiting Areas D and E share
(A) overlapping territories
(B) overlapping home ranges
(C) a portion of defended land
(D) the same food source
(E) the same ecological niche

151. Of the following, Area D most likely belongs to a
(A) field mouse
(B) beaver
(C) doe
(D) rabbit
(E) bobcat

152. The territories claimed by each animal are indicated in the diagram by
(A) dark circles only
(B) open spaces only
(C) cross-hatches and dark circles only
(D) open spaces and dark circles only
(E) cross-hatches, open spaces, and dark circles

153. Which of the following areas is most likely associated with a poor habitat?
(A) Area A
(B) Area B
(C) Area C
(D) Area D
(E) Area E

154. An animal is most likely to defend an area of land against other members of its species if the
(A) defended area is extensive and has far-ranging borders
(B) defended area contains an evenly dispersed food source that is also available elsewhere
(C) defended area contains a concentrated food source that is difficult to locate
(D) benefit derived from exclusive use of the area is equal to the cost in energy of defending the area
(E) density of the animal's population continues to increase

GO ON TO THE NEXT PAGE.

Questions 155-158 refer to the following table.

| | 16h 8h | 8h 16h | 8h 16h |
|---|---|---|---|
| Plant I | – – – | + + + | – – – |
| Plant II | + + + | + + + | + + + |
| Plant III | + + + | – – – | + + + |

(+ + + = flowering; – – – = absence of flowering)
(☐ = light; ■ = dark)

The photoperiodic response of three different types of plants were recorded by observing flowering responses to varying lengths of light and dark. The photoreceptor responsible for flowering of plants is phytochrome. Phytochrome undergoes an allosteric change upon absorption of red light having a specific wavelength. The $P_R$ form of phytochrome absorbs red light of wavelength 660 nm; the $P_{FR}$ form absorbs red light of wavelength 730 nm. $P_{FR}$ spontaneously converts back to $P_R$ in the absence of light. During daylight hours $P_{FR}$ is more prevalent than $P_R$; during nighttime hours $P_R$ is the more prevalent. $P_{FR}$ induces flowering in long-day plants and inhibits flowering in short-day plants.

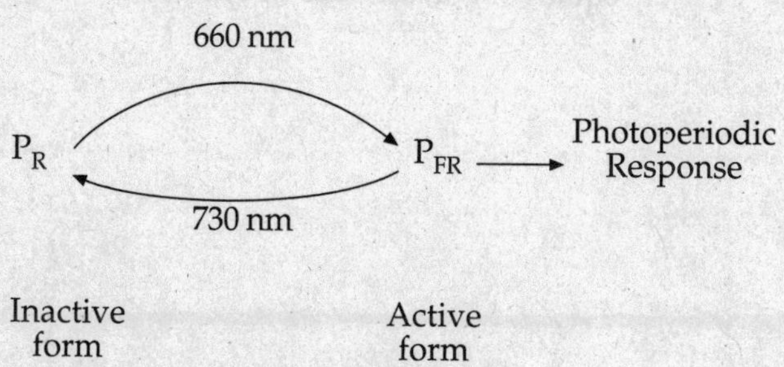


155. Based on the flowering responses exhibited by the plants in the experiment, Plant III most likely is
(A) a short-day plant
(B) a long-day plant
(C) a day-neutral plant
(D) unable to produce the $P_R$ in the dark
(E) unable to produce the $P_{FR}$ in the light

156. The critical factor in eliciting a flowering response in Plant II appears to be
(A) number of hours of daylight
(B) number of hours of darkness with brief interrupted exposure to light
(C) number of hours of darkness uninterrupted by brief exposure to light
(D) equal lengths of light and darkness
(E) light and dark periods do not trigger flowering in these plants

157. Which of the following statements is the most reasonable conclusion concerning the influence of alternative forms of phytochrome on flowering by the study plants?
(A) $P_{FR}$ inhibits flowering in Plant I.
(B) $P_{FR}$ induces flowering in Plant I.
(C) $P_R$ inhibits flowering in Plant I.
(D) $P_{FR}$ inhibits flowering in Plant III.
(E) $P_{FR}$ induces flowering in Plant II.

158. Certain seeds germinate when subjected to light of wavelength 660 nm. When briefly exposed to light of wavelength 660 nm followed by brief exposure to light of wavelength 730 nm, they fail to germinate. When briefly exposed to light of wavelength 660 nm followed by exposure to light of wavelength 730 nm followed by exposure to light of 660 nm, they germinate. The most likely interpretation of these results is that
(A) exposure to light of wavelength 660 nm converts $P_R$ to $P_{FR}$
(B) exposure to light of wavelength 730 nm converts $P_R$ to $P_{FR}$
(C) exposure to light of wavelength 730 nm activates the phytochrome pigment
(D) germination in seeds displaying photoperiodism is influenced by the seeds' final exposure to red light
(E) germination in these seeds is not influenced by photoperiod

GO ON TO THE NEXT PAGE.

Questions 159-161

A graph of population growth is shown below for two different animal species, *X* and *Y*, each of which produces a characteristic growth curve.

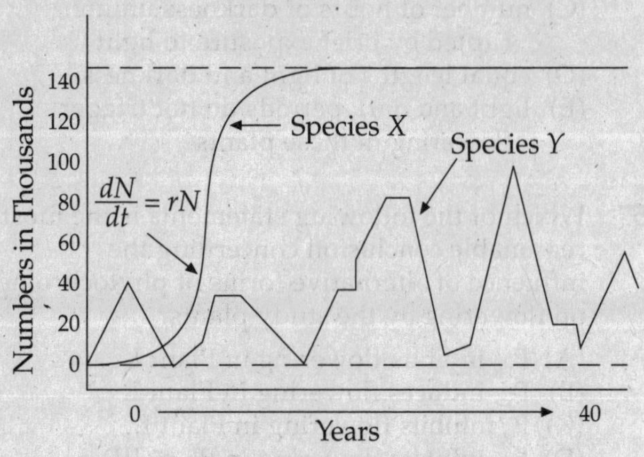


159. The equation associated with the portion of the curve belonging to species *X* located between 0 and 140,000 individuals indicates that at that segment
    (A) the net growth rate is negative
    (B) growth occurs in the absence of environmental restraints
    (C) birth and death rates are constant
    (D) exponential decay occurs from the initial population
    (E) negative feedback is in effect

160. The difference between populations belonging to an r-selected species and those from a k-selected species is that
    (A) populations from an r-selected species tend to increase in size exponentially in the absence of environmental restraints
    (B) populations from a k-selected species tend to inhabit unstable environments
    (C) populations from r-selected species have an equilibrium density at or near the carrying capacity of the environment
    (D) populations from an r-selected species are better adapted to survive periods of stress
    (E) populations from a k-selected species are better adapted to colonize a new environment

161. Which of the following statements is best supported by the data?
    (A) Species *X* is characterized by a negative feedback control mechanism.
    (B) Species *X* is representative of an r-selected species.
    (C) Species *Y* is representative of a k-selected species.
    (D) The number of individuals in the population of species *X* has surpassed the carrying capacity of the environment once it reached a density of 140,000 individuals.
    (E) At year 25, the birth rate in species *Y* equals the death rate in species *Y*.

GO ON TO THE NEXT PAGE.

Questions 162-164

Bcl-2 is a mitochondrial surface protein whose expression is associated with rescue from apoptosis (cell disintegration into particles that are then phagocytosed). Mice that are transgenic for the bcl-2 gene (a proto-oncogene) have been mated with nontransgenic mice. The transgene is inserted in such a way that allows it to be co-expressed with surface immunoglobulin. Blood samples from the offspring of the transgenic versus nontransgenic mating are analyzed and the results of the lymphocyte and polymorphonuclear cells is shown.

| Sample No. | Lymphocytes/ml | Polymorpohonuclear Cells (PMN)/ml |
|---|---|---|
| 1 | $14 \times 10^6$ | $3 \times 10^6$ |
| 2 | $8 \times 10^6$ | $5 \times 10^6$ |
| 3 | $55 \times 10^6$ | $4 \times 10^6$ |
| 4 | $30 \times 10^6$ | $35 \times 10^6$ |
| 5 | $11 \times 10^6$ | $5 \times 10^6$ |
| 6 | $52 \times 10^6$ | $6 \times 10^6$ |
| 7 | $71 \times 10^6$ | $6 \times 10^6$ |
| 8 | $12 \times 10^6$ | $3 \times 10^6$ |
| 9 | $92 \times 10^6$ | $4 \times 10^6$ |
| 10 | $49 \times 10^6$ | $3 \times 10^6$ |

162. The offspring most likely to have received the transgene are

(A) 3, 4, 6, 7, 9, and 10
(B) 1, 2, 5, and 8
(C) 4 only
(D) 3, 6, 7, 9, and 10
(E) 2, 5, and 7

163. The elevation in mouse number 4's lymphocytes and polymorphonucleocytes is most likely due to

(A) bcl-2 transgene expression
(B) an error in the count
(C) malignancy
(D) adverse drug reaction
(E) cannot be determined from the information given

164. If the proto-oncogene c-myc (associated with proliferation of cells) was inserted as a transgene rather than bcl-2 (same location), and the same blood counts were obtained from the same backcross of transgenic to nontransgenic mice, which offspring would be most likely to have received the transgene?

(A) 3, 4, 6, 7, 9, and 10
(B) 3, 6, 7, 9, and 10
(C) 4 only
(D) 1, 2, 5, and 8
(E) none of the mice

GO ON TO THE NEXT PAGE.

Questions 165-167 refer to the following experiment in which an experimental plot of nettles was provided with alternate intensities of light exposure with and without supplemental phosphorus. Phosphorus was supplied to the soil. Nettle productivity was measured in milligrams of dry weight following administration of both variables. Results are shown in the table below.

| | Phosphate Supplement | |
|---|---|---|
| Light Intensity | None | 5 g/m$^2$ |
| Low | 2.0 | 10.5 |
| High | 15.2 | 177.7 |

165. The increase in plant productivity shown by the nettle dry weight measuring 177 mg indicates that

(A) of the two variables, phosphate is the only limiting factor to nettle growth
(B) of the two variables, sunlight is the only limiting factor to nettle growth
(C) adequate levels of sunlight and phosphate provide for optimal plant growth
(D) neither sunlight nor phosphate is an essential element for nettles
(E) phosphate is a nonessential nutrient in nettles

166. To determine if an element is essential to a plant's growth, which of the following approaches would be best?

(A) Grow the plant in a solution that contains all known essential elements minus the suspected essential element and observe whether it develops normally
(B) Grow the plant in a solution containing only the suspected essential element and observe whether it develops normally
(C) Grow the plant in soil and measure its rate of growth against that of a plant in which the element is not essential
(D) Grow the plant in soil, measure the amount of the suspected essential element present in the soil, and chart those amounts against the plant's growth
(E) Grow the plant in the soil, supplement the soil with added amounts of the suspected essential element, and chart those amounts against the plant's growth

167. The phosphorus taken up by the root hairs of the nettles is likely to be incorporated into all of the following compounds EXCEPT

(A) deoxyribonucleic acid
(B) ribonucleic acid
(C) adenosine triphosphate
(D) phospholipids
(E) carbohydrates

GO ON TO THE NEXT PAGE.

Questions 168-171 refer to the following experiment.

| Effect on Population Growth and Survival of Two Populations, *A* and *B* | | | | | |
|---|---|---|---|---|---|
| Interaction | When Not Interacting *A* | *B* | When Interacting *A* | *B* | Outcome of Interaction |
| I | 0 | 0 | 0 | 0 | Neither *A* nor *B* Affects The Other |
| II | 0 | 0 | – | – | Population Most Affected is Driven from Niche |
| III | – | – | + | + | Interaction is Obligatory for *A* and *B* |
| IV | 0 | 0 | + | + | Interaction Favorable to *A* and *B*, but Not Obligatory |
| V | – | 0 | + | 0 | Obligatory for *A*; *B* Unaffected |
| VI | 0 | 0 | – | 0 | *A* Inhibited; *B* Unaffected |
| VII | – | 0 | + | – | Obligatory for *A*; *B* is Inhibited |
| + = population growth increases<br>– = population growth decreases<br>0 = population growth remains the same | | | | | |

Interactions between species may have a neutral effect upon the interacting populations, or they may act to increase or decrease the population sizes. The effects of different interspecies interactions possible between a two populations (populations *A* and *B*) on population size, relative to the respective population sizes in the absence of the interactions, are presented in the chart above.

168. Which of the following interspecies interactions is represented by commensalism?

(A) I
(B) II
(C) IV
(D) V
(E) VI

169. It can be inferred from the chart that in interaction VII, population *A* may be

(A) a host
(B) a predator
(C) prey
(D) a partner
(E) not enough data is presented to characterize population *A*

170. Interaction II characterizes interspecies competition between populations *A* and *B*. What results are expected according to Gause's competitive exclusion theory?

(A) If populations *A* and *B* compete for the same limited resources, one population will succeed in gaining access to the resources and the other population will be excluded.
(B) If populations *A* and *B* compete for the same limited resources, the population that succeeds in gaining access to the resources establishes a new niche for itself.
(C) If populations *A* and *B* compete for the same limited resources, neither will be excluded, so that both eventually will co-occupy the same niche.
(D) If populations *A* and *B* compete for slightly different resources, the more fit population will cause the exclusion of the less fit population from the area.
(E) If populations *A* and *B* compete for slightly different resources, both populations will eventually become locally extinct.

171. Examples of the obligatory relationship between populations *A* and *B* cited for interaction III include each of the following EXCEPT

(A) algae and fungi
(B) rumen bacteria and cattle
(C) zooflagellates and termites
(D) fly orchids and flies
(E) canines and ticks

GO ON TO THE NEXT PAGE.

Questions 172-173 refer to the following circumstances.

A small, isolated population of moths are nearly decimated by a tornado. The few surviving moths by chance happened to be located in an area tangential to the direct path of the tornado when it touched down. Thirty percent of the tangential-path moths survived in the tornado's wake. Those moths that happened to be in the direct path of the tornado weren't as fortunate: only 1% of their original number survived.

172. Which of the following is true of the subpopulation of tangential-path moths which survived in the greatest numbers?

(A) They were more fit than the subpopulation of direct-path moths that suffered the greater losses.
(B) They were acted upon by natural selection while the direct-path moths were not.
(C) They demonstrated Darwinian competition with regard to the direct-path members of their species.
(D) Their higher rate of survival compared to the direct-path moths was due to chance.
(E) Their higher rate of survival compared to the direct-path moths suggests that natural selection is a random process.

173. Which of the following forces is most compatible with the results of the scenario presented?

(A) The Hardy-Weinberg law
(B) Genetic drift
(C) Allen's rule
(D) The optimality theory
(E) Gause's competitive exclusion principle

Questions 174-176

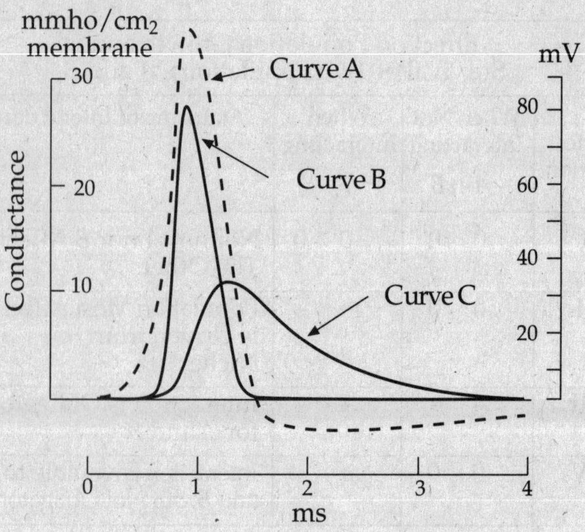


The graph above shows the changing conductances of the giant squid axon to two different ions during the course of an action potential.

174. Which of the following may be concluded based on the data?

(A) Curve A represents the action potential.
(B) Curve A represents conductance to potassium.
(C) Curve B represents conductance to chloride.
(D) Curve C represents conductance to sodium.
(E) Curve C represents the action potential.

175. In curve B, the change in conductance is in response to an initial

(A) polarization
(D) depolarization
(C) repolarization
(D) hyperpolarization
(E) not enough information is presented to answer the question

176. During a nerve action potential, axonal membrane conductance to chloride

(A) increases
(B) decreases
(C) increases and then decreases
(D) decreases and then increases
(E) does not increase or decrease

GO ON TO THE NEXT PAGE.

Questions 177-179

Caroline and James are seeking genetic counseling because they have a history of albinism in their families. Albinism is an autosomal recessive disorder. Following their consultation with the genetic counselor, the following pedigree analysis was established for this trait. Only two alleles at a single locus are responsible for albinism. Circles represent females, squares represent males, and darkened figures represent family members having albinism.

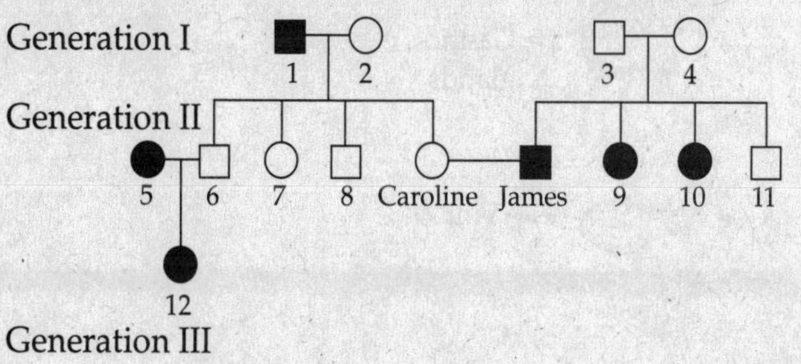


177. Based on the pedigree analysis, what is the percentage chance that James and Caroline's first child will be an albino?

(A) 0%
(B) 25%
(C) 50%
(D) 75%
(E) 100%

178. According to the pedigree, which of the following is a correct statement about the family members shown?

(A) Individual 1 is heterozygous for albinism.
(B) Individual 2 is heterozygous for albinism.
(C) Individual 4 is homozygous for albinism.
(D) Individual 8 is homozygous for albinism.
(E) Individual 11 is heterozygous for albinism.

179. What are the genotypes of James' mother (I-4) and both of James' sisters (II-9 and II-10), respectively?

(A) *aa* and *Aa*
(B) *Aa* and *AA*
(C) *AA* and *Aa*
(D) *aa* and *aa*
(E) *Aa* and *aa*

GO ON TO THE NEXT PAGE.

Questions 180-181

Presumptive lung epithelium was removed from the endodermal tubes of a mammalian embryo and cultured in appropriate media both in the absence (1) and presence (2-6) of mesenchymal cells. The mesenchymal cells were chosen from specific locations in the embryo. The goal of the experiment was to ascertain if and in what ways patterns of epithelial differentiation varied in response to regional source of the mesenchymal inductive tissue. Results of the cell cultures are shown in the diagram below.

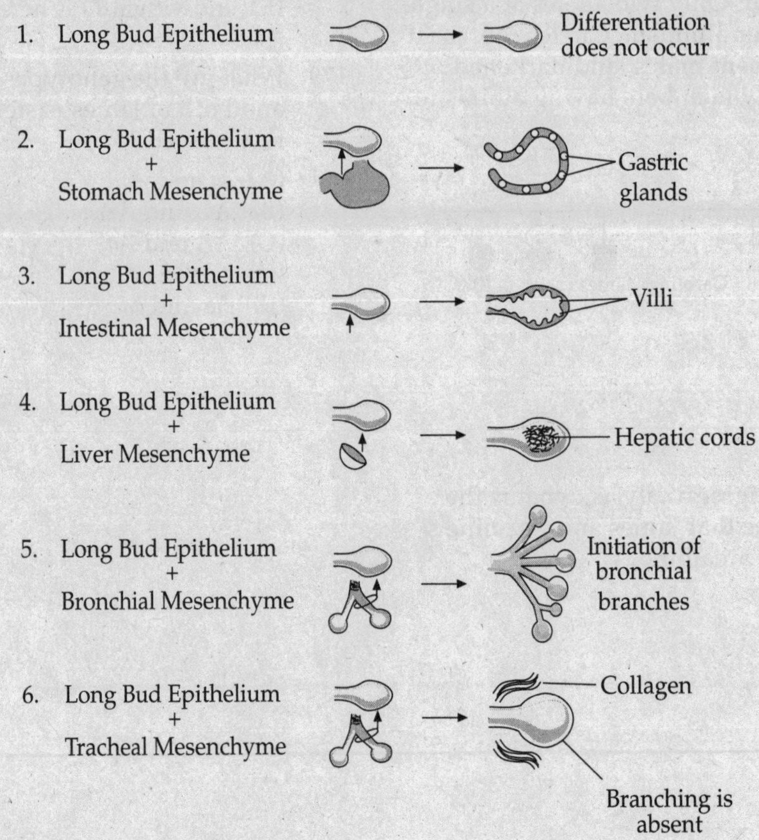


180. Which of the following statements is best supported by the results of the experiment?

(A) Presumptive lung epithelium will be induced only by regionally specific mesenchyme.
(B) The inductive effect of mesenchymal cells on presumptive lung epithelium is region-specific depending on the source of mesenchyme.
(C) Reciprocal induction occurs between regionally specific mesenchyme and presumptive lung epithelium.
(D) Regionally specific mesenchyme cells are induced by presumptive lung epithelium to become specific structures.
(E) Epithelio-mesenchymal interactions are not a prerequisite for differentiation of presumptive lung epithelium.

181. Under appropriate conditions, endodermal presumptive lung epithelium is most likely able to develop into each of the following EXCEPT

(A) the pancreas
(B) the gall bladder
(C) the thyroid
(D) the lungs
(E) the blood vessels

Questions 182-183 refer to the following diagram.

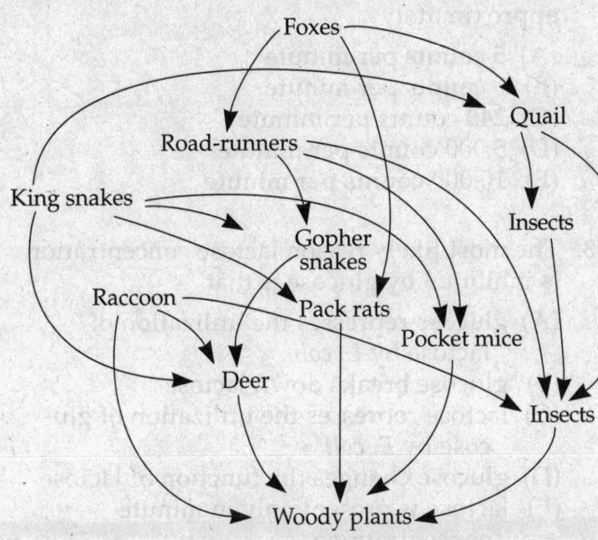


A food web is a more accurate representation of the interrelationships of predator and prey species than is a food chain. In a California chaparral, a select group of resident producers and consumers were observed in the field and a food web was compiled based on their interactions. The diagram above indicates the interrelationships between the organisms studied. Golpher snakes were noted to occasionally scavenge in addition to hunting their prey.

182. As the trophic levels represented become successively higher, which of the following takes place?

(A) Total biomass increases.
(B) Amount of available energy increases.
(C) Numbers of organisms increase.
(D) Nonbiodegradable pesticide residues become less concentrated.
(E) Home range requirements of predators increase.

183. If the woody plants utilize 1% of available solar energy, what amount of available solar energy is utilized by the foxes belonging to the food chain woody plants–deer mice–gopher snakes–road-runners–foxes?

(A) 1.0%
(B) .01%
(C) .001%
(D) .0001%
(E) .00001%

Questions 184-185 refer to the following observations involving two embryos, *A* and *B*, during their respective developmental stages.

Embryo *A* and embryo *B* both were observed to possess visceral clefts at a stage early in their respective development. Later in their developmental stages, the visceral cleft in embryo *A* developed into a eustachian tube and the visceral cleft in embryo *B* formed gills.

184. Embryos *A* and *B* both possess visceral clefts during early stages of their respective development because

(A) all developing embryos exhibit visceral clefts at some stage of their development
(B) the visceral clefts represent analogous structures
(C) all invertebrates exhibit visceral clefts at some stage of their development
(D) both embryos have a common ancestor which possessed visceral clefts as an embryo
(E) both embryos will exhibit features that are common to their species during early development

185. The observation that visceral clefts initially present in both embryos later diverge into structures different from one another can best be explained by the fact that

(A) natural selection acted to modify a common ancestral feature
(B) the embryos underwent convergent evolution
(C) induction produces a morphological change in the tissue it influences
(D) different germ cell layers give rise to different structures
(E) each embryo expressed a different allele for a common trait

GO ON TO THE NEXT PAGE.

Questions 186-189

The rate of *Escherichia coli* reproduction was examined using two different broth media, one containing only glucose, and the other containing equal concentrations of glucose and lactose. As *E. coli* replicated, samples were removed and subjected to 10-fold dilutions and plated on a nutrient petri dish. The number of bacterial colonies (colonies forming units) were calculated. Curve *A* represents the growth kinetics of bacteria grown with glucose only. Curve *B* shows bacterial growth when glucose and radiolabeled lactose were utilized. Curve C represents radiolabeled carbon dioxide that appears after the second phase of the growth curve. The results demonstrate that glucose inhibits the utilization of lactose in the medium.

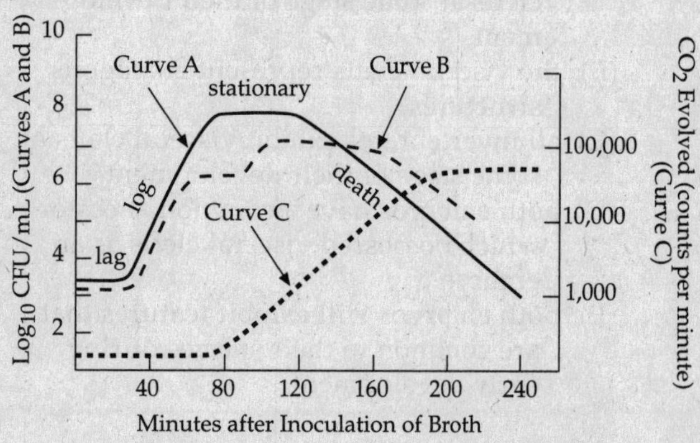


186. During replication, the increase in the bacterial population is exponential because the bacteria are reproducing by

(A) sporulation
(B) budding
(C) binary fission
(D) regeneration
(E) vegetative propagation

187. The rate of carbon dioxide evolved three hours after inoculation of the broth is approximately

(A) 5 counts per minute
(B) 8 counts per minute
(C) 240 counts per minute
(D) 5,000 counts per minute
(E) 10,000 counts per minute

188. The most likely reason lactose concentration is inhibited by glucose is that

(A) glucose represses the utilization of lactose by *E. coli*
(B) glucose breaks down lactose
(C) lactose represses the utilization of glucose by *E. coli*
(D) glucose changes the function of lactose
(E) lactose is present only in minute concentrations

189. The latter phase of curves *A* and *B* represent

(A) the log phase of the growth curve
(B) a high metabolic rate of the bacterial population
(C) a release of toxic metabolic wastes
(D) an increase in the growth rate of the bacterial colonies
(E) an increase in the number of bacterial colonies present

GO ON TO THE NEXT PAGE.

<u>Questions 190-192</u> refers to the following experiment.

An experiment was conducted to determine the effects of digitalis on the plasma membranes of heart muscle. Digitalis was found to strengthen the heartbeat by increasing the pumping action of the heart. Two membrane channels were examined: the sodium-potassium pump and the sodium-calcium channel. Digitalis was found to slow down the action of the sodium-potassium pump.

190. If digitalis acts to slow down the action of the sodium-potassium pump, then sodium will
(A) increase in the extracellular fluid
(B) increase in the interior of muscle cells
(C) achieve equal concentrations inside and outside of the cell
(D) passively move out of the cell
(E) passively move into the cell

191. During active transport, what is the ratio of sodium to potassium ions exchanged by the sodium-potassium pump?
(A) 1:1
(B) 3:2
(C) 2:3
(D) 1:2
(E) 2:1

192. A decrease in the rate of exchange in the sodium-potassium pump would have which of the following effects on sodium-calcium antiport conducted in heart cells?
(A) A lower concentration of incoming sodium ions would produce a lower concentration of incoming calcium ions.
(B) A lower concentration of outgoing sodium ions would produce a lower concentration of incoming calcium ions.
(C) A lower concentration of outgoing calcium ions would produce a lower rate of incoming sodium ions.
(D) A lower concentration of outgoing sodium ions would produce a lower concentration of outgoing calcium ions.
(E) A lower concentration of incoming sodium ions would produce a lowered concentration of outgoing calcium ions.

GO ON TO THE NEXT PAGE.

Questions 193-196

Peripheral blood samples were taken from infants under the age of two months and analyzed for various types of immunologically active cells and antibody titers (levels). CD4+ CD3+ cells are helper T cells; CD8+ CD3+ cells are cytotoxic T cells; CD19+ cells are B cells. Results of the analysis for each subject are recorded in the table below.

| | Subject | | | |
|---|---|---|---|---|
| Sample # | 1 | 2 | 3 | 4 |
| Total Lymphocyte Count | nl | nl | nl | d |
| Polymorphonuclear Cell Count | nl | ee | nl | nl |
| CD4+ CD3+ | nl | nl | d | d |
| CD8+ CD3+ | nl | nl | nl | d |
| CD 19+ | nl | nl | e | d |
| Serum IgG | nl | nl | e | d |
| Serum IgM | e | nl | e | d |
| Serum IgA | nl | nl | e | d |
| (e = elevated; d = decreased; nl = normal) | | | | |

193. The only immunoglobulin type able to cross the placenta is

(A) IgA
(B) IgD
(C) IgM
(D) IgG
(E) IgE

194. The site of origin of T lymphocytes is (are) the

(A) spleen
(B) appendix
(C) thymus
(D) red blood cells
(E) lymph nodes

195. Which of the following may be concluded about patient number 3?

(A) He suffers from a B-cell defect.
(B) He suffers from a T-cell defect.
(C) He has an intrauterine infection.
(D) He has acquired immunological deficiency syndrome (AIDS).
(E) He suffers from a stem-cell defect.

196. Patient number 4 most likely suffers from

(A) acquired immunological deficiency syndrome (AIDS)
(B) intrauterine infection
(C) stem-cell defect
(D) adhesion protein defect
(E) T-cell defect

Questions 197-200

A graph of blood glucose levels for normal, hyperglycemic and hypoglycemic individuals is given below. The values in the graph represent averaged data from 10 subjects for each condition.

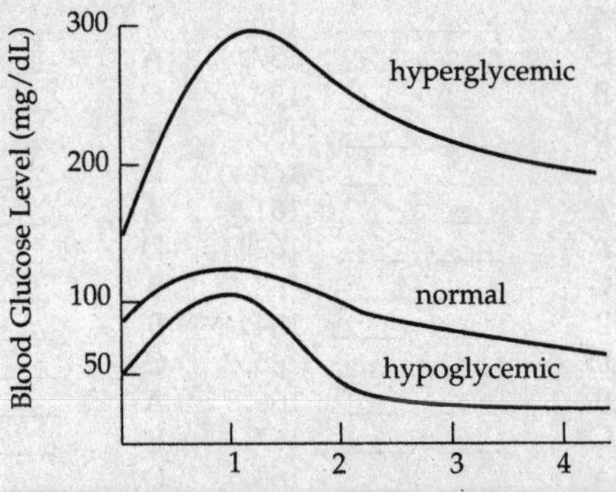


A glucose tolerance test was administered to evaluate the glucose levels in the blood of experimental subjects. Subjects were asked to fast for 12 hours, were administered glucose at time 0, and then had blood samples drawn to assess blood glucose levels. Glucose concentration was monitored every 30 minutes for a total of 5 hours. If the blood glucose concentration exceeded 130 ml/dL, the subject was considered hyperglycemic. Typically, hyperglycemic patients exhibit symptoms such as thirst, increased appetite, and weight loss.

197. The maximum glucose level for the hypoglycemic subjects in the experiment is:
(A) 50 ml/dL
(B) 100 ml/dL
(C) 120 ml/dL
(D) 200 ml/dL
(E) 300 ml/dL

198. Why would a physician prescribe a diet consisting of several small meals to hypoglycemic individuals?
(A) To rapidly decrease the concentration of glucose
(B) To increase the blood glucose concentration to the same level as those found in hyperglycemic individuals
(C) To maintain a steady concentration of glucose in the blood
(D) To increase the conversion of glucose to glycogen
(E) To cause the pancreas to release more glycogen

199. Approximately how many minutes does it take for the hypoglycemic individuals to reestablish their initial blood glucose concentration?
(A) 1.5
(B) 45
(C) 90
(D) 110
(E) 180

200. The condition diabetes mellitus may occur when the pancreas does not produce a sufficient amount of insulin. This causes
(A) glucose concentration in the cells to increase
(B) glucose concentration in the bloodstream to increase
(C) glucose to be rapidly converted into glycogen
(D) glucose concentration in the bloodstream to approach 100 ml/dL
(E) hypoglycemia in the patient

**STOP**

IF YOU FINISH BEFORE TIME IS CALLED, YOU MAY CHECK YOUR WORK ON THIS SECTION ONLY. DO NOT WORK ON ANY OTHER SECTION IN THE TEST.

# ANSWERS TO THE PRINCETON REVIEW GRE BIOLOGY SUBJECT TEST

| Quest. # | Correct Ans. | Right | Wrong | Quest. # | Correct Ans. | Right | Wrong | Quest. # | Correct Ans. | Right | Wrong | Quest. # | Correct Ans. | Right | Wrong |
|---|---|---|---|---|---|---|---|---|---|---|---|---|---|---|---|
| 1. | D | | | 53. | D | | | 105. | A | | | 156. | E | | |
| 2. | A | | | 54. | C | | | 106. | C | | | 157. | A | | |
| 3. | C | | | 55. | E | | | 107. | B | | | 158. | D | | |
| 4. | B | | | 56. | C | | | 108. | B | | | 159. | B | | |
| 5. | C | | | 57. | C | | | 109. | C | | | 160. | D | | |
| 6. | C | | | 58. | B | | | 110. | A | | | 161. | A | | |
| 7. | D | | | 59. | E | | | 111. | A | | | 162. | D | | |
| 8. | E | | | 60. | D | | | 112. | C | | | 163. | B | | |
| 9. | C | | | 61. | A | | | 113. | B | | | 164. | B | | |
| 10. | A | | | 62. | A | | | 114. | D | | | 165. | C | | |
| 11. | C | | | 63. | C | | | 115. | B | | | 166. | A | | |
| 12. | E | | | 64. | E | | | 116. | C | | | 167. | E | | |
| 13. | A | | | 65. | A | | | 117. | A | | | 168. | D | | |
| 14. | C | | | 66. | B | | | 118. | B | | | 169. | B | | |
| 15. | D | | | 67. | E | | | 119. | E | | | 170. | A | | |
| 16. | C | | | 68. | E | | | 120. | A | | | 171. | E | | |
| 17. | D | | | 69. | A | | | 121. | C | | | 172. | D | | |
| 18. | E | | | 70. | C | | | 122. | B | | | 173. | B | | |
| 19. | B | | | 71. | A | | | 123. | E | | | 174. | A | | |
| 20. | D | | | 72. | B | | | 124. | A | | | 175. | B | | |
| 21. | C | | | 73. | A | | | 125. | C | | | 176. | E | | |
| 22. | A | | | 74. | A | | | 126. | C | | | 177. | C | | |
| 23. | E | | | 75. | D | | | 127. | C | | | 178. | E | | |
| 24. | B | | | 76. | B | | | 128. | D | | | 179. | E | | |
| 25. | A | | | 77. | A | | | 129. | C | | | 180. | B | | |
| 26. | D | | | 78. | E | | | 130. | D | | | 181. | E | | |
| 27. | E | | | 79. | B | | | 131. | A | | | 182. | E | | |
| 28. | B | | | 80. | E | | | 132. | D | | | 183. | D | | |
| 29. | B | | | 81. | C | | | 133. | C | | | 184. | D | | |
| 30. | C | | | 82. | E | | | 134. | C | | | 185. | A | | |
| 31. | A | | | 83. | E | | | 135. | B | | | 186. | C | | |
| 32. | D | | | 84. | E | | | 136. | D | | | 187. | E | | |
| 33. | D | | | 85. | E | | | 137. | C | | | 188. | A | | |
| 34. | D | | | 86. | A | | | 138. | B | | | 189. | C | | |
| 35. | A | | | 87. | E | | | 139. | A | | | 190. | B | | |
| 36. | E | | | 88. | C | | | 140. | B | | | 191. | C | | |
| 37. | E | | | 89. | E | | | 141. | B | | | 192. | C | | |
| 38. | A | | | 90. | B | | | 142. | C | | | 193. | D | | |
| 39. | E | | | 91. | D | | | 143. | A | | | 194. | C | | |
| 40. | A | | | 92. | D | | | 144. | A | | | 195. | D | | |
| 41. | C | | | 93. | B | | | 145. | C | | | 196. | C | | |
| 42. | C | | | 94. | A | | | 146. | D | | | 197. | B | | |
| 43. | A | | | 95. | D | | | 147. | E | | | 198. | C | | |
| 44. | B | | | 96. | E | | | 148. | D | | | 199. | D | | |
| 45. | E | | | 97. | B | | | 149. | C | | | 200. | B | | |
| 46. | B | | | 98. | E | | | 150. | B | | | | | | |
| 47. | D | | | 99. | C | | | 151. | E | | | | | | |
| 48. | A | | | 100. | B | | | 152. | A | | | | | | |
| 49. | C | | | 101. | C | | | 153. | B | | | | | | |
| 50. | D | | | 102. | E | | | 154. | C | | | | | | |
| 51. | A | | | 103. | C | | | 155. | B | | | | | | |
| 52. | C | | | 104. | D | | | | | | | | | | |

# HOW TO SCORE THE PRINCETON REVIEW GRE BIOLOGY SUBJECT TEST

When you take the real exam, the proctors will collect your text booklet and bubble sheet and send your answer sheet to New Jersey where a computer (yes, a big old-fashioned one that has been around since the '60s) looks at the pattern of filled-in ovals on your answer sheet and gives you a score. We couldn't include even a small computer with this book, so we are providing this more primitive way of scoring your exam.

## Determining Your Score

**STEP 1** Using the answers on the next page, determine how many questions you got right and how many you got wrong on the test. Remember, questions that you do not answer don't count as either right answers or wrong answers.

**STEP 2** List the number of right answers here. (A) ______

**STEP 3** List the number of wrong answers here. Now divide that number by 4. (Use a calculator if you're feeling particularly lazy.) (B) ______ ÷ 4 = ______

**STEP 4** Subtract the number of wrong answers divided by 4 from the number of correct answers. Round this score to the nearest whole number. This is your raw score. (C) (A)______ – (B) ______ = ______

**STEP 5** To determine your real score, take the number from Step 4 above and look it up in the left column of the Score Conversion Table on page 232; the corresponding score on the right is your score on the exam.

| RAW SCORE | SCALED SCORE | %-ILE |
|---|---|---|
| 168–200 | 990 | 99 |
| 166–167 | 980 | 99 |
| 163–165 | 970 | 99 |
| 161–162 | 960 | 99 |
| 158–160 | 950 | 99 |
| 155–157 | 940 | 99 |
| 153–154 | 930 | 99 |
| 150–152 | 920 | 99 |
| 148–149 | 910 | 99 |
| 145–147 | 900 | 99 |
| 143–144 | 890 | 99 |
| 140–142 | 880 | 99 |
| 137–139 | 870 | 99 |
| 135–136 | 860 | 98 |
| 132–134 | 850 | 98 |
| 130–131 | 840 | 97 |
| 127–129 | 830 | 97 |
| 124–126 | 820 | 96 |
| 122–123 | 810 | 95 |
| 119–121 | 800 | 94 |
| 117–118 | 790 | 93 |
| 114–116 | 780 | 92 |
| 112–113 | 770 | 90 |
| 109–111 | 760 | 89 |
| 106–108 | 750 | 87 |
| 104–105 | 740 | 85 |
| 101–103 | 730 | 83 |
| 99–100 | 720 | 81 |
| 96–98 | 710 | 79 |
| 93–95 | 700 | 76 |
| 91–92 | 690 | 74 |
| 88–90 | 680 | 71 |
| 86–87 | 670 | 68 |
| 83–85 | 660 | 66 |
| 80–82 | 650 | 63 |
| 78–79 | 640 | 59 |
| 75–77 | 630 | 56 |
| 73–74 | 620 | 53 |
| 70–72 | 610 | 49 |
| 68–69 | 600 | 46 |
| 65–67 | 590 | 43 |
| 62–64 | 580 | 39 |
| 60–61 | 570 | 36 |
| 57–59 | 560 | 33 |
| 55–56 | 550 | 30 |
| 52–54 | 540 | 27 |
| 49–51 | 530 | 24 |
| 47–48 | 520 | 21 |
| 44–46 | 510 | 19 |
| 42–43 | 500 | 16 |
| 39–41 | 490 | 14 |
| 37–38 | 480 | 12 |
| 34–36 | 470 | 10 |
| 31–33 | 460 | 9 |
| 29–30 | 450 | 8 |
| 26–28 | 440 | 6 |
| 24–25 | 430 | 5 |
| 21–23 | 420 | 4 |
| 18–20 | 410 | 3 |
| 16–17 | 400 | 2 |
| 13–15 | 390 | 2 |
| 11–12 | 380 | 1 |
| 8–10 | 370 | 1 |
| 6–7 | 360 | 1 |
| 3–5 | 350 | 1 |

# PART VIII

# Explanations

## ABOUT THE AUTHOR

Deborah Guest holds a bachelor of science degree from Columbia University, where she also spent two years as a teaching assistant in the Biological Sciences. She has worked as a research assistant at the Psychiatric Institute of New York where she worked with SAD (seasonal affective disorder) patients, and as an associate editor at Genetic Engineering News. She has written, edited, and tutored for the Princeton Review since 1989.

She is currently a freelance writer and editor specializing in medicine and biology.

# THE PRINCETON REVIEW WORLDWIDE

Each year, thousands of students from countries throughout the world prepare for the TOEFL and for U.S. college and graduate school admissions exams. Whether you plan to prepare for your exams in your home country or the United States, The Princeton Review is committed to your success.

INTERNATIONAL LOCATIONS: If you are using our books outside of the United States and have questions or comments, or want to know if our courses are being offered in your area, be sure to contact The Princeton Review office nearest you:

- CANADA (Montreal) 514-499-0870
- HONG KONG 852-517-3016
- JAPAN (Tokyo) 8133-463-1343
- KOREA (Seoul) 822-508-0081
- MEXICO (Mexico City) 525-564-9468
- PAKISTAN (Lahore) 92-42-571-2315
- SAUDI ARABIA 413-584-6849 (a U.S. based number)
- SPAIN (Madrid) 341-323-4212
- TAIWAN (Taipei) 886-27511293

U.S. STUDY ABROAD: *Review USA* offers international students many advantages and opportunities. In addition to helping you gain acceptance to the U.S. college or university of your choice, *Review USA* will help you acquire the knowledge and orientation you need to succeed once you get there.

*Review USA* is unique. It includes supplements to your test-preparation courses and a special series of *AmeriCulture* workshops to prepare you for the academic rigors and student life in the United States. Our workshops are designed to familiarize you with the different U.S. expressions, real-life vocabulary, and cultural challenges you will encounter as a study-abroad student. While studying with us, you'll make new friends and have the opportunity to personally visit college and university campuses to determine which school is right for you.

Whether you are planning to take the TOEFL, SAT, GRE, GMAT, LSAT, MCAT, or USMLE exam, The Princeton Review's test preparation courses, expert instructors, and dedicated International Student Advisors can help you achieve your goals.

For additional information about *Review USA*, admissions requirements, class schedules, F-1 visas, I-20 documentation, and course locations, write to:

The Princeton Review • Review USA
2315 Broadway, New York, NY 10024
Fax: 212/874-0775

# NOTES

# NOTES

# NOTES

# NOTES

# NOTES

# NOTES

# NOTES

# NOTES

# NOTES

# NOTES

## NOTES

# NOTES

# NOTES

# NOTES

**DO NOT USE INK**

SIDE 1

## THE PRINCETON REVIEW GRADUATE RECORD EXAMINATIONS - GRE - SUBJECT TEST

Use only a pencil with soft, black lead, (No. 2 or HB) to complete this answer sheet. Be sure to fill in completely the space that corresponds to your answer choice. Completely erase any errors or stray marks

**1. NAME** Enter your last name, first name, initial (given name), and middle initial, if you have one. Omit spaces, apostrophes, Jr., II., etc.

Last Name only (Family or Surname) - first 15 letters | First Name initial | Middle initial

A B C D E F G H I J K L M N O P Q R S T U V W X –

BE SURE EACH MARK IS DARK AND COMPLETELY FILLS THE INTENDED SPACE AS ILLUSTRATED HERE: ●

YOU MAY FIND MORE RESPONSE SPACES THAN YOU NEED. IF SO, PLEASE LEAVE THEM BLANK.

| | | |
|---|---|---|
| 1 Ⓐ Ⓑ Ⓒ Ⓓ Ⓔ | 37 Ⓐ Ⓑ Ⓒ Ⓓ Ⓔ | 73 Ⓐ Ⓑ Ⓒ Ⓓ Ⓔ |
| 2 Ⓐ Ⓑ Ⓒ Ⓓ Ⓔ | 38 Ⓐ Ⓑ Ⓒ Ⓓ Ⓔ | 74 Ⓐ Ⓑ Ⓒ Ⓓ Ⓔ |
| 3 Ⓐ Ⓑ Ⓒ Ⓓ Ⓔ | 39 Ⓐ Ⓑ Ⓒ Ⓓ Ⓔ | 75 Ⓐ Ⓑ Ⓒ Ⓓ Ⓔ |
| 4 Ⓐ Ⓑ Ⓒ Ⓓ Ⓔ | 40 Ⓐ Ⓑ Ⓒ Ⓓ Ⓔ | 76 Ⓐ Ⓑ Ⓒ Ⓓ Ⓔ |
| 5 Ⓐ Ⓑ Ⓒ Ⓓ Ⓔ | 41 Ⓐ Ⓑ Ⓒ Ⓓ Ⓔ | 77 Ⓐ Ⓑ Ⓒ Ⓓ Ⓔ |
| 6 Ⓐ Ⓑ Ⓒ Ⓓ Ⓔ | 42 Ⓐ Ⓑ Ⓒ Ⓓ Ⓔ | 78 Ⓐ Ⓑ Ⓒ Ⓓ Ⓔ |
| 7 Ⓐ Ⓑ Ⓒ Ⓓ Ⓔ | 43 Ⓐ Ⓑ Ⓒ Ⓓ Ⓔ | 79 Ⓐ Ⓑ Ⓒ Ⓓ Ⓔ |
| 8 Ⓐ Ⓑ Ⓒ Ⓓ Ⓔ | 44 Ⓐ Ⓑ Ⓒ Ⓓ Ⓔ | 80 Ⓐ Ⓑ Ⓒ Ⓓ Ⓔ |
| 9 Ⓐ Ⓑ Ⓒ Ⓓ Ⓔ | 45 Ⓐ Ⓑ Ⓒ Ⓓ Ⓔ | 81 Ⓐ Ⓑ Ⓒ Ⓓ Ⓔ |
| 10 Ⓐ Ⓑ Ⓒ Ⓓ Ⓔ | 46 Ⓐ Ⓑ Ⓒ Ⓓ Ⓔ | 82 Ⓐ Ⓑ Ⓒ Ⓓ Ⓔ |
| 11 Ⓐ Ⓑ Ⓒ Ⓓ Ⓔ | 47 Ⓐ Ⓑ Ⓒ Ⓓ Ⓔ | 83 Ⓐ Ⓑ Ⓒ Ⓓ Ⓔ |
| 12 Ⓐ Ⓑ Ⓒ Ⓓ Ⓔ | 48 Ⓐ Ⓑ Ⓒ Ⓓ Ⓔ | 84 Ⓐ Ⓑ Ⓒ Ⓓ Ⓔ |
| 13 Ⓐ Ⓑ Ⓒ Ⓓ Ⓔ | 49 Ⓐ Ⓑ Ⓒ Ⓓ Ⓔ | 85 Ⓐ Ⓑ Ⓒ Ⓓ Ⓔ |
| 14 Ⓐ Ⓑ Ⓒ Ⓓ Ⓔ | 50 Ⓐ Ⓑ Ⓒ Ⓓ Ⓔ | 86 Ⓐ Ⓑ Ⓒ Ⓓ Ⓔ |
| 15 Ⓐ Ⓑ Ⓒ Ⓓ Ⓔ | 51 Ⓐ Ⓑ Ⓒ Ⓓ Ⓔ | 87 Ⓐ Ⓑ Ⓒ Ⓓ Ⓔ |
| 16 Ⓐ Ⓑ Ⓒ Ⓓ Ⓔ | 52 Ⓐ Ⓑ Ⓒ Ⓓ Ⓔ | 88 Ⓐ Ⓑ Ⓒ Ⓓ Ⓔ |
| 17 Ⓐ Ⓑ Ⓒ Ⓓ Ⓔ | 53 Ⓐ Ⓑ Ⓒ Ⓓ Ⓔ | 89 Ⓐ Ⓑ Ⓒ Ⓓ Ⓔ |
| 18 Ⓐ Ⓑ Ⓒ Ⓓ Ⓔ | 54 Ⓐ Ⓑ Ⓒ Ⓓ Ⓔ | 90 Ⓐ Ⓑ Ⓒ Ⓓ Ⓔ |
| 19 Ⓐ Ⓑ Ⓒ Ⓓ Ⓔ | 55 Ⓐ Ⓑ Ⓒ Ⓓ Ⓔ | 91 Ⓐ Ⓑ Ⓒ Ⓓ Ⓔ |
| 20 Ⓐ Ⓑ Ⓒ Ⓓ Ⓔ | 56 Ⓐ Ⓑ Ⓒ Ⓓ Ⓔ | 92 Ⓐ Ⓑ Ⓒ Ⓓ Ⓔ |
| 21 Ⓐ Ⓑ Ⓒ Ⓓ Ⓔ | 57 Ⓐ Ⓑ Ⓒ Ⓓ Ⓔ | 93 Ⓐ Ⓑ Ⓒ Ⓓ Ⓔ |
| 22 Ⓐ Ⓑ Ⓒ Ⓓ Ⓔ | 58 Ⓐ Ⓑ Ⓒ Ⓓ Ⓔ | 94 Ⓐ Ⓑ Ⓒ Ⓓ Ⓔ |
| 23 Ⓐ Ⓑ Ⓒ Ⓓ Ⓔ | 59 Ⓐ Ⓑ Ⓒ Ⓓ Ⓔ | 95 Ⓐ Ⓑ Ⓒ Ⓓ Ⓔ |
| 24 Ⓐ Ⓑ Ⓒ Ⓓ Ⓔ | 60 Ⓐ Ⓑ Ⓒ Ⓓ Ⓔ | 96 Ⓐ Ⓑ Ⓒ Ⓓ Ⓔ |
| 25 Ⓐ Ⓑ Ⓒ Ⓓ Ⓔ | 61 Ⓐ Ⓑ Ⓒ Ⓓ Ⓔ | 97 Ⓐ Ⓑ Ⓒ Ⓓ Ⓔ |
| 26 Ⓐ Ⓑ Ⓒ Ⓓ Ⓔ | 62 Ⓐ Ⓑ Ⓒ Ⓓ Ⓔ | 98 Ⓐ Ⓑ Ⓒ Ⓓ Ⓔ |
| 27 Ⓐ Ⓑ Ⓒ Ⓓ Ⓔ | 63 Ⓐ Ⓑ Ⓒ Ⓓ Ⓔ | 99 Ⓐ Ⓑ Ⓒ Ⓓ Ⓔ |
| 28 Ⓐ Ⓑ Ⓒ Ⓓ Ⓔ | 64 Ⓐ Ⓑ Ⓒ Ⓓ Ⓔ | 100 Ⓐ Ⓑ Ⓒ Ⓓ Ⓔ |
| 29 Ⓐ Ⓑ Ⓒ Ⓓ Ⓔ | 65 Ⓐ Ⓑ Ⓒ Ⓓ Ⓔ | 101 Ⓐ Ⓑ Ⓒ Ⓓ Ⓔ |
| 30 Ⓐ Ⓑ Ⓒ Ⓓ Ⓔ | 66 Ⓐ Ⓑ Ⓒ Ⓓ Ⓔ | 102 Ⓐ Ⓑ Ⓒ Ⓓ Ⓔ |
| 31 Ⓐ Ⓑ Ⓒ Ⓓ Ⓔ | 67 Ⓐ Ⓑ Ⓒ Ⓓ Ⓔ | 103 Ⓐ Ⓑ Ⓒ Ⓓ Ⓔ |
| 32 Ⓐ Ⓑ Ⓒ Ⓓ Ⓔ | 68 Ⓐ Ⓑ Ⓒ Ⓓ Ⓔ | 104 Ⓐ Ⓑ Ⓒ Ⓓ Ⓔ |
| 33 Ⓐ Ⓑ Ⓒ Ⓓ Ⓔ | 69 Ⓐ Ⓑ Ⓒ Ⓓ Ⓔ | 105 Ⓐ Ⓑ Ⓒ Ⓓ Ⓔ |
| 34 Ⓐ Ⓑ Ⓒ Ⓓ Ⓔ | 70 Ⓐ Ⓑ Ⓒ Ⓓ Ⓔ | 106 Ⓐ Ⓑ Ⓒ Ⓓ Ⓔ |
| 35 Ⓐ Ⓑ Ⓒ Ⓓ Ⓔ | 71 Ⓐ Ⓑ Ⓒ Ⓓ Ⓔ | 107 Ⓐ Ⓑ Ⓒ Ⓓ Ⓔ |
| 36 Ⓐ Ⓑ Ⓒ Ⓓ Ⓔ | 72 Ⓐ Ⓑ Ⓒ Ⓓ Ⓔ | 108 Ⓐ Ⓑ Ⓒ Ⓓ Ⓔ |

**2. YOUR NAME:** ______________________
(Print) Last Name (Family or Surname) First Name (Given) M.I.

**MAILING ADDRESS:** ______________________
P.O. Box or Street Address

City State or Province

Country Zip or Postal Code

**CENTER:** ______________________
City State or Province

Country Center Number Room Number

**3. DATE OF BIRTH**

Month: Jan. Feb. Mar. April May June July Aug. Sept. Oct.

Day: 0 1 2 3 / 0 1 2 3 4 5 6 7

Year: 0 1 2 3 4 5 6 7

**4. SOCIAL SECURITY NUMBER** (U.S.A. Only)

0 1 2 3 4 5 6 7

**5. REGISTRATION NUMBER** (from your admission ticket)

0 1 2 3 4 5 6 7

**6. TITLE CODE** (on back cover of your test book)

0 1 2 3 4 5 6 7

**7. TEST NAME** (on back cover of your test book)

**FORM CODE** (on back cover of your test book)

**8. TEST BOOK SERIAL NUMBER** (red number in upper right corner of front cover of your test book)

## SIDE 2

## SUBJECT TEST

BE SURE EACH MARK IS DARK AND COMPLETELY FILLS THE INTENDED SPACE AS ILLUSTRATED HERE: ⬬

YOU MAY FIND MORE RESPONSE SPACES THAN YOU NEED. IF SO, PLEASE LEAVE THEM BLANK.

109 Ⓐ Ⓑ Ⓒ Ⓓ Ⓔ
110 Ⓐ Ⓑ Ⓒ Ⓓ Ⓔ
111 Ⓐ Ⓑ Ⓒ Ⓓ Ⓔ
112 Ⓐ Ⓑ Ⓒ Ⓓ Ⓔ
113 Ⓐ Ⓑ Ⓒ Ⓓ Ⓔ
115 Ⓐ Ⓑ Ⓒ Ⓓ Ⓔ
116 Ⓐ Ⓑ Ⓒ Ⓓ Ⓔ
117 Ⓐ Ⓑ Ⓒ Ⓓ Ⓔ
118 Ⓐ Ⓑ Ⓒ Ⓓ Ⓔ
119 Ⓐ Ⓑ Ⓒ Ⓓ Ⓔ
120 Ⓐ Ⓑ Ⓒ Ⓓ Ⓔ
121 Ⓐ Ⓑ Ⓒ Ⓓ Ⓔ
122 Ⓐ Ⓑ Ⓒ Ⓓ Ⓔ
123 Ⓐ Ⓑ Ⓒ Ⓓ Ⓔ
124 Ⓐ Ⓑ Ⓒ Ⓓ Ⓔ
125 Ⓐ Ⓑ Ⓒ Ⓓ Ⓔ
126 Ⓐ Ⓑ Ⓒ Ⓓ Ⓔ
127 Ⓐ Ⓑ Ⓒ Ⓓ Ⓔ
128 Ⓐ Ⓑ Ⓒ Ⓓ Ⓔ
129 Ⓐ Ⓑ Ⓒ Ⓓ Ⓔ
130 Ⓐ Ⓑ Ⓒ Ⓓ Ⓔ
131 Ⓐ Ⓑ Ⓒ Ⓓ Ⓔ
132 Ⓐ Ⓑ Ⓒ Ⓓ Ⓔ

133 Ⓐ Ⓑ Ⓒ Ⓓ Ⓔ
134 Ⓐ Ⓑ Ⓒ Ⓓ Ⓔ
135 Ⓐ Ⓑ Ⓒ Ⓓ Ⓔ
136 Ⓐ Ⓑ Ⓒ Ⓓ Ⓔ
137 Ⓐ Ⓑ Ⓒ Ⓓ Ⓔ
138 Ⓐ Ⓑ Ⓒ Ⓓ Ⓔ
139 Ⓐ Ⓑ Ⓒ Ⓓ Ⓔ
140 Ⓐ Ⓑ Ⓒ Ⓓ Ⓔ
141 Ⓐ Ⓑ Ⓒ Ⓓ Ⓔ
142 Ⓐ Ⓑ Ⓒ Ⓓ Ⓔ
143 Ⓐ Ⓑ Ⓒ Ⓓ Ⓔ
144 Ⓐ Ⓑ Ⓒ Ⓓ Ⓔ
145 Ⓐ Ⓑ Ⓒ Ⓓ Ⓔ
146 Ⓐ Ⓑ Ⓒ Ⓓ Ⓔ
147 Ⓐ Ⓑ Ⓒ Ⓓ Ⓔ
148 Ⓐ Ⓑ Ⓒ Ⓓ Ⓔ
149 Ⓐ Ⓑ Ⓒ Ⓓ Ⓔ
150 Ⓐ Ⓑ Ⓒ Ⓓ Ⓔ
151 Ⓐ Ⓑ Ⓒ Ⓓ Ⓔ
152 Ⓐ Ⓑ Ⓒ Ⓓ Ⓔ
153 Ⓐ Ⓑ Ⓒ Ⓓ Ⓔ
154 Ⓐ Ⓑ Ⓒ Ⓓ Ⓔ
155 Ⓐ Ⓑ Ⓒ Ⓓ Ⓔ

156 Ⓐ Ⓑ Ⓒ Ⓓ Ⓔ
157 Ⓐ Ⓑ Ⓒ Ⓓ Ⓔ
158 Ⓐ Ⓑ Ⓒ Ⓓ Ⓔ
159 Ⓐ Ⓑ Ⓒ Ⓓ Ⓔ
160 Ⓐ Ⓑ Ⓒ Ⓓ Ⓔ
161 Ⓐ Ⓑ Ⓒ Ⓓ Ⓔ
162 Ⓐ Ⓑ Ⓒ Ⓓ Ⓔ
163 Ⓐ Ⓑ Ⓒ Ⓓ Ⓔ
164 Ⓐ Ⓑ Ⓒ Ⓓ Ⓔ
165 Ⓐ Ⓑ Ⓒ Ⓓ Ⓔ
166 Ⓐ Ⓑ Ⓒ Ⓓ Ⓔ
167 Ⓐ Ⓑ Ⓒ Ⓓ Ⓔ
168 Ⓐ Ⓑ Ⓒ Ⓓ Ⓔ
169 Ⓐ Ⓑ Ⓒ Ⓓ Ⓔ
170 Ⓐ Ⓑ Ⓒ Ⓓ Ⓔ
171 Ⓐ Ⓑ Ⓒ Ⓓ Ⓔ
172 Ⓐ Ⓑ Ⓒ Ⓓ Ⓔ
173 Ⓐ Ⓑ Ⓒ Ⓓ Ⓔ
174 Ⓐ Ⓑ Ⓒ Ⓓ Ⓔ
175 Ⓐ Ⓑ Ⓒ Ⓓ Ⓔ
176 Ⓐ Ⓑ Ⓒ Ⓓ Ⓔ
177 Ⓐ Ⓑ Ⓒ Ⓓ Ⓔ
178 Ⓐ Ⓑ Ⓒ Ⓓ Ⓔ

179 Ⓐ Ⓑ Ⓒ Ⓓ Ⓔ
157 Ⓐ Ⓑ Ⓒ Ⓓ Ⓔ
180 Ⓐ Ⓑ Ⓒ Ⓓ Ⓔ
181 Ⓐ Ⓑ Ⓒ Ⓓ Ⓔ
182 Ⓐ Ⓑ Ⓒ Ⓓ Ⓔ
183 Ⓐ Ⓑ Ⓒ Ⓓ Ⓔ
184 Ⓐ Ⓑ Ⓒ Ⓓ Ⓔ
185 Ⓐ Ⓑ Ⓒ Ⓓ Ⓔ
186 Ⓐ Ⓑ Ⓒ Ⓓ Ⓔ
187 Ⓐ Ⓑ Ⓒ Ⓓ Ⓔ
188 Ⓐ Ⓑ Ⓒ Ⓓ Ⓔ
189 Ⓐ Ⓑ Ⓒ Ⓓ Ⓔ
190 Ⓐ Ⓑ Ⓒ Ⓓ Ⓔ
191 Ⓐ Ⓑ Ⓒ Ⓓ Ⓔ
192 Ⓐ Ⓑ Ⓒ Ⓓ Ⓔ
193 Ⓐ Ⓑ Ⓒ Ⓓ Ⓔ
194 Ⓐ Ⓑ Ⓒ Ⓓ Ⓔ
195 Ⓐ Ⓑ Ⓒ Ⓓ Ⓔ
196 Ⓐ Ⓑ Ⓒ Ⓓ Ⓔ
197 Ⓐ Ⓑ Ⓒ Ⓓ Ⓔ
198 Ⓐ Ⓑ Ⓒ Ⓓ Ⓔ
199 Ⓐ Ⓑ Ⓒ Ⓓ Ⓔ
200 Ⓐ Ⓑ Ⓒ Ⓓ Ⓔ